Trials, Tremors and Hope

Political Economy of Contemporary Nepal

Author

Ram Sharan Mahat

ADROIT

Adroit Publishers

NEW DELHI • KATHMANDU

ISBN : 978-81-87393-75-7

2020

Published by
ADROIT PUBLISHERS 4675/21, Ganpati Bhawan, Ansari Road,
Daryaganj, New Delhi-110 002 Phone : 011-23266030
adroitpublishers@gmail.com

Typeset in Garamond Premier Pro by Arun Sharama,
Akriti Graphic Solution, Delhi-110081 E-mail: arun263923@gmail.com,
Ph: 9999414390

Dedicated to all Nepali men and women who are devoted to honest and creative hard work for the nation's socioeconomic transformation in a democracy.

Contents

Preface

Nepal has entered a new political phase with the promulgation of the new constitution, marking a sharp departure from the past, towards greater pluralism and broader inclusiveness in representation and devolution in the exercise of power. The country has freed itself from the monarchical rule and unitary structure of governance that lasted for nearly 250 years. In recent decades, the country underwent political turmoil and upheavals with frequent regime change and governments within.

Nepal opened up to external influence and engagement after 1951 when it transitioned from the century-long Rana family oligarchy to a democratic order cut short by a royal takeover in 1960. Only in 1990 did Nepal embrace parliamentary democracy with constitutional monarchy, following a popular uprising. Soon after, this change of regime also came under assault from both the extreme left (Maoists) and the extreme right represented by an absolute but discredited monarch. In 2006, a peace accord was signed which enabled the mainstreaming of the insurgents into national politics and the founding of a new republic. The peace process helped usher the democratic polity into a secular, federal order, enshrined firmly in the new constitution promulgated in September 2015.

The country's economic policy has shifted from state-centrism towards liberalism, in stride with the ethos of broad political freedoms attained after 1990. Despite changes in regime, however, Nepal's development imperatives and contemporary international practices were visionary and ensured that there has been no major change in the fundamental economic orientation of the country.

This book is an attempt to review and chronicle some aspects of the country's contemporary political economy. It summarizes the impact and implications of political travails, trials and tribulations, particularly the Maoist conflict and the turmoil of the 2015 earthquake disaster. The principal features and implementation constraints of the new constitution are covered. The document incorporates many progressive elements to help create an equitable and just society and a decentralized federal structure with three tiers of government. Its major challenge is that it presupposes a robust economic strength and a capable and efficient state committed to the rule of law and good governance.

The commitment to create the foundation for socialism is another conspicuous feature of the constitution, even though this goal is subject to varying interpretations. The socialist objectives are to be met through democratic norms and values including competitive plural politics, as well as an elaborate list of fundamental rights including those related to social protection, the security of property rights, among others.

This book begins with a review of the evolution of socialist thinking in response to emerging challenges and realities, culminating in the form prevailing in the contemporary world as adopted by countries that exhibit elements of socialist philosophy in its full continuum, from communism to social democracy. The choice in the modern world is no longer Stalin-style centralized planning with collective ownership of the means of production, nor the complete laissez-faire free market economy in the classical sense. Adoption of a mix of pragmatic policies that converge the two systems, choosing positive elements of both and addressing shortcomings of each is the way forward. Today we see communist China adopting features of a market economy and leaders of the US Democratic Party such as Bernie Sanders and Elizabeth Warren advocating democratic socialist programs, once considered radical in capitalist America.

Most countries in the world today pursue a market-oriented path to resource allocation and economic prosperity, with a desire for a strong regulatory state to curb possible abuses and distortions, while providing social justice and protection for the underprivileged.

Nepal cannot be aloof from this trend, which is recognized as a necessity based on the country's own experience. The economic and social transformation of the country is an unfinished agenda, acknowledged by all segments of Nepali society. The country's past progress in the social sector and reduction of poverty and hunger, despite modest income growth under adverse conditions of conflict, turbulent politics, has received widespread international recognition and appreciation. This was made possible on the foundation of economic reforms set in motion in the early nineties. The challenge at present is to accelerate economic growth by capitalizing on the comparative advantage possessed by the country in clean energy, biodiversity, eco-tourism, together with cultural heritage, strategic geo-political location between China and India, and the goodwill accorded to Nepal by the international community. Only with the strengthening of the economy, steered prudently by an efficient federal and sub-national administration, will it be possible to meet popular expectations, together with state obligation to ensure socio-economic justice. The immediate development agenda is to manage the post-graduation transition of Nepal from the status of Least Developed Country (LDC) following the triennial review at the UN in 2021, and meeting of the Sustainable Development Goals, including a respectable middle-income status, by 2030.

To attain these goals, the country has to work vigorously by initiating new reforms and solving entrenched implementation bottlenecks. The book suggests several priority tasks in this regard. The requirement is to improve the efficiency of public sector investment which should focus more on capital formation and infrastructure building by putting a cap on unproductive recurrent spending which is rising as a result of competitive populism.

The excessive preoccupation with political issues on the national scene has percolated and infested practically all aspects of civic and social life. There is an urgent need for better governance, together with stress on higher productivity, entrepreneurship and creativity to capitalize on the country's potentials by enticing external private investment.

The mixture of hard work and thrift is considered to be the essence of a work culture amenable to putting the country on a high growth trajectory. Only by attracting more private investment, including FDI laden with better technology and know-how, will the country be able to leverage its natural and human resource endowment. For this, a better investment climate, improved infrastructure, efficient and investment-friendly public administration are simultaneously necessary. Another requirement is to raise factor productivity by improving the Nepali work ethic and discipline. The country presently suffers from a highly politicized work culture that rewards partisan affiliations to meritocratic performance and delivery.

Managing the new federal structure is an un-tested but daunting challenge. The multiple levels of governance in a relatively small country with a history of centralized administration creates problems of overlap, ambiguity and conflict of authority. These cannot simply be dismissed for much longer as simply the birth pangs of a new republic. The priority in the new context should be the clarity on working guidelines and procedures on the jurisdiction and responsibilities across different levels of government, and creation and strengthening of institutions to make them capable of performing functions entrusted by the constitution. All this demands new sets of skills on the part of the leadership to set the right vision and to faithfully execute constitutional mandates within a robust democratic system undergirded by quality governance.

This book is a result of the use of my free time over the past year. Having won four consecutive parliamentary elections from Nuwakot since 1994, I lost the last one in 2018. Friends and well-wishers urged me to utilize the time that became available to produce a sequel of sorts to my earlier book, *In Defence of Democracy: Dynamics and Fault Lines of Nepal's Political Economy*, which had come out in 2005 countering the claims of the royal regime that was striving hard to discredit the previous parliamentary democratic rule to justify the power takeover by the king in October 2002.

I take this opportunity to express my sincere gratitude to various institutions and individuals who provided materials and data for this effort. It is not possible to name them all here. The book also draws on inputs from my earlier publications, including newspaper articles and presentations at various forums. I wish to thank Swarnim Wagle in particular for going through the entire draft manuscript and making substantive comments as well as editorial improvements. The book has also benefitted from consultations with Madhu Raman Acharya, Surya Dhungel, Arjun Karki and Tula Raj Basyal on specific issues in their respective fields. Thanks, are also due to Arun Mahat and Pravin Nepal for their patient assistance on the technical and logistical fronts, and Dishebh Shrestha for cover design of the book. Appreciation is also due to my wife Roshana and family members for continued inspiration and providing me relief from domestic responsibilities to facilitate the completion of this exercise, together with meeting the obligations of my public life. Lastly, I wish to extend my thanks to the Adroit Publishing House and the associated editor for their contribution in bringing the book to this shape.

Chapter One

Socialism in the Changing World

Socialism has now been a political currency in Nepal for nearly seventy years since it got rid of feudal oligarchy and moved towards a governance system of people's rule in 1951. In recent years, it assumed heightened importance and became a buzzword during and after the promulgation of the new constitution. The Constitution of Nepal in 2015 committed itself to the goal of socialism through the adoption of democratic values based on competitive multiparty politics—including periodic election, adult franchise, press freedom, civil liberty and an independent and impartial judiciary.

The semantic renaissance of 'socialism' is not just a Nepali phenomenon, but a global one. In 2015, after the former US Presidential candidate Bernie Sanders positioned himself as a 'democratic socialist', it was the most searched term on Merriam-Webster's site.[1] If a former Maoist guerilla from the mountains of Nepal and a senator from the world's largest capitalist economy both swear by socialism, it must be a maelstrom, meaning different things to different people at various times. Indeed, C.E.M. Joad, an English philosopher, remarked many decades ago that socialism was like a hat that had lost its original shape because everybody wore it.

Socialism has been an all-weather ideology professed by rulers ranging from communists, fascists and Western democrats to leaders of newly liberated developing countries after the Second World War. It would be useful to review the evolution of the concept and the shape it has come to take in the modern era.

Origin

According to BP Koirala, the first Nepali revolutionary leader who advocated the socialist philosophy in Nepal, its roots lie in the human mind—out of empathy, compassion and concern towards human suffering, deprivation and injustice, and a desire to seek a solution to remedy social evil. He saw elements of socialist thinking in Hindu, Buddhist and Christian philosophies, as well as in the works of the early Greek philosophers like Socrates, Plato and Aristotle.

Traditionally, the essence of socialism was associated with shared ownership or communal possession of public goods, as the institution of private property was perceived to be at the root of greed, exploitation and inequality. Communal ownership of land and houses was seen as a way of controlling the sins of pride, greed, and envy. In Plato's *Republic*, he envisages an austere society with communal ownership in which men and women of the ruling class share with each other not only material goods but also spouses and children. The Christian community, in the olden days, practiced monasticism which too involved the sharing of possessions and the fruits of labor.

On a continuum of beliefs, socialism is a philosophy opposed to capitalism, which is based on individual ownership of the means of production and allowing the market to determine the choice of goods and services for production and distribution. The traditional socialists believed that capitalism leads to unfair concentration of wealth and power which in turn is used to reinforce the dominance of a narrow elite. Therefore, they advocated social control over the means of production and natural resources for a fairer distribution of economic outcomes.

The socialist movement was conditioned in response to the mounting inequality and excessive poverty stemming from the early days of the Industrial Revolution. There was deep moral outrage at the pauper-like living conditions of the working class following the Revolution. This produced radical critics of industrial capitalism, in favor of a utopian philosophy with which to create a new and glorious society. Subsequently, a transformation of the existing body politic into small communities without private property was advocated by Utopian philosophers like Robert Owen, Saint Simon and Fourier.

Marxist socialism

The Marxist understanding of socialism, adopted by the communists, originated from the works of Karl Marx and Friedrich Engels in the middle of the nineteenth century. Marx called the early socialists 'utopians': their vision was considered egalitarian and idealist, but not grounded in material conditions and lacking consideration of the means and methods to achieve such a society. Unlike Marx, the utopians did not contemplate a class struggle and a revolution to beget socialism.

According to Marxist theory, the contradictions in the material interests between the oppressed working class and the bourgeoisie—who own the means of production and exploit the working labor class—would lead to a social rupture. There is an accumulation of wealth through the extraction of surplus value produced by the proletariat, which would inevitably lead to class struggle. This will culminate in a proletarian revolution to overthrow the capitalist system and establish a socialist order. Marxist socialism imagines a socioeconomic system based on the collective ownership of the means of production, and production, not to garner profit, rather directly for use. The advancement of productive forces under this system would ultimately lead to the emergence of a communist society which would be classless and stateless based on common ownership, with the underlying principle of 'each according to his ability and to each according to need.'

Marx categorized history into various stages: primitive socialism, slave society, feudalism, capitalism and socialism, based on the principle of dialectical materialism. Each passing stage of history is an advancement, ushered at the decline and eventual fall of preceding epochs because of internal contradictions arising due to a clash of material interests. As the first three stages of history had long passed, Marx devoted special attention to the capitalist period which emerged with the rise of the bourgeoisie. The capitalist stage is superior to feudalism, he argued, but a system guided by market forces and profit-motive would lead to a concentration of means of production through the exploitation of labor.

Chartism and revisionism

Around the same time, the Chartist movement started emerging in Britain. The Chartists demanded the extension of suffrage (at the time limited only to property-owners) to all male adults, equitable distribution of income and better living conditions for the working class. This movement which began in 1838 and continued until 1858, involved mass meetings and petitions presented to the House of Commons signed by millions of workers, and also witnessed some insurrectionary activities. The demands for reforms, called the People's Charter, were varied: universal manhood voting right, a secret ballot, absence of property qualification for contesting in the parliamentary elections, introduction of payment to MPs, constituencies based on equal population and annual parliamentary elections. The wage cut following the depression of 1842 gave further momentum to the movement. There were strikes and an outbreak of violence with an additional demand for restoration of wages. Although the movement lasted for a long period, it did not directly generate reforms because of state persecution and conflicting views of Christian preachers concerning Christians and their role in politics. With the onset of relative prosperity in mid-Victorian Britain, the movement lost steam after 1848. Nonetheless, the demands of the Chartist movement started gaining acceptance among the parliamentarians in the 1850s; the franchise was extended to working men in 1867, with other reforms being implemented in subsequent years. The universal suffrage was enacted only in 1928. A raised awareness of political rights was also a legacy of the movement, as were strident writings and public speaking which helped undermine the power of the ruling elite.

Chartism is considered an important factor heralding the notion of moderate and constitutional means to attain socialist goals, as opposed to violence. The Fabian socialism built on the foundation of Chartism, exercised considerable influence over the philosophy of the British Labour Party that believed in gradualism and peaceful means, instead of violent class-warfare to bring about socialism. Prominent Fabians included Bernard Shaw, Sidney and Beatrice Webb, Graham Wallas and H.G. Wells, who favored persuasion and education through trade unions and existing political parties to head towards socialism. Indeed, they were all behind the establishment of the London School of Economics in 1895.

Foremost among the philosophers behind this revisionist approach to socialism in the late nineteenth century, who saw flaws in Marxian thinking, was Eduard Bernstein of Germany. He was exposed to the Fabians when he was living in exile in England to escape the harassment and persecution under Bismarck's regime in Germany. He challenged the Marxist materialistic interpretation of history and saw the possibility of achieving socialism through peaceful legislative reforms without violence. He observed that the Marxian prediction of increasing pauperization of the working class had been falsified—largely as a result of trade union activity, an extension of adult franchise, and burgeoning elements of a welfare state. This led him to believe in the desirability of a peaceful and gradual route of transformation to socialism (*Evolutionary Socialism*, 1899), as opposed to the revolutionary path with the potentially tyrannical dictatorship of the proletariat. Although the Bernstein philosophy drew sharp criticism from other SPD (Social Democratic Party) comrades in Germany like Karl Kautsky, Rosa Luxemburg and other Marxist revolutionaries, the revisionist philosophy eventually triumphed in SPD which abandoned the revolutionary approach.

Revolutionary vs democratic

Viewed from the above perspective, two dominant strands of socialism exist: revolutionary and democratic. The communists believe in orthodox Marxian approach of class struggle to overthrow capitalism, although the revolutions led by the communist parties till date have taken place only in countries with a largely feudal and agrarian setting, and not in mature capitalist economies. The first communist revolution took place in Russia when it was a semi-feudal country with only rudimentary industrial development, without the historical genesis of capitalism.

The standard position of classical Marxism considered capitalism as a necessary stage of historical development for the proletarian revolution. The hardship and suffering of the Russian people inflicted by the First World War created an opportunity for the Bolshevik revolution of 1917, leading to the collapse of the Tsarist regime, and takeover of power by the communist party led by Vladimir Lenin. Some classical Marxists like Rosa Luxemburg termed this new development as a dictatorship of the communist party rather than the Marxist vision of the dictatorship of the proletariat. Lenin had little faith in the revolutionary potential of the proletariat who he thought would only fight for better wages and living conditions when left to themselves. He believed in the need for a strong and disciplined vanguard party of revolutionaries. The communist revolution in China also took place in an agrarian economy under the leadership of Mao Zedong. The same pattern was seen later in countries like Cuba, Vietnam and North Korea which had an agrarian base. Capitalism continues to survive and evolve in industrially advanced countries in Europe and elsewhere, falsifying the Marxian theory of historical determinism which predicted the downfall of capitalism leading to socialism and eventually communism.

Contrary to the path of class conflict and violent revolution to attain socialist goals, the proponents of democratic socialism believe in peaceful and democratic means. The SPD which in an early stage comprised of both Marxist revolutionaries and evolutionary socialists eventually moderated its line through progressive reforms. The Labour party of Great Britain grew out of the trade union movement that focused on labor rights. Clause IV of the Labour Party constitution stressed national planning and nationalization of industry as a tool and called for common ownership of the means of production, distribution and exchange. The idea of social justice was put into practice through social protection measures for the disadvantaged, poor, unemployed and aged; guaranteed representation to industrial workers; trade union rights and collective bargaining; minimum working hours; unemployment benefits and other welfare reforms. Labor and the other under-classes held increasing amounts of power, as a result of the practice of periodic election and universal suffrage under democratic polity and the introduction of progressive tax and increasing social expenditure in favor of the underprivileged, old and unemployed. This helped transform the exploitative face of capitalism and brought improvement in the living conditions of the previously oppressed class. The institution of democracy and democratic practices empowered the working class (through voting power and other socio-economic rights and entitlements), which made the notion of class conflict less relevant.

The success of legislative reforms under the democratic constitution—in changing the exploitative character of capitalism and ameliorating the living conditions of the working class—prompted the leaders of the newly decolonized nations to follow a similar path to achieve humanitarian and socialist goals. Significantly, the leaders of the newly liberated nations with a long history of the struggle for independence, or against domestic autocracy and oligarchy, were committed to political liberty and economic justice. Exposed to the philosophy and principles of the French Revolution like liberty, fraternity and equality, and 'No Taxation without Representation' of the American War of Independence, they were not ready to abandon their faith in liberal democracy in favor of an autocratic one-party rule. Therefore, most of these newly independent nations and democracies followed the path of democratic socialism rejecting the path of class warfare.

In 1951, a worldwide association of democratic socialist, social democratic and labor parties was formed under the name of Socialist International (SI), which acted as a successor to the Labor and Socialist International and parallel to the Comintern of communist parties with antecedents in the nineteenth century. The SI has grown into an organization of 153 member parties from over one hundred countries. Many of them have been governing parties in their countries, mostly in Europe. From the South Asian region, the member parties are the Nepali Congress, Indian National Congress and the Pakistan Peoples' Party.

Historically, socialism has been associated with largely state-centric policies that stood for public control and management of basic industries and services, and socialization of the means of production. Setting up state-owned enterprises and nationalization of privately-owned industries, particularly the basic industries were part of post-war economic policy in both developed and developing countries. Therefore, socialist parties in both advanced and developing countries followed this policy of promotion of state-run industries and increased public expenditure for welfare activities. After 1945, the Labour government in Britain nationalized key industries like railway, steel and electricity. Most of the nationalized industries were natural monopolies. Large sections of banking, mining and shipping came under government control. A third of the British industry was taken into public ownership after the Second World War. India nationalized airlines, insurance and major banks, coal and oil industries after Independence. Pakistan, under Bhutto's Pakistan Peoples' Party (PPP) regime, nationalized all major industries including iron and steel, heavy engineering, petrochemicals, cement and public utilities. The phenomenon of nationalization, government control through proprietorship, strong regulation and control of industries in the post-war period was not confined to socialist economies.

One of the arguments favoring this policy was the belief that the profit generated therefrom would go to the state treasury for welfare spending and equitable distribution, rather than to private pockets further accentuating economic disparities. Moreover, it was also believed that the state-run industries would be managed in the best public interest generating externalities under public and social pressure. But with the passing of time, this experiment did not turn out to be satisfactory. Publicly owned entities were generally found to be suffering from political pressure, inefficiency, overstaffing and high production cost. They were not required to meet any efficiency criteria and were protected from competition. Huge losses accumulated by the public sector enterprises started placing a heavy burden on the treasury and the taxpayers, leading to increases in tax and public borrowing. Furthermore, restrictive policies imposed on the private sector due to excessive regulations drove away potential investors resulting in low investment and economic growth. In fact, the annual loss from public undertakings amounted to around four billion sterling pounds in England. This phenomenon gave impetus to the emergence of the Tory government of Margaret Thatcher, coming to power in 1979, which was committed to the policy of denationalization. Starting with the privatization of Jaguar, British Telecom, Cable and Wireless, British Aerospace and British Gas, the Tory government pushed the privatization policy aggressively, becoming an example for the rest of the world.

Shifting paradigm

The relative success of the pro-market policy and denationalization did not prevent the Labour Party from continuing the liberal economic policy after coming to power in 1997. Tony Blair's government further pushed the policy of state downsizing and privatization, with the intention of making industries more efficient and modern, with greater private sector access to the capital market and by employing modern management methods. The new policy of privatization generated huge revenue for the UK treasury while allowing tax cuts and creating an environment for other reforms.

The early influence on this policy of New Labour was the legacy of Anthony Crosland, a prominent socialist intellectual and Labour Party minister in the 1960s and 70s. His landmark book *The Future of Socialism* (1956) argued against Marxism and orthodox socialism of expanding public ownership. He questioned the rationale of classical socialist thinking favoring state ownership and control over the means of production. Alternatively, he advocated the end of poverty and improved public services as the priority objectives. He reformulated the old socialist thinking in response to the changing British society. This revisionist policy rejected the old view of socialism as state ownership of the means of production. His 'revisionism' pleaded for a market-oriented mixed economy with the central role of capitalism and entrepreneurship.

In 1959, Hugh Gaitskell, the leader of the Labour Party who lost the general elections, reached the conclusion that the party's policy of nationalization and collective ownership of the means of production had scared the voters away. He proposed to amend Clause IV of the original Labour Party constitution of 1918 that made a commitment to the 'common ownership' or nationalization of the means of production, distribution and exchange. Gaitskell failed, and the Labor party had to wait until 1995 to amend this clause under the leadership of Tony Blair.

The amended Clause IV removed the phrase 'common ownership of the means of production, distribution and exchange' drafted in 1917 by Sidney Webb, a great Fabian of the Labour Party's intellectual wing of the early days. Tony Blair went on to convey: '*What was mainstream leftist thinking in the early twentieth century had become hopelessly unreal, even surreal, in the late-twentieth-century world in which, since 1989, even Russia had embraced the market.*'[2] The new Labour Party declared itself to be a democratic socialist party that believed in creating '*the means to realize true potential in which power, wealth, and opportunity are in the hands of many, not the few.*' This revised thinking of the traditional postulates of socialism had its influence not only in Britain but across Europe and elsewhere, including South Asia.

The economy of India, following its Independence from the British rule, was guided by the socialist policy of Nehru, who had co-led the liberation movement. He espoused the cause of farmers and laborers against zamindars, landed interests and princely states. It followed the policy of mixed economy, considered to be superior to both capitalism and communism. Inspired by the philosophy of Fabian socialism and the Russian model of heavy industrialization, Nehru believed in the policy of a large public sector of basic industries and followed an inward-looking import substituting policy with excessive regulation and control over private sector potentials. Foreign capital and competition were discouraged, which prevented the country from reaping the benefits of technology and world-class competition. The government introduced land reform measures and nationalized major industries, banks and insurance companies. Under Indira Gandhi's premiership, the fourteen largest commercial banks in India were nationalized in 1969 to divert the credit flow to the neglected sectors. In the same year, she enacted the Monopolies and Restrictive Trade Practices (MRTP) Act, placing a ceiling on industrial assets that debarred industries from expanding the business.

After nearly four decades of experimentation, policymakers began to realize the need to check and reverse the state-centric policy. The reason for the same was the failure of the policy of suppressing economic liberty to not only generate reasonable economic growth but also to reduce poverty, especially in comparison to countries that had adopted a more liberal outward-oriented economic policy. The dismal performance of the Indian economy against various socioeconomic and human indicators was in sharp contrast to the achievements of East and South East Asian economies. The country started massive reforms in 1991 liberalizing the economy under Prime Minister Narasimha Rao—reversing the previously inward-oriented economic policy with central planning accompanied by extensive regulatory control over the economy—drawing appropriate lessons from the success stories of East Asian economies. The reform measures included the relaxation of equity limit on foreign investment, the abolition of restrictive trade barriers, removal of the industrial licensing system, privatization and disinvestment of public enterprises and others reforms related to taxation, foreign exchange convertibility and the banking sector.

Furthermore, the increasing prosperity of Communist China after 1978 following liberal economic reforms was another eye-opener. The reforms in China and the former Soviet Union to transition away from the traditional communist philosophy were landmark developments in shaping a new form of socialism based on private initiatives, market-based resource allocation and outward orientation of the economy. The communist revolution in both countries resulted in centrally planned economies under the dictatorship of the communist party. Chinese economic reforms spearheaded by Deng Xiaoping de-collectivized agriculture, fostered rural and urban private enterprises and opened up the economy to direct foreign investment. He also implemented price reforms, set up special economic zones and introduced corporatization of state-owned enterprises. The new policy led to phenomenal investment growth in China attracting an average of $12 billion foreign direct investment (FDI) annually until 2006, rising to US$135 billion in 2018. This unleashed the creative potential of Chinese entrepreneurship making the nation one of the fastest growing major economies, with an average annual growth rate of nine percent for decades. From an underdeveloped and an overwhelmingly agricultural economy, China's standing has now been elevated to that of a global economic power.

The new economic policy in China is called market socialism, while the Chinese leaders call it 'socialism with Chinese characteristics.' In the case of Russia, the reform program was launched after the fall of the Berlin Wall and the collapse of communism in the former Soviet Union in 1989, following which Russia committed itself to become a capitalist market economy. Under Boris Yeltsin, policy reforms included the legalization of private property, removal of price controls, promotion of competition and opening up of the economy to international trade and finance.

Privatization of state-owned enterprises (SOEs) was another phenomenon that swept the post-1990 world, especially in central and Eastern Europe. Towards the end of the millennium, more than 75,000 SOEs were privatized in more than a hundred countries in all continents.[3] The mass privatization program in Russia in the early 1990s transferred ownership of more than 15,000 factories via the voucher system. They accounted for two-thirds of the industrial output and 60 percent of the industrial workforce. The privatization drive also covered 85,000 small businesses, shops, restaurants and services establishments representing 70 percent of the national total. Everything from sawmills to rolls of barbed wire were auctioned off.[4] China also followed the privatization policy in a big way from the mid-nineties, as most of the SOEs were deeply in debt incurring huge losses; in fact, by 1994, close to half of the SOEs had zero or negative equity. As the firms were relying on 70-80 percent of bank credit, the banks were saddled with uncollectible loans of around US$200 billion, accounting for around a quarter of all outstanding bank loans. Between 1995 and 2005, close to 100,000 firms with 11.4 trillion RMB worth of assets were privatized, comprising two-thirds of SOEs and state assets, making China's privatization by far the largest in history. China adopted multiple approaches of privatizing SOEs; these included share-issue privatization, joint ventures with foreign firms, management buyouts and sales to outsiders.[5]

Concluding remarks

The character and nature of socialism has undergone a deep transformation with new developments and progress of human society since its origin two centuries ago. Capitalism has shed its murky, exploitative character of yesteryears after the introduction of universal suffrage, periodic elections, legislated welfare and progressive socio-economic reforms within a democratic polity. The enactment of trade union rights, collective bargaining, labor participation in management and other reforms—including the implementation of the minimum wage, social security, old age pension and other forms of social insurance—gave a human face to the capitalist order, rendering the Marxist dream of proletariat revolution irrelevant.

At the same time, the lack of political freedom under communism, in addition to its failure to uplift and grow the economy and improve the living conditions of the people at par with countries which adopted a market economy, created compelling conditions to revise their orthodox ideologies. The evolutionary and peaceful approach to achieve social democracy and set up a welfare state (within the framework of liberal democracy and market economy) received wide acceptance compared to the revolutionary approach of class warfare associated with the Marxist doctrine. Many previously communist regimes in Eastern Europe and the developing world with one-party rule have now transformed into liberal democracies and market economies. Similarly, the third-world liberal democratic countries that adopted state-centric policies with nationalization and state control of the means of production also shifted their policy towards market competition and capitalist development. Hence the imperative of the modern-day socialist approach is the combination of both political and economic democracy. There is an increasing realization that a market-oriented approach to generating wealth and achieving growth also enables it to redress social disparities and injustice, through fiscal redistribution and legislative reforms aimed at social protection.

Some important features of the modern day socialist society include equal work opportunities for everybody with rewards based on the result of their work and elimination of exploitation; social welfare and security with special assistance for the disabled to lead a dignified life; civil rights and freedom to all citizens through representative democracy; sustainable development and strategic planning through economic tools and indicative targets.

The reality of the twenty-first century is the narrowing of differences between capitalist and socialist systems, with a move towards a political economy paradigm that values individual freedoms and ventures, but calls on the state to check excesses in market-based outcomes. The role of the market is increasing in traditionally socialist economies; at the same time the role of the state in directing economic development outcomes, such as in the aftermath of the 2008 Global Financial Crisis, is increasing in capitalist economies. Capitalist and socialist systems are adopting features of each other based on social and economic imperatives, giving credence to convergence theory.

Highlighting the relevance of socialism even in modern times, the Italian philosopher Vittorio Bufacchi remarks,[6] 'When the Berlin Wall fell in November 1989, socialism was proclaimed dead and the triumph of capitalism was hailed as the end of history. Today though, things are much different. Socialism in the 21st century has never been in a better state of health.' As socialism is once again a global force to be taken seriously, it is time to assess what socialism is, and what it is not. Clarifying some of the misconceptions about both, Bufacchi says that socialism is not the annihilation of individual freedom under the diktat of impersonal, centralized state institutions. Socialism is not even against the market system—notwithstanding its distortion with potential for exploitation and injustice, as the state is empowered to regulate and control improper actions to ensure social justice. Neither is socialism driven by violent and vengeful revolution; instead, it is committed to democratic, gradualist and reformist policies. Contrary to what many think, Bufacchi asserts that socialism is not synonymous with strict equality or with coerced uniformity but stands against excessive inequality. The burgeoning model of socialism is liberal, democratic and market-oriented, but not market dictated.

Obviously, the essence of the two systems is to address each other's shortcomings. Brian Barry of the London School of Economics and Columbia University further clarifies that socialism does not mean the rejection of the market system, rather the core of its philosophy is to overcome the undesirable consequences of individual action and modify the market to accommodate the legitimate interest of people such as workers, consumers, and above all citizens.

The socialist thinking of the contemporary world is also interpreted as the third way political and economic philosophy whose essence is economic rationalism that combines the features of market-based economic order with redistributive policies. At the time of its refounding in 1951, the Socialist International had spoken of the Third Way, as distinct from American Capitalism and Soviet Communism. The philosophy received prominence in the early 1990s, the most notable practitioners being Tony Blair with New Labour in the UK, Bill Clinton with New Democrats putting the "people first" agenda in the USA, German SPD under Gerhard Schroder, and others including many leaders in the developing world. According to Anthony Giddens, the prominent third-way philosopher, this school of thought represents an attempt to transcend old-style social democracy and neoliberalism. The centrist approach utilizes the dynamism of the market but with the public interest in mind, involving the balance between regulation and deregulation, on a transnational, as well as national and local levels.[7] Elaborating the imperative for his country USA, consistent with the essence of third way and social democracy, the Nobel Prize -winning economist Joseph E Stiglitz pleads for Progressive Capitalism with the comprehensive agenda to restore growth and shared prosperity that would exploit the benefits of market while taming their excesses to ensure that market works for the people, not the other way around. The new social contract should involve the commitment that every individual has the opportunity to live up fully to his or her potential and every person's voice is heard in a democratic regime.[8]

Notes

1. Towler, Callum. (2015, December 21). 'Socialism' is 2015's most looked-up word – so what should its modern definition be? *New Statesman.* Retrieved from https://www.newstatesman.com/2015/12/socialism-2015-s-most-looked-word-so-what-should-its-modern-definition-be
2. The words had actually been written in an attempt to avoid a more Bolshevik language from the further Left of those days. See Blair, Tony (2010). *A Journey: My Political Life,* (p. 77). Alfred A Knopf: New York.
3. Nellis, John (June 1999). Time to Rethink Privatization in Transition Economies? *Finance and Development,* Volume 36, Number 2.
4. Edwards, Mike (March 1993). Russian Privatization and Oligarchs. *Facts and Details.* Retrieved from http://factsanddetails.com/russia/Economics_Business_Agriculture/sub9_7b/entry-5169.html
5. Gan, Jie (2009), Privatization in China, Experiences and Lessons. Hongkong University of Science and Technology. Retrieved from http://cn.ckgsb.com/Userfiles/doc/Privatization%20in%20China.pdf
6. Bufacchi, Vittorio (2017, October 17). The Rebirth of Socialism. *RTE.* Retrieved from https://www.rte.ie/brainstorm/2017/1011/911510-the-rebirth-of-socialism/
7. Giddens, Anthony (1998). *The Third Way: The Renewal of Social Democracy,* Chapters 1 and 4. Polity Press: Oxford, UK.
8. Stiglitz, Joseph E, *People, Power and Profits, Progressive Capitalism for the Age of Discontent.* Penguin Random House, UK, 2019.

Chapter Two

BP Koirala, Socialism and the Nepali Congress

BP Koirala was the first socialist leader of Nepal with international stature and a vision to democratize and modernize the country. He founded the Nepali National Congress in 1947, which merged with the Nepali Democratic Congress to become the Nepali Congress in April 1950. Immediately afterwards, the revolution of 1950 was started under his leadership against the feudal Rana oligarchy that had held absolute power in Nepal since 1846. The original declaration of the Nepali Congress was to establish democracy with an equitable social order in the country by fighting against the prevailing political oppression and economic exploitation under the Rana oligarchy. The end of the Rana rule in early 1951 was, however, followed by frequent changes in government where the king had an upper hand in the formation of the cabinet until March 1959.

After the end of the Rana autocracy, there was power-sharing between the Ranas and the Nepali Congress in the first government. This government did not last long because of mutual distrust and suspicion. The subsequent cabinet of Nepali Congress too was short-lived due to an intense internal power struggle and fragmentation among and within political parties that ultimately strengthened the hands of the monarch. Nepali Congress itself was split into two factions. The Interim Government Act—which was announced in April 1951 to provide a political framework for the country's governance—was further amended to consolidate the royal authority; the amendment restored the king to the position of a traditional monarch with sovereign power.

The evolving circumstances forced the Nepali Congress to announce the formation of United Democratic Front which launched Satyagraha in 1958 demanding the recognition of the principle of people's sovereignty, holding an early election and government formation with a popular mandate. The new development compelled the king to announce the general election in March

1959 which brought the Nepali Congress to power with an overwhelming majority under the leadership of BP Koirala. The first elected government in Nepal took office in May 1959 under his premiership.

Democratic Socialism

Influenced mainly by contemporary thinking of the nations, newly independent from colonial rule, with emphasis on political liberty, social justice and equality, the policy of the Nepali Congress was guided by socialist philosophy from its earliest days. This was reflected in its policy measures announced by their short-lived governments in the early 1950s. The formal announcement of its commitment to democratic socialism was made in its sixth general convention held in Birgunj in January 1956. For BP, the core human value is the principle of equality which can be attained by democracy and socialism. While democracy establishes political equality, socialism ensures economic equality. The convention declared its commitment to constitutional monarchy with parliamentary democracy where the cabinet will be accountable to popularly elected representatives. The other elements of BP's democratic plank included universal adult franchise, unicameral legislature, decentralized administration, fundamental rights without discrimination based on caste, creed, gender and tribe; independent judiciary, public service commission and auditor general; and abolition of hereditary feudal lords. On the economic front, the first emphasis was on land reform to improve the lives of farmers by restructuring ownership patterns and raising productivity. The main policy components were nationalization of Birta and forest land, abolition of Zamindari system, introduction of ceiling on land ownership and land redistribution to tillers. It was believed that the productivity of land would increase when its ownership is transferred to actual cultivators and tillers. It was government responsibility to provide other services like irrigation, improved seeds and easy credit by extricating the farmers from the clutches of usurious money lenders. Other policies included the consolidation of small landholdings, promotion of cooperative farming and state-funded farming on newly reclaimed land.

The Nepali Congress's policy document stated that improved living condition of farmers was also linked with the prospect of market creation for domestic industries. On industrialization, the emphasis was on encouraging domestic capital for the promotion of consumer goods and small and cottage industries. Large and basic industries including power, transport and mining sectors would be owned and managed by the government. In view of limited domestic savings, it would accept development assistance from friendly countries without compromising national sovereignty. The resolution also proposed the introduction of progressive taxation leading to the creation of a welfare state and improvement of monetary management to bring price stability. The other policy prescriptions mentioned in the document were universal and free primary education, road development, technical training and progressive labor laws to set the minimum wage and to facilitate the participation of workers in corporate management.

The commitments made in the resolution of democratic socialism at the Birgunj convention was largely reflected in the manifesto of the Nepali Congress prepared for the first-ever multi-party general elections held in Nepal in 1959. The party went on to win an overwhelming majority, securing seventy-four out of 109 seats in parliament.

In view of the party's socialist orientation and commitment to social democratic values since its formation, Nepali Congress had been participating in the meetings of Asian socialist parties since 1953, when its umbrella organization Asian Socialist Conference was established. The Nepali delegation to the first historic Yangon meeting of January 1953 was led by BP Koirala, comprising of KP Bhattarai, Sushila Koirala and Rajeshwori Prasad Upadhyaya as members. The meeting saw participation by international socialist leaders like Jayaprakash Narayan of India, Clement Attlee of UK, and Milovan Djilas and Aleš Bebler of Yugoslavia. In his address to the conference, Koirala interpreted socialism as a living doctrine and a way of life—rather than a mere economic philosophy to reduce poverty, exploitation and inequality—helping to liberate the society not just from orthodox conservative oppression, but also from new modes of communist suppression and autocracy.[1] BP Koirala also participated in the bureau meeting of the Asian Socialist Conference held in Tokyo in December 1954.

After the formal self-declaration as a democratic socialist party, the sixth general convention of the Nepali Congress passed a resolution authorizing the party central committee to formally become the member of the Asian Socialist Conference. Subsequently, it became a full member of the Asian Socialist Conference in October 1956, while participating in its second plenary meeting held in Bombay. Nepali Congress also hosted in Kathmandu the bureau meeting in March 1958 in which socialist parties from India, Pakistan, Burma, Vietnam, Indonesia, Israel, Lebanon and Japan participated. At the sideline of the silver jubilee occasion of Indian Socialist Party in 1959 in Bombay, the Asian Socialist Conference also held its working committee meeting in which BP Koirala was invited. As BP was unable to attend the meeting because of preoccupation with official work at home, Nepali Congress was represented by Shree Bhadra Sharma and Yogendra Man Sherchan with the message from BP. Shree Bhadra Sharma, later on, recalled in his memoir the loud applause to the message, along with the overwhelming accolades expressed in the meeting by all socialist leaders in honor of BP, who happened to be the only elected socialist Prime Minister in the region during that time.[2] Nepali Congress was awarded observer status by the Socialist International in 1960, and eventually full membership by the SI XX1 Paris Conference in 1999. Even when political parties were outlawed in Nepal by the king during the autocratic Panchayat regime, after his release from the prison BP was invited to address the 1980 Congress of the Socialist International in Madrid, and the 1981 Asia Pacific Socialist Conference in Sydney.

Progressive reforms

Genuine reforms aimed at greater social justice by helping the downtrodden and marginalized working class started in earnest only after the political change of 1951. When the first post-Rana government took power in 1951, the state of the economy was extremely rudimentary, with only 1.4 megawatts of power supply, one airfield, fifty-one miles of narrow-gauge railways, 50,000 hectares of irrigated land, one hundred post offices and 300 telephone lines. The education system comprised of one college, eleven secondary schools and 200 primary schools. A total of 649 hospital beds and fifty doctors represented the entire health system of the country. There was one financial institution in the form of Nepal Bank Ltd, a commercial bank. The national currency was only in partial circulation, as the Indian currency remained the dominant medium of exchange in the Tarai region. The economy was purely agricultural where feudal order prevailed. A few industries, which were established under the stimulus of scarcity conditions during and before the Second World War, existed in the border towns of Birgunj and Biratnagar. These consisted of two jute mills, a sugar mill, two match factories and a few food processing industries.

Against this backdrop of the poor state of the economy and the absence of modern institutions of governance, the priority of the new government was to create democratic institutions and lead socio-economic reforms to break from age-old feudal traditions.

One of the first acts of the post-Rana government led by the Nepali Congress was to announce a series of socio-economic reforms aimed at creating a new political-economy and a modern administration, effectively ending an extremely extractive feudal order. The measures included the abolition of the Jhara system and the practice of free state allowances and land to the Rana family and their favorites. The Jhara system represented the practice of state-arranged compulsory labor used for services such as transportation of arms and ammunition, food, military supplies, maintenance and repair of public works like road, canals, bridges and forts. The entire male population except for the members of the nobility and high officials were conscripted to render these services under state diktat. Another landmark announcement was the acceptance in principle to abolish Birta landholdings. Birta land was a state grant to private individuals for their subsistence and enrichment as a reward based on political, economic and religious patronage. As a first step, transfer of such land beyond twenty-five Ropani by sale or mortgage was outlawed. Other agrarian reforms included a guarantee of tenancy right to land cultivators. The policy stipulated that landlords could not extract more than fifty percent of the land produce from the cultivators, and the interest rate was fixed at ten percent.

The monopoly of the Rana family in high positions of government and army was brought to an end. A notification was issued requiring all government and government-supported schools to admit students of the 'untouchable' community. Civil services were reorganized into modern ministries and departments, and a meritocratic examination system was introduced to recruit civil servants. Singh Durbar, the massive government building used as the official residence of the Rana Prime Ministers was converted into the central government secretariat.

There was no practice of announcing the annual budget—an estimate of national income and expenditures—during the Rana regime. The state treasury was treated almost as a means of personal enrichment. Revenue surplus created by increasing revenue from sources like land revenue, sale of timber, customs duty and others and minimizing public spending was appropriated by the Prime Minister. Nobody, except the ruling beneficiary, quite knew how much was raised, spent, and stolen until 1951.

The end of the Rana regime saw the introduction of modern budgetary practices in Nepal. Suvarna Shamsher Rana, the first finance minister of Nepal representing the Nepali Congress, announced the first budget of Nepal. He detailed a statement of the government's financial position with all assets and liabilities inherited from the Rana regime. The total balance left over from the Ranas in the forms of gold, silver, coins and foreign currency was valued at eighty million rupees. He presented a budget of fifty-two and a half million of which twenty-two million represented the deficit to be covered partly from the reserves. While allocating the budget, priority was given to the construction of roads and airports, postal development and radio communication, and the promotion of health and education. The government announced a policy of mixed economy, promising space for private enterprises without allowing exploitation of any class or individual.

The decade following the overthrow of the Rana regime also witnessed the beginning of international assistance to Nepal. The United States started the US Operational Mission (USOM), the precursor of the USAID, to provide assistance in rural development, agriculture, health, education, malaria eradication and the ambitious Rapti Doon Valley Project that opened up the Chitwan district, allowing mass migration from the hills.

The Indian assistance started with the construction of Gauchar airport and Kathmandu-Raxaul highway. Assistance was also extended for irrigation, drinking water, and manpower training in Indian universities. Other external sources that started development partnerships with Nepal were the United Nations, People's Republic of China, Soviet Union and Switzerland. UN technical assistance focused on malaria eradication, dairy development, nurses training and geological surveys. The Swiss helped pioneer modern dairy development, and Chinese assistance was provided in the form of cash and commodities. The Soviet assistance started with the construction of a fifty-bed hospital. Even philanthropic entities like the Ford foundation assisted in cottage industries and handicrafts training.

Breaking the feudal order

After leading the Nepali Congress to a thumping victory in 1959, the charismatic BP Koirala hit the ground running with bold, progressive policies anchored in democratic socialism. His first economic priority was to break the backbone of feudal practice in landholdings that was characterized by large concentration of ownership in the hands of few, and exploitation of cultivators and tillers. The socialist orientation of the government policy was further articulated by Finance Minister Suvarna Shamsher in his budget speech of August 1959. The main objectives outlined were to increase the national income, bring a fundamental change in agriculture, redistribute wealth and reduce income disparities, solve the problem of unemployment and launch social welfare programs. The immediate task of the new government was to expedite the implementation of the First Five Year Plan started in 1956 and formulate a new Plan. A new Planning Board was created under the chairmanship of the Finance Minister, who was also the Planning/Development Minister. Given the limited planning capacity of the government, a negotiation was held with the Ford Foundation to enhance the technical capacity of the Planning Board. Thus, the formulation of the ambitious Second Plan began, aiming for a radical upliftment of the economy. The Second Five Year Plan, with an estimated outlay of Rs. 1,960 million, was proposed to start in 1962 from mid-July, with the objective of raising the national income by thirty percent and creating 500,000 jobs. Priorities were given to industrial projects, road building and agricultural production.[3]

To raise resources for the implementation of the government's periodic plans, a number of friendly countries and institutions including the US, India, China, Soviet Union, Great Britain, Switzerland, Australia, New Zealand and the United Nations were taken into confidence. In the presentation of the second annual budget in 1960, overtures were made to attract foreign investment in the form of aid and private investment. On May 18, 1960, Finance Minister Suvarna Shamsher signed an agreement with the United States, aimed at encouraging private American investment in Nepal by providing safeguards for such investments. On October 27, Prime Minister Koirala appealed to Indian businessmen and industrialists in Bombay to invest in Nepal, and assured them full guarantees and 'industrial peace for the next ten years.'[4]

Confronted with popular aspirations and demands, the government also focused on meeting the basic needs of the people in education, health transportation and communication services. A separate ministry was created to handle local development needs. The government launched a program to set up 2,200 primary schools throughout the country, ensuring at least one in each polling center. Out of this total, 1,600 were established in a single year. Another program to establish 109 hospitals and dispensaries was launched, at least one in each parliamentary constituency. District Development Boards headed by the

District Development Officers (DDOs) were set up in all districts to execute and expedite development work at the local level. Flagship road construction projects were begun to connect Banepa with Sindhuli, and Kathmandu with Hetauda (known as Kantipath), together with a number of other projects to improve connectivity between different parts of the country.

Along with mobilizing external assistance, the Congress government initiated reforms to mobilize domestic revenue by introducing new tax measures and widening the tax base. Taxes were introduced on income, urban property, foreign investment, trade profits and Birta land. Water taps and radio receivers were also required to pay user fees. The rates were modest and the revenue contributed a negligible amount, an estimated two and a half million rupees in total. Another scheme introduced to mobilize internal resources was the flotation of government bonds with five-year maturity (at an estimated value of twenty million rupees).

Furthermore, the Nepali Congress government in 1960 worked to bring about exchange rate stability and end the dual currency system prevailing in the country. The exchange rate was fixed after careful consideration and continued until 1966 when it had to be readjusted following the massive devaluation of the Indian rupee against other currencies. The Foreign Exchange Control enacted in 1960 prohibited foreign dealings in currency other than Nepali rupees except by authorized dealers under the strict conditions imposed by the Nepal Rastra Bank.

Bold measures and royal takeover

Pressed by the Congress party in the first Rana-Congress coalition, the abolition of the Birta system was agreed to in principle in 1951. The Birta land occupied more than one-third of the total farmland in the country, a large proportion of which was owned by the Rana family. The onus of translating this bold measure into legislation ultimately fell on the popularly elected Congress government. It lost no time in introducing the bill in the House of Representatives to convert all Birta land into Raikar. The bill became law in October 1959, within six months of the Party coming into power, converting all registered tenants into owners. Another important legislation passed in May 1960 was the abolition of the Rajya Courts, integrating their functions into regular courts. The Rajya system allowed the hereditary feudal rulers in some principalities in Western Nepal to have semi-autonomous authority in the maintenance of law and order and in the dispensation of justice. The government also nationalized all privately-owned forests.

These bold measures of the Congress government met with stiff resistance from the traditional forces that had vested interest in the old order. The charismatic and progressive image of the Prime Minister had been a matter of envy to the ambitious monarch who instigated opposition to the government policy. Organizations like *Jan Hit Sangh* (Public Welfare Union) sprung overnight inciting general strike in the Kathmandu valley to oppose new taxation and land reforms. A letter from the Palace secretariat responding to the petition from the Sangh openly supported the continuation of the agitation. A royalist-religious party named Karmabir Mahamandal led by Yogi Naraharinath incited people in the Gorkha region to oppose the Birta liquidation measure. Indeed, that the Yogi had links with the palace was an open secret.

The ill intention of King Mahendra towards the Koirala government was becoming amply clear as a result of these developments. The Prime Minister was, however, undeterred. Responding to the demonstration by the Sangh, he strongly defended in a public meeting on 11 December 1960 the progressive measures of the government, a replacement of old values by new ones in favor of the downtrodden people who had been suppressed for centuries.

Four days after this speech, the king dissolved the eighteen-month-old government, imprisoned the Prime Minister, cabinet members and party leaders. The king started direct rule abrogating the parliamentary constitution. Political parties were outlawed, and civil liberty and press freedom curtailed. The nation came under monarchial autocracy that lasted for three decades. Ironically, after a few years of the takeover, the royal regime gave continuity to some of the land reform measures announced by the Congress government. The Land Reform Act of 1964 had provisions including the fixation of land ceiling, guarantee of tenancy right to cultivators, fixation of maximum interest on agricultural loans and compulsory savings scheme. The measures were obviously aimed at gaining popular support and acceptability of the regime; nonetheless, the actual implementation of these progressive reforms was far from satisfactory, as it suffered from shortcomings and loopholes aimed at preserving the interest of the feudal elements close to the monarch.

Congress policy in the 1990s

The popular uprising in 1990 launched by the Nepali Congress, and subsequently aided by other forces including the communist parties, brought an end to the royal rule. An interim government was formed under the leadership of Congress President Krishna Prasad Bhattarai consisting of representatives from the Left Front, royal nominees and independents with the mandate to draft a new democratic constitution and hold a general election within one year. A new constitution was promulgated in time, the basic political elements of which comprised of multiparty parliamentary democracy and constitutional monarchy. The constitution guaranteed fundamental rights and declared Nepal a multi-ethnic, multi-lingual, democratic, sovereign and Hindu monarchial kingdom. The election held subsequently in May 1992 returned the Nepali Congress to power with 110 seats out of 205 in the House of Representatives. The party assigned its General Secretary, Girija Prasad Koirala, to lead the government as the Prime Minister.

When the new government took office, the economy was in poor shape with a GDP of Rs. 130.7 billion. Agriculture represented the principal economic sector accounting for more than 50 percent of Gross Domestic Product (GDP) and 81 percent of employment. Adult literacy stood at 40 percent and life expectancy at fifty-three years. Population with access to electricity and improved drinking water stood at 9 percent and 46 percent respectively. The total road length of the country comprised of 7,036 kilometers. There was no motorable road access to most hill and mountain districts of the country.

In the face of this weak economic reality, the government was confronted with rising expectations of the people. The task of the new government was also to modernize the economy in line with global developments while pursuing the goal of social justice and equitable development. The priority objectives of the Congress government as presented in the royal address and subsequently the budget in the joint session of parliament were as follows:

- Commitment to social justice in favor of the underprivileged, poor and destitute.
- Emphasis on meeting the basic needs of the citizens in rural areas such as drinking water, access roads, irrigation and environmental protection.
- Production growth with an emphasis on equitable distribution and productive employment opportunities.

- Emphasis on macro-economic stabilization, price control and revenue growth.
- Review of ongoing development projects in line with national priorities.
- Emphasis on investment-friendly policies in economic activities and disinvestment of state-owned loss-making commercial public enterprises.

A conspicuous paradigm shift in policy was the emphasis placed on private investment and market-friendly policies. A host of new legislations were announced to open various sectors of the economy to private, non-government and cooperative sectors. The government also pressed ahead with the decentralization of power to local bodies, off-loading of shares through open competitive bidding of some sick government industrial enterprises that had been a burden on the government treasury and restructuring of public expenditure in favor of the social sector. The details of the new reform measures undertaken by the post-Panchayat Congress government are described in the next chapter.

The Eighth Plan of Nepal (1992-97) prepared by the new government reiterated the commitment by highlighting that the development approach of the government would be guided by the philosophy of democratic socialism, the principal objective of which would be the amelioration of living conditions of deprived citizens through inclusive economic growth. The document further clarified that socialism, as conceived by the Nepali Congress, was not an orthodox form of statist socialism, where the government owned and dictated most aspects of production, distribution and exchange in the economy.

The Nepali Congress sought to establish its democratic socialist credentials by harnessing the potential of private initiatives to enlarge the size of the national economy before the distributionist functions could be assumed. The end goal of fostering social justice remained; however, the means for increasing production, creating jobs, and uplifting the socially and economically deprived demanded fresh approaches.

It was evident from the collapse of communism that the traditional state-directed socialism was no longer suited to the global scenario of the time. Concurrently, the Eighth Plan of the government also disapproved of the efficacy of the traditional trickle-down approach in ensuring proper distribution of development benefits to the lower rungs of the economic ladder. It called for targeted development assistance in areas and among people who were less likely to benefit from new-found economic momentum in the country. It observed that 'the experience of several developing countries has demonstrated the fallacy of the concept that a high economic growth rate automatically benefits the people.'

The new policy stressed the expansion of the government's role in the development of physical infrastructure and social sector, including education, health care and drinking water, institutional and technical improvements in agricultural systems, creation of employment opportunities for the rural population, alleviation of poverty and environmental protection. Private sector investment was encouraged in business and commercial sectors in a competitive environment. The policy emphasized the expansion of not just the private sector in a narrow sense, but creating an environment conducive to tapping and unleashing the creative energy of all sections of the society including non-government organizations, local authorities and grass-roots community organizations.

Understanding BP

Some aspects of the new policies, particularly those related to the promotion of the private sector and disinvestment in loss-making public enterprises, were interpreted by some critics as a deviation from the commitment to socialist philosophy of the Nepali Congress and its founder BP Koirala. They thought that the post-1990 economic policy of the Nepali Congress contradicted the socialist philosophy he propounded. This author had the privilege of engaging in long conversations with BP during the last days of his life that helped me to understand his thinking more closely. At the same time, a glance at the party resolutions and government actions under his leadership, and the views expressed by BP in various statements and interviews at different occasions enables one to understand his development philosophy and political vision.

According to BP, the essence of socialism is equality, both political and economic. Human society is not divinely ordained but created in the material world. Socialism aims to maximize human welfare and security. Representative democracy represents the political facet of equality that implies sovereign authority vested in the people and elected government, the main features of which are individual liberties including the right to form political parties, universal franchise and periodic election, a government accountable to parliament and the rule of law. On the economic front, socialism implies liberation from exploitation, poverty and injustice. Socialism is opposed to economic disparity and aims at ensuring decent living conditions for all. The attainment of this goal depends on the productive capacity of the economy, which is not created overnight. Therefore, the primary step towards socialism in an underdeveloped country like Nepal is an enhancement of production and income which calls for economic freedom to promote creativity and entrepreneurship. BP was adamant that 'abundant production' must precede distribution. He said, figuratively, that the goal is to distribute 'one glass of milk' each to all citizens, 'not a spoonful.' Socialism could never be seen as 'distribution of poverty.'[5] Quoting Marx, he considered capitalist development as a historical necessity to raise productive capacity. Differentiating socialism from communism, he once observed that socialism is communism *with* democracy, while communism is socialism without democracy. Given the contradictions between the two philosophies, it was obvious that communism and democracy in combination is not practicable in the real world. The essence of his remark, therefore, was to incorporate the positive elements of the two systems into a middle ground philosophy of democratic socialism.

For BP, given the extremely backward and poverty-stricken state of a predominantly rural Nepal, improvement in living conditions was paramount. He believed that any development that takes care of urban amenities and neglects rural people is no development.[6] Towards attaining the goal of uplifting the living condition of rural dwellers, his first priority was to destroy the feudal order, the traditional strength of which was based on land ownership. Therefore, he launched measures to break the exploitative production relation—institutionalized in various land tenure systems including the Zamindari, Birta and exploitative tenant-cultivator relationships—fight untouchability and social discrimination and adopt democratic values in politics. He further emphasized the basic needs of poor village folk, such as drinking water, rural access roads, small irrigation, primary health care and education. He often contrasted these needs with 'mega' development projects like big highways and international airports that may not have an immediate payoff for the poor. BP presented a 'middle-income' rural family akin to his own as a goal to strive for within fifteen years. He wanted, symbolically, to possess a milking cow, a pair of oxen, and access to basic socio-economic services including education and health care. Quoting a UNICEF report, he once told me that as 70 percent of diseases affecting children in Nepal were water-borne, socialism ought to start with a basic supply of potable water, not expensive hospitals.

BP Koirala was not an ivory tower idealist, but a practical politician who understood the dynamics of the modern world and how state-centric economies were faring worldwide. Unlike some contemporary thinkers, he did not believe in state control of the means of production, but on the creativity of individual. I was amazed by his knowledge of the poor productivity of collective farming in comparison to the highly productive kitchen farms in the Soviet Union of those days.

He was aware of the magic of incentives in economic life. In his view, socialism is a living doctrine, which should be suitably adjusted according to time and circumstances. He also declared that Nepal cannot accept the principle of socialism at the cost of individual liberty. Joshi and Rose, who had closely observed the developments of Nepal's politics and economy in the 50s and 60s and authored the classic book *Democratic Innovations in Nepal,* rightly said, 'BP was a pragmatic politician and his socialist policies and measures in Nepal was animated more by a pragmatic awareness of the country's problems than by the doctrinaire commitment to a partisan ideology.'[7] Therefore, the economic policy adopted by Nepali Congress in the 1990s was in general conformity to BP's pragmatic thinking to promote creativity and entrepreneurship of human mind, with the state performing the role based on its capacity and national needs in response to changing times circumstances.

Towards the end of his life, BP gravitated towards the philosophy of Gandhi and Schumacher and emphasized a village-based self-sufficient economy with a focus on intermediate technology and attainment of basic needs. He always prioritized the improvement of rural life with the use of intermediate technology, rather than sophisticated technology of the West in agriculture, to improve productivity with minimal investment. He opined that the economic philosophy based on Henry Ford's model of mass production, being emulated worldwide including in the Soviet Union, would exhaust the finite resources of Earth. He said with 6 percent of the global population, the US was consuming more than 30 percent of the resources of the earth. He considered this model unsustainable, hence gravitated towards an alternative development model based on Gandhian thought. This was the theme of his speech at a gathering at

Tribhuvan University, Kirtipur in the early 1980s. He expressed similar views at the Asia Pacific Socialist Conference in Sydney in 1981 and at Columbia University.

During my conversations with BP, I raised doubt about the feasibility of the Gandhian model for adoption by a small economy like Nepal in an interdependent world of today, when even a big country like India did not follow Gandhian economic thought. Gandhi himself chose Jawaharlal Nehru, who had no faith in his mentor's development philosophy, as his political successor and the leader of independent India. Being a pragmatic thinker and leader, BP did not claim his new thinking to be the final truth, but rather only an idea to be placed as an agenda for discussion among development practitioners and experts. He urged that his ideas be vetted and scrutinized for their viability and utility.

It may be noted that the 1970s saw the publication of the Club of Rome's controversial *Limits to Growth* report and the emergence of new thinking such as the Triage and Life Boat theories. These raised questions about the Earth's capacity to support the growing needs of mankind, emphasizing the need to exercise restraint on unbridled growth and human aspirations for sustainable development without jeopardizing the interest of future generations. This view had also entered into the development debate of the time.

The essence of BP's views was being against the pursuit of unrestrained growth driven by excessive greed, joblessness and disproportionate use of the Earth's finite resources leading to unsustainable and irreversible consequences. This concern is shared by the world today which is facing the problem of climate change and other negative implications of fossil-fuel propelled industrialization.

In hindsight, it could be argued that he was prescient in anticipating a development-environment trade-off. He foresaw the era of Sustainable Development that we live in today. He would have affirmed the global consensus that the course of today's development must not jeopardize the interest of future generations. He would have endorsed mandatory restrictions on greenhouse gas emissions through various means to protect humanity from the existential threats posed by global warming and the degradation of ecosystems.

Notes

1. Basnet, Purushottam (2066 v.s.). *Nepali Congressko Aitihasik Prarup*, (pp. 445-46). Kathmandu.

2. Adhikari, Surya Mani (2056 v.s.). *Nepali Congressko Itihas*, (p. 340). Kathmandu: Bhundipuran Prakashan.
3. Joshi, Bhuban Lal, and Rose, Leo E. (2004). *Democratic Innovations in Nepal; A Case of Political Acculturation*, (p. 350). Mandala Publications: Kathmandu.
4. Joshi and Rose. Ibid. Quoted from *The Hindustan Times*. (2006, October 28).
5. Koirala, B. P. (2066 v.s.). *Garibi-Kangaliko Bitaran Samajbad Hoina*. In P. Giri (Ed.), *B P Koirala: Rajnitik Abhilekh*. Kathmandu. This was based on Yagya Bahadur Thapa's interview with B. P. Koirala for Kaski district Nepal Vidyarthi Sangh's magazine in 1980.
6. See BP Koirala's last interview with Bhola Chatterjee. In Sushil Koirala (Ed.), (1982). *B.P Koirala: Democracy Indispensable for Democracy*. Kathmandu.
7. Joshi and Rose. Ibid. (p. 310).

Chapter Three

Economic Reforms and Impact

The failure of the inward-oriented and state-centric economic policy in promoting growth and reducing poverty—compared to the progress made by economies following outward-oriented strategies—encouraged the start of liberal reforms beginning in the 1970s across the developing world. Chronic crisis in some state-dominated economies and the collapse of the Communist bloc at the end of the 80s gave further momentum to this reform process. There was a renewed focus on the primacy of individual economic rights and freedom, liberal foreign investment, the rule of law, an increased role of the government in the social sector, macro-economic stability and regulation of unfettered commerce.

South Asian overview

In the aftermath of Independence, South Asia's dominant economies—India and Pakistan—adopted state-centric policies. To sustain an import substitution strategy, both the governments ran industries, erected high tariff walls and introduced a web of permits, licenses and other regulatory measures to maintain tight control in the production and distribution of goods and services. Leaders in the subcontinent who were exposed to Fabian socialism, and were also awed by Soviet-style central planning, aimed to match political independence with economic self-reliance. Even smaller economies like Nepal which had never come under British rule adopted a similar inward-looking model of development between 1950 and 1980. In hindsight, when compared with East Asian economies, this inward-looking economic model failed to promote high growth and raise the living conditions of the masses. East Asian countries like South Korea, Taiwan, Hong Kong and Singapore which followed a market-oriented open-economic policy emerged as 'Asian economic tigers. They achieved rapid growth following the economic boom and graduated to the status of developed countries within a single generation. Subsequently, after the late 70s, unnerved by imminent crises and the example of their peers, South Asian economies were forced to revise their development paradigms.

Sri Lanka is credited with being a pioneer of economic reforms in South Asia. In 1977, through IMF assistance, Sri Lanka brought together a stabilization package coupled with structural measures in trade and finance. Nepal started the stabilization and structural-adjustment program in the mid-80s in response to the precarious situation threatening fiscal and monetary viability. Bangladesh initiated similar programs in 1987, which continued well into the 90s. Pakistan saw a macroeconomic and structural-adjustment program implemented in 1990 that further accelerated in 1993.

The most transformative reforms in South Asia were undertaken in the largest economy, India, after the assumption of power by Narasimha Rao in 1991 in response to an unprecedented balance of payments crisis.[1] The package of reforms included a stabilization phase where government expenditures were reined in, followed by a structural-adjustment phase which removed controls and restrictions through deregulation and privatization. The licensing system and public sector monopolies in several industries ended, and automatic approval of Foreign Direct Investment (FDI) was introduced for several sectors. Furthermore, import and export policies were liberalized. Such historic reforms in an economy which accounted for about 80 percent of the regional GDP provided further impetus to the acceleration of reforms elsewhere.

Growth in India had actually started picking up in the 1980s. This uptick can be traced to the economic reforms carried out under Rajiv Gandhi's administration in the mid-80s when he freed up capital goods imports, started rolling back the 'license raj' and promoted the growth of telecommunications and software industries. Just three decades prior to this, the country's growth rate averaged 3.5 percent, with per capita income growth rate of a meager 1.3 percent.

Despite possessing a rich cultural heritage and immense potential, South Asia was an economic laggard in the twentieth century. The region with 24 percent of the world's population accounted for 40 percent of all the people living in extreme poverty, and generated only 1.3 percent of the world income in 1995. The *Human Development in South Asia Report 1997* authored by the late Mahbub Ul Haq characterized the region as the poorest, the most illiterate, the most malnourished, and the least gender-sensitive—indeed, the most deprived region in the world. He further lamented that the neglect of basic social services and mass poverty went hand in hand.[2]

Today, South Asia is a region on the move; in recent years, it has consistently been the fastest-growing region in the world. A large share of the credit for this burgeoning economic dynamism goes to the economic reforms that liberalized the economy and unleashed the forces of private capital, entrepreneurship and creativity. After decades of stagnation, it was the success of export-led development strategies across East and Southeast Asia that served as a model for South Asia. Despite sub-regional differences, the current regional growth rate in South Asia is around 7 percent, led mainly by the robust growth of the Indian economy. Unlike other regions, the growth in South Asia is largely internally driven where export accounts for only around 10 percent of the regional GDP. On the other hand, East Asia's export accounts for 20 percent of its GDP and represents an important driver of growth. In Europe and Central Asia, the ratio is even higher, exceeding 30 percent of GDP.

This growth has predictably made a mark on human development and poverty reduction: South Asia reduced its extreme poverty rate from over 47 percent in 1990 to 12 percent in 2015, which shows that the region is a major contributor to sustained poverty reduction worldwide. South Asia's share of the world's poor has now gone down from 40 percent in 1995 to 33 percent in 2017. According to the *Human Development Report 2015*, the growth rate in Human Development Index (HDI) during 1990–2014 in South Asia was 1.4 percent, the highest among all regions. The region's potential for accelerated growth in the short to medium term is now widely recognized, which also translates into continued poverty reduction. Between 1990 and 2015, the world experienced a drop of 25 percent in extreme poverty, against a 35 percent drop in South Asia.[3]

Reforms in Nepal

After fits and starts in the mid-80s, economic liberalization gained meaningful momentum after the successful People's Movement of 1990 which ended the three-decade-old Party-less Panchayat monarchial autocracy. The liberalization of the economy thus followed the nation's liberalized polity. The first elected government of Nepali Congress in 1991, led by Girija Prasad Koirala, under the new democratic constitution vowed to place Nepal on a path of rapid economic change. Through liberal reforms, it emphasized macro-economic stability, increased national production, development of backward areas and social justice in favor of the underprivileged. The liberal economic policy of the new democratic government underscored the role of private and non-government sectors and represented a paradigm shift from the excessively regulated economic regime of the past with state control in economic and social spheres.

Countering the allegation of incompatibility of the new policy shift with the philosophy of democratic socialism advocated by the Nepali Congress, the Eighth Plan document (prepared immediately after assuming power) stated that the new liberal policy was aimed at not just promoting the private sector in a narrow sense, but creating an environment to allow the unleashing of the initiative and energy of all sections of the society including non-governmental organizations, cooperatives, local bodies and grassroots organizations.[4] The declared objective was the amelioration of living conditions of deprived citizens by increasing production, creating employment and launching special programs to uplift the socially and economically marginalized.

The Eighth Plan committed itself to dismantling the overbearing regulatory edifice of the past. The principle role assigned to the government was in the development of physical infrastructure and social services such as health care, education, drinking water, environmental protection, social security and poverty alleviation. The government would also create conditions for the private sector to flourish. Through taxes and job creation, this would further the aim of achieving the democratic socialist objective.

The first wave of reforms in the early 90s focused largely on macro-economic challenges including stabilization measures, trade, industry, monetary and fiscal reforms. The restrictive trade regime of the past through tariff walls, quantitative restriction, foreign exchange control and licensing was dismantled. The tariff structure was rationalized by reducing peak tariff rates from 225 percent in 1991 to 110 percent in 1994. A large number of tariff slabs were consolidated into only six clusters by the Finance Act of 1994. The practice of setting quotas on the import of consumer goods and foreign exchange auction for import of raw materials was terminated. All imports except for those in the negative list were placed under open generalized licensing. Facilities of duty drawback, bonded warehouse and a simpler documentation system were introduced to facilitate exports.

The dual foreign exchange rate in practice was brought to an end with the introduction of full convertibility in the current account in 1993, thus relaxing the government's stranglehold over foreign currency. Other allied reforms included allowing commercial banks to maintain foreign exchange accounts abroad and permitting Nepali citizens to maintain foreign exchange accounts of their earnings in local banks.

Sweeping changes took place to remedy the maladies in the tax system which suffered from low elasticity, a narrow tax base and problems of administrative arbitrariness. The most important policy reform in taxation was the bold introduction of the Value Added Tax (VAT) in 1997 which caused widespread controversy, criticism and market shut-down for several days. Today, the VAT is the backbone of Nepal's public revenue, accounting for more than one rupee for every four rupees raised.

Reforms were made in excise, customs and income tax as well. The excisable items were brought down from thirty-eight in 1991 to six in 1996. The excise administration based on physical control gave way to a system of self-removal. The income tax rate, as well as the number of slabs, were reduced both at the corporate and personal levels; only two rates remained. Another landmark legislative action was the Income Tax amendment bill of 2002 which brought all income tax provisions under a single umbrella, broadening the tax base by eliminating various exemptions and tax holidays and introducing capital gains tax. The bill encouraged self-assessment and offered a liberal deduction system that allowed for carrying losses forward or backwards. To strengthen the tax administration, all inland tax offices were brought under the Inland Tax Department, revenue offices were fully computerized and the customs offices started using Automated System of Customs Data (ASYCUDA).

The banking system was dominated by the public sector even though three private joint-venture banks had been permitted to operate since 1985. Following the reforms in the early 90s, there was a massive expansion of banking and financial institutions in the private sector. Reform measures included the raising of the minimum capital requirement, introducing call money market to facilitate inter-bank transactions, deregulation of the interest rate, partial offloading of shares of publicly-owned banks and finally the standardization of regulatory norms with respect to loan classification, provisioning requirements, liquidity, capital adequacy and discounting of treasury bills. Steps were also undertaken to strengthen the regulatory and supervisory capacity of the central bank and to build a strong banking and non-banking financial sector. New legislations were enacted to improve the legal and judicial aspects of the financial system, improve accounting and auditing standards and to promote financial discipline.

One component of the reform program was the restructuring of the two ailing government banks that accounted for 60 percent of total deposits. Services of expatriate management teams were procured to execute the restructuring and proposed reforms in these banks. The reforms in the capital market were carried out with the enactment of legislation to create a regulatory body. The Securities Board as a regulatory body was established in June 1993, as was the Nepal Stock Exchange for trading in January 1994. The stock exchange provided a trading floor for secondary and primary issues, creating opportunities for common citizens to invest in companies by buying shares.

Deregulation in the industrial sector started with the codification of the Industrial Enterprise Act in 1992 that abolished licensing to set up industries (except those related to defense and with the potential of causing an adverse impact on health and environment). The new arrangement dealt a death blow to those profiteering from the sheltered market for certain goods by restricting new entry through cronyism. This helped to eliminate the deep-rooted rent-seeking opportunism embedded in a discretionary license system which had been an important source of bureaucratic corruption.

The Foreign Investment and Technology Act of 1992 was another landmark legislation that allowed 100 percent foreign investment in industries, provided guarantees against nationalization, and defined terms and conditions for repatriation of profits and proceeds from the sale of investment assets.

The hydropower sector was opened up to domestic and foreign private investment. The Act was further amended in 1996 paving way for foreign investment in all areas including the services sector except those in the negative list. A 'One Window' mechanism was established to provide all government-related services including taxation, foreign exchange and utilities. The state monopoly in telecommunications and aviation sectors was also ended by allowing domestic and foreign direct investment. These reform measures including the enactment of new legislation were intended to remove hurdles to start business and encourage investment, changing the government's role from being a 'process stopper' to 'process facilitator' where they treat businesses like businesses treat their customers.[5]

Economic reforms also comprised of a review of government-owned enterprises particularly those incurring heavy losses and absorbing a disproportionate share of domestic credit. They posed a budgetary burden due to excessive regulations, inefficiency, over-staffing and poor management. The cumulative loss of these state-owned enterprises amounted to more than eleven billion rupees in 1991.[6] The privatization policy was announced to set the criteria for selecting enterprises and methods of privatization. Soon, legislation was enacted to elaborate on the modalities, process, and institutional arrangements—such as the formation of the privatization committee representing all stakeholders including the opposition party in parliament—to take policy decisions on privatization proposals. To ensure transparency, a press release was made mandatory at every step of the privatization process. Three enterprises were privatized in the first stage and seven in the second stage. By the end of 2003, twenty-four enterprises were either privatized or liquidated using various modalities depending on the nature of the concerned entity. The modalities included a public sale of bulk or partial shares, management contracting or leasing of assets through open competitive bidding. In the case of fully privatized enterprises, provision was made to sell 25 percent of shares to the general public and 5 percent to the employees mandatorily. The policy of privatization of bulk share or management contract was executed with respect to only those enterprises that could operate in a competitive market.

Other policy reforms

These economic measures were accompanied by other reforms in administration, public expenditure restructuring, and decentralization to improve overall governance. The Administration Reform Commission constituted in 1992 identified deficiencies in the prevailing administrative structure and systems and made far-reaching recommendations. These included limiting the government functions, restructuring ministries, departments and government offices, increasing the delegation of decision-making power to lower levels and improvement of government working procedures and financial regulations, corruption control and human resource management. The most prominent recommendation was to cut down the size of civil service by 25 percent, from 102,744 to 77,000. Many of these recommendations were implemented. A new phase of administrative reform was started in 2003 with the objective of making the civil service more accountable, efficient and transparent.

These initiatives included the restructuring of public expenditure to be more in favor of the social sector, infrastructure and rural development. Emphasis was given to expand access of rural areas to basic infrastructure facilities including road, electricity, irrigation and other social services. Nepal Army was also mobilized to expand road access to remote districts of the country. The primary health care network was expanded to cover all of the approximately 4,000 village development committees. The increased budgetary allocation in the education sector was channeled to expand primary and secondary education to ensure easier access in all remote areas.

The government also formed the Public Expenditure Review Commission to streamline government expenditure by minimizing unproductive administrative expenses. Based on the recommendation of the Commission, the number of government offices was reduced at the central, regional and local levels through closure, amalgamation and restructuring. Some centrally administered services were transferred to local authorities. Legislation was brought into effect in 1991 and 1999 to institutionalize, regulate and empower the village, municipal and district-level bodies with devolution of fiscal and administrative authority vis a vis the delivery of basic services. Local bodies were empowered to collect land revenue and other local taxes, as part of the fiscal decentralization scheme. Cash grant was provided to local bodies to launch development activities at their discretion. A Rural Development Fund was created to provide 70 percent matching funds for projects chosen and managed by local users and contributed up to 30 percent by themselves in the form of labor participation or cash. This was aimed to enhance local participation and management in rural development in partnership with local authorities, private and non-government organizations. The most prominent sector where the participatory approach was applied and extended was in the field of forest management by local communities for conservation and sustainable use of the resources. Leasehold forestry program also was introduced with the aim of supporting the livelihood of people living below the poverty line.

The investment pattern of the government expenditure was also influenced by the Agriculture Perspective Plan (APP) that recommended the concentrated investment in a package of selected priority inputs. These comprised of controlled year-round irrigation, a grid of agricultural roads, rural electrification, fertilizer, technical know-how and extension services, with the larger objective of modernizing and commercializing the country's subsistence-based agriculture. The APP initiated by the National Planning Commission in 1993was completed after two years of rigorous exercise by experts from APROSC under the guidance of an internationally reputed agricultural economist John Mellor. The Plan aimed at starting a technology-based green revolution to reduce rural poverty and create conditions for economic prosperity. It had also proposed separate strategies for Tarai and hill agriculture, and high-value seeds, horticulture and livestock products and basic food.

Various special programs were launched for poverty alleviation and upliftment of target groups including scheduled tribes and classes, remote and backward region, Kamaiyas, the historically neglected and oppressed, the downtrodden, women, and the old, the handicapped and victims of natural calamities. To encourage the Dalit community to send their children to school, a monthly stipend was provided from 1995 to every Dalit child going to government primary school. A similar arrangement was made to encourage girls to join schools in economically weak and deprived communities and in districts where girl education remained low. Various schemes of stipend for students (including those of the marginalized caste groups) up to secondary level and for meritorious students up to higher education have also been provided for. Provisions such as the payment of monthly cash allowance to senior citizens above 70, widows, handicapped, and free healthcare and medical services medical care to senior citizens, disabled and helpless people were started as part of the social security measures. Provision was also made for maternity allowance during the delivery period and for food supplements for malnourished children and lactating mothers of economically deprived families. In recent years, the universal health insurance scheme against thirty-nine diseases has been launched in phases. Initially started on a pilot basis in three districts, it now covers nearly a million households in thirty-nine districts. Additionally, there is a provision for cash subsidy for low-income citizens suffering from fatal diseases relating to heart, cancer, kidney, Parkinson's, Alzheimer, spinal injury and head injury.

Similarly, other forms of target-oriented poverty alleviation programs were begun to create income opportunities for economically deprived communities and districts. The programs include the Poverty Alleviation Fund supported by the World Bank, the chain of micro-credit institutions targeted at the poorest of the poor and women based on the principle of group liability and various other subsidized credit schemes such as the Small Farmers Bank and youth self-employment scheme. A scheme for 'one family one job' was started on a pilot basis for the country's most remote and backward Karnali zone from the fiscal year 2006/07; the objective was of giving relief to families unable to get job opportunities anywhere—including those from self-employment and development and construction projects carried out by the government. Such families would be provided with an allowance equivalent to minimum cash wage for a hundred days in a year.

The liberal democratic polity of the post-Panchayat era thus helped to reduce the grip of government regulations over economic and social activities. The social sector was made much more open to non-governmental and community-based organizations whose access, flexibility and creative energy were deemed suitable for service delivery at the local level. The cooperative sector and microcredit organizations were encouraged through new legislation as a means of promoting income-generating activities in rural areas. The government role shrank in production and other business activities but became much wider in extending education, health and other basic facilities, infrastructural development, antipoverty programs, upliftment of the deprived and marginalized communities and environmental protection. This was made possible mainly because of the increasing internal revenue generated from the growing economy that resulted from the new policy shift. Furthermore, the disinvestment of loss-making state enterprises released the government money previously expended in them to be used afterwards in priority sectors. Emphasis was also placed on maintaining macroeconomic stability and reducing budget deficit through greater mobilization of internal resources and better expenditure management. Another notable policy development was the implementation of a gender-responsive budget since 2006/07. Nepal is considered as one of the pioneering third world countries in pushing this concept in budget implementation.

Impact of reforms

The broad set of reforms aimed at reducing poverty through market reforms, investment in the social sector and target oriented social welfare and security programs made a positive impact on the economy. The growth rate in the 90s accelerated to around 5 percent, which was and still remains the highest decadal average recorded in Nepal's economic history. The non-agricultural sectors grew as the economy became open and diversified. Improvement was recorded in macro and fiscal indicators. Overall investment ratio increased to 23 percent of the GDP from 20 percent of the preceding decade, attributed mainly to increased private investment. Industrial investment picked up resulting in an increased share of the manufacturing sector to reach a peak of nearly 10 percent of GDP. The number of industrial enterprises including direct foreign investments registered in the Department of Industry rose significantly in the 1990s. The fiscal year 1992/93 witnessed the establishment of 606 industries with employment generation of 89,351 jobs, a record in Nepal's industrial history of recent decades. In the decade of nineties, the exports to GDP ratio increased from six to fourteen percent, and export to import ratio from 30 to around 50 percent. Gross domestic savings rose from 10.5 percent to 15 percent in 2001. The static occupational structure of the economy with heavy dependence on agriculture started declining from 81 percent of the population in 1981 to 66 percent in 2001. Reforms in the financial sector increased competition and efficiency in the banking sector, but also expanded, diversified and deepened the reach of the middle class and the poor to modern banking services. New services including the issuance of debit and credit cards, Automated Teller Machines (ATMs) along with a variety of deposit and loan options were introduced. This led to increased mobilization of public savings in the banking system together with a dramatic increase in the access to capital financing for the private sector.

Despite a promising start, the positive impact of the sweeping reforms on investment and growth was cut short with the onset of political turbulence and instability. The Maoist insurgency started in 1996 and intensified after 2001, leading to a serious deterioration of the security situation across large parts of the country. Nepal passed through one of the most tumultuous periods in its modern history with a series of unstable governments, widespread violence, suspension of democratic institutions and royal takeover in October 2002. Growth momentum slowed and the investment climate suffered from lack of security, labor unrest and work disruptions due to the civil conflict. Furthermore, the phasing out of quotas for the export of garments under the WTO Agreement on Textiles and Clothing (which ended the Multi-fiber Arrangement) resulted in a rapid decline of Nepal's major export.

Peace returned following the start of negotiations and political compact reached with the Comprehensive Peace Agreement and subsequent passing of an interim constitution. This brought some normalcy but the expected peace dividend did not materialize because the political transition was protracted. It took about eight years with two constituent assembly elections to draft and announce the constitution of federal democratic republican Nepal in 2015. The post-conflict transitional period after 2006 saw ten Prime Ministers with ten governments, mirroring the scenario of the period after the mid-90s. Furthermore, the two devastating earthquakes in April 2015, followed immediately by an undeclared trade blockade from the Indian side that lasted four and a half months resulted in a dismal economic growth rate of near zero percent in 2015-2016.

In the troubled period of armed conflict and the protracted transition, meaningful reforms could not be continued or initiated. The country began witnessing an epic outmigration of young citizens, pushed away by conflict, turbulent politics and limited domestic job opportunities, and lured by a commodities-fueled boom in the Middle East and East Asia. The increasing labor migration is a phenomenon that was also enabled by a liberal passport and migration regime since the mid-90s. Prior to that, travelling abroad was extremely difficult for common citizens because of a restrictive passport policy.

A decadal growth average of around 4 percent in the 2000s was lower than that of peer economies, making Nepal an economic laggard in the region. The latest data of the year 2017/18 shows that the share of manufacturing has plunged to 5.4 percent of GDP. The export sector slowed down while imports have ballooned, resulting in the unprecedentedly high trade deficit relative to the size of the economy. Fueled by economic reforms of the 90s and rising remittance inflows, the size of the services sector has grown dramatically to account for over half of GDP, followed by agriculture which contributes less than a third.

Despite sluggish investment in manufacturing, there has been a remarkable surge of private investment in education, health, tourism, telecommunications, hydropower and aviation. After the opening up to the private sector, there has been an increase in private investment in sectors like electricity, telecommunications and civil aviation which were previously state monopolies, treated as commanding heights of the economy. The latest data show that the private sector accounts for about half of power production and telecommunication services of the country. In civil aviation, around one and a half dozen airlines are in operation accounting for 95 percent of domestic air traffic. The growth of these sectors has not only helped in improving the socio-economic lives of the people but also contributed significantly to government revenue making an increased investment in priority social sectors possible.

Nepal's revenue to GDP ratio which was 9 percent in 1991 currently stands at around 24 percent, the highest in South Asia. As a result, the actual reliance on external assistance has declined from around one-third of annual expenditure in the early 90s to around 12 percent at present; the level of indebtedness remains low. The total public borrowing currently stands at 30 percent of GDP of which external debt represents around 60 percent. The foreign exchange reserve stood at around US$10 billion in 2018, sufficient to cover the import of goods and services for nearly eight months. A few years back, the reserve had reached a level sufficient to cover up to eleven months of imports.

The forestry sector has undergone an important transformation, particularly with the dramatic expansion of the community sector throughout the country. By mid-July 1917, the number of forests managed by local communities stood at approximately 20,000, covering the total forest area of 1.9 million hectares. The total households involved in the management of forests numbered 2.5 million.[7] The total area covered by 7,500 leasehold forests is estimated at 4,300 hectares made available to 72,000 households. The success of these programs, particularly the community forestry scheme has contributed in transforming the landscape of most hills into green land that had previously suffered from forest denudation, excessive landslides and soil erosion leading to the unwanted flow of topsoil. This led to a situation where the country was earning the notorious reputation of being an environmental hotspot with fragile mountains.

Despite the slowdown in economic growth in the 2000s, momentum continued with respect to poverty reduction and social sector development. In the education sector, the number of primary schools increased from 17,842 in 1990 to 35,211 in 2017, and the secondary schools from 1,959 to 9,171. The net enrollment ratio at the primary level stood at 97 percent and at the secondary level (class 11-12) at 44 percent, with an equal ratio between boys and girls, in 2017. In the higher education, the total enrollment of students in different universities and affiliated colleges stood at 453000, and the production of graduates at 82000 in that year. The enrollment in medical and engineering colleges reached approximately 45000 in 2017 from around 1600 in 1990. The production of medical and engineering graduates at various levels of higher education from Tribhuvan University alone numbered 2000 and 2400 respectively. The total number of medical specialists registered in Nepal Medical Association stood at 6137.

Significant progress in the health sector is reflected by the reduction of maternal mortality rate from 53.9 persons to 23.9 per 10,000 births, under-5 child mortality from 158 to 30 per 1,000 live births and total fertility rate from 5.3 to 2.10 between 1991 and 2017.

Although the value of its human development index in 2017 was only 0.574 lower than the South Asian average of 0.638, it is ranked higher than Afghanistan and Pakistan. Nepal's average life expectancy at birth is 70.6 years, higher than the South Asian average of 69.3 years. The infant mortality rate per 1,000 live births has come down from 106 in 1990 to 28 in 2017, lower than that of India, Bangladesh, Pakistan and Afghanistan and the overall SAARC ratio. The progress made in the past decades in reducing under-5 child mortality is also noteworthy.[8] Nepal attained almost all of the Millennium Development Goal targets ahead of schedule; it is ranked twenty-second among seventy-seven developing economies in the Inclusive Development Index of the World Economic Forum (2018). According to the 2017 World Hunger Index released by International Food Research Institute, Nepal holds the top position among South Asian countries in hunger reduction due to a sharp decline in undernourishment, child stunting and child mortality. The Human Development Report of 2010 ranked Nepal as one of the top ten fast movers globally in non-income human development index because of impressive progress in health and education despite modest income growth.

Nepal's consumption-based poverty rate stands at below 20 percent, a sharp drop from 49 percent 25 years ago. The headcount survey between 1996 and 2011 shows poverty reduction at an annual average of 2.2 percent, one of the fastest regionally. Multidimensional poverty has also declined by half between 2006 and 2014. The consumption of the bottom 40 percent grew almost twice faster than the consumption level of the top 60 percent showing progress in shared prosperity. The World Bank Country Memorandum of 2017 terms Nepal as a 'leader in poverty alleviation, but a laggard in growth.' Together with sustained public spending over three decades, an important factor behind the modest growth but sharp poverty reduction and improved living conditions has been the export of human capital and the money remitted back home. Among populous countries, Nepal is the largest recipient of remittances relative to the size of the economy, equivalent to over one-fourth of the GDP. Nepal, a late economic development starter with difficult topography in South Asia also made steady progress in providing economic services, particularly following the reforms and rising public investment in priority areas facilitated by impressive growth in government revenue. Access of households to basic economic services like education and health services, drinking water, transport, communications and irrigation and banking facilities has increased significantly, due to the opening up of the economy and the restructuring of public expenditure in favor of social sector and infrastructure creation.

Another remarkable beneficiary of the reforms is the financial sector. As of 2018, the total number of the banks and other financial institutions (after the acquisition and merger policy adopted by the central bank to consolidate the banking sector) stands at 153 (28 commercial banks, 36 development banks, 25 finance companies and 64 microfinance institutions) from 7 in 1990. Together they have nearly 5,848 branches serving, on average, 5,000 people each. This expansion has helped broaden the reach of over 40 percent of households to modern banking instruments. In addition, there are 32,633 cooperatives (with five million members) of which 13,460 are savings and credit cooperatives providing financial service to rural and non-formal sector serving 21 percent of the households. All these developments have contributed to better access to financial instruments resulting from significant progress in financial deepening indicators such as broad money supply, debt flow to the private sector and deposit to GDP ratio. The broad money supply to GDP ratio is 94 percent, the ratio of debt flow to the private sector in relation to GDP is 76.8 percent and the total deposit to GDP ratio is 82.7 percent in 2017/18.[9]

Commendable progress has also been made in the construction of roads, irrigation and drinking water and sanitation. The total road network has surged from a meager 7,000 kilometers in 1991 to more than 88,000 kilometers in 2018 of which more than two-thirds is built by local bodies with state funding, which are largely fair-weather earthen roads. The total cultivable area under irrigation has risen by almost three times to reach 1.5 million hectares, and access to safe and improved drinking water has more than doubled to reach 85 percent of households over the past two decades.

The telecommunications sector has undergone a massive transformation in the last two and a half decades, aided mainly by the opening up of the sector leading to fresh investment, and innovation of modern technologies evolving from the telegraph to today's mobile technology. The introduction and penetration of new technologies have brought significant change in the social and economic lives. According to the Nepal Telecommunications Authority, telephone density in Nepal in 2017 was 130.3 percent with 381.6 million telephone users; the number of mobile users in Nepal was 372.97 million, 34 percent higher than the total population.[10]

Concluding remarks

Economic reforms in Nepal were driven mainly by the realization of the failure of the past inward-looking policy in promoting growth and reducing poverty. The stranglehold of government regulations over social and economic lives giving limited space to private capital and market forces resulted in low productivity, sluggish economic growth and poor revenue generation. Prodded by the lessons learnt from the international experience, South Asian countries including Nepal started liberal economic reform processes since the late 80s, which accelerated in the 90s. In Nepal, the liberalization process received meaningful momentum after the assumption of power by the elected government of the Nepali Congress in 1991. The new policy reforms covered a host of aspects including macroeconomy, taxation, bank and finance, cooperatives, non-government sector, private investment, trade liberalization, disinvestment of loss-making state-owned enterprises. This was coupled with the restructuring of public investment in favor of the social sector, infrastructure creation, development of backward areas, target-oriented poverty alleviation and social justice measures for the marginalized and underprivileged towards achieving the socialist goal of economic and social justice. Economic reforms were undertaken in tandem with governance reform measures including administrative changes and authority decentralization at the local level.

The positive impact of the reforms was felt in increased investment in the industrial and services sector, export growth, financial stability and higher growth rate for about a decade, but could not be sustained with the onset of the Maoist insurgency, turbulent politics and a prolonged political transition. Despite the modest growth rate in subsequent years, progress continued in a remarkable manner in internal revenue generation which made it possible to raise public investment in priority areas and reduce external dependence. Notable progress was made in poverty reduction and human development, and in the infrastructure sector like transport, communications, drinking water and sanitation, irrigation and others because of increased public spending. A study on the assessment of poverty situation during the period between 1995-96 and 2003-4, undertaken by the Central Bureau of Statistics, in collaboration with development partners including the World Bank, DFID and Asian Development Bank, has characterized the all-round improvements in economic and human development during the period as remarkable amidst turbulence. The report entitled Resilience Amidst Conflict called the achievements very impressive, given that they took place in a politically difficult and conflict-ridden period.[11]

Against this backdrop, the future challenge remains to raise the growth rate through both public and private investment. The reform process should be a continuous endeavor. An intermittent and piecemeal approach could produce growth spurts, but cannot sustain it over long periods. Therefore, some measures such as the legislation on Special Economic Zone, financial sector reforms and labor policy were undertaken in the recent post-conflict years as part of the resumption of the past reform process. Nepal's public investment in recent years is not only low at around five percent of GDP, but also inefficient as reflected in the high incremental capital-output ratio (ICOR). Unstable politics in the past took its toll in the quality of public administration. The task now is to tackle the governance deficit, which calls for redressal by the state authority with a popular mandate, capable of rising above partisan interest. Furthermore, there is a fresh political context of a new federal and decentralized constitution that calls for a more careful and rational approach with an emphasis on austerity, efficiency and productivity growth.

The challenge in the days ahead is, quite simply, to build upon the set of past achievements to launch a fresh wave of economic reforms by reclaiming the same spirit of ambition and purpose that was seen in Nepal in the 90s.

Notes

1. The economy faced the serious crisis when the foreign exchange reserve had gone down equivalent to two weeks of imports that forced the government to approach IMF for a bail out with a $2.2 billion loan for which a part of the country's gold reserve was flown to London to serve as collateral. The government also devalued the Indian rupee by 20 percent. See Das, Gurucharan (2002). *India Unbound- From Independence to the Global Information Age*, (p. 215). Penguin Books: New Delhi.
2. Haq, Mahabub ul (1997). *Human development in South Asia 1997*, Chapter 1, (p. 2). The Human Development Center Karachi, Oxford University Press: Karachi.
3. Jolliffe, Dean In PTI. (2018, September 19). Pace of extreme poverty reduction in S Asia faster than rest of the world: World Bank. *The Economic Times Business News*. Retrieved from https://economictimes.indiatimes.com/news/international/business/pace-of-extreme-poverty-reduction-in-s-asia-faster-than-rest-of-the-world-world-bank/articleshow/65875618.cms

4. National Planning Commission. (1992). *Eighth Plan (1992-1997) – Summary*, (p. 12-18).
5. Shakya, Sujeev (2009). *Unleasing Nepal*, (p. 58). Penguin Books: New Dehi.
6. The Ministry of Finance. (2051 b.s.). *Privatization Unit on the Evaluation of Privatization of Public Enterprises, (p. 4).*
7. Ministry of Finance. (2018). *Economic Survey 2017/18*, (p. 62).
8. *UN Inter-agency Group for Child Mortality Estimation 2018 and the CIA World Factbook* for 2016 and 2017 Estimations.
9. Ministry of Finance. (2018). *Economic Survey 2017/18*, (p. 36).
10. Ibid. (p. 100).
11. The Central Bureau of Statistics, National Planning Commission, Government of Nepal (2006), *Resilience Amidst Conflict: An ASSESSMENT OF poverty IN Nepal, 1995-96 AND 2003-04.* In collaboration with the World Bank, DFID and ADB, September 2006.

Chapter Four

Maoist Conflict and the Peace Process

Nepal suffered a long period of Maoist War, formally waged on 13 February 1996 with raids against police stations and capture of small farmers' bank offices in isolated hill districts of rural Nepal. Inspired by the guerilla warfare of 'Shining Path' in Peru, the brutal armed rebellion under the name of People's War was launched with the objective of establishing a 'New Democratic Republic' by removing 'bureaucratic-capitalist class, uprooting semi-feudalism and driving out imperialism.' They adopted the Maoist strategy of establishing bases in rural and remote areas with an eventual aim of surrounding urban centers and capturing state power. This protracted People's War passed through different phases including what they called 'strategic offence' and 'strategic balance'. Their tactical menu involved the development of base areas, declaration of guerilla zones, the capture of arms and ammunition and physical attacks to annihilate 'class enemies' and security forces. Encouraged by some initial success, the Maoists also installed parallel administrations in some remote districts.

At a later stage, they formed the People's Army and began a series of military offensives. On 25 September 2000, they launched a ferocious attack against government security forces in Dunai, the district headquarters of Dolpa, resulting in a heavy human toll and destruction. Even more daring attacks were mounted against other army barracks and police stations with greater casualties and loss on both sides. A year later, they renamed their militia outfit the People's Liberation Army and established central headquarters and a chain of command. They also boasted of forming three army divisions, nine brigades and twenty-nine battalions equipped with semi-automatic self-loading rifles (SLR) and rocket launchers which had been robbed from state army and police. Meanwhile, the country continued to suffer from a large number of guerilla raids, sabotage, annihilations, ambushes, kidnappings, and widespread intimidation of civilians.

Enabling condition and tactics

The deep-rooted poverty in the rural countryside characterized by rugged and difficult terrain provided a fertile ground for an insurgency, however misguided. The gains from a few years of democratic rule were too modest to make a meaningful dent on the vast ocean of backwardness and youth unemployment. The democratic rule was also marked by a period of rising expectations fueled by frequent elections, free press, an explosion of mass media and the information revolution and the growth of civil society and national and international human rights organizations. Freedom of expression allowed people to pursue a radical agenda and organize themselves to fight for rights, raising popular aspirations and expectations. Although these developments were legitimate from a democratic perspective, they placed heavy stress on a young fledgling democracy.

The Communist Party of Nepal (Maoists) also took advantage of the deep-seated structural cleavages and fault-lines of the Nepali society to advance their cause and recruit fighters. In a multi-ethnic and multi-cultural country with more than a hundred languages and dialects and even more ethnic groups, they argued that the political power structure was highly centralized and monopolized by 'high caste' Hindus. They blamed that social, economic and cultural lives were also dominated by a few ethnic and caste groups. There were also complaints of subjugation and neglect of the Dalits, indigenous ethnic groups, the Madhesis and women in various degrees.

The Dalits that constitute twelve percent of the population represented the extreme case of discrimination and marginalization. Furthermore, the spatial disparities and extreme poverty of people living in remote neglected districts of Far-Western and Mid-western region without even basic networks of transport and communications created the enabling ground for the Maoists to expand their membership swiftly. Shrewd exploitation of these structural cleavages was apparent from their promise to grant autonomy and the right of self-determination along ethnic lines to these communities which had been historically neglected and economically and culturally marginalized. This opportunistic narrative helped the Maoist insurgency spread: they formed various ethnic and 'national liberation fronts' for communities like Kirats, Magars, Newars, Tamangs, Tharus, and Madhesis and the Karnali region (where the Khas originated) to launch ethno-regional movements, taking advantage of the frustration and a sense of injustice felt in the communities. They also tried to appease the non-Hindu communities by advocating cow slaughter and attacking Hindu religious symbols. The objective was to polarize the Nepali society to incite class warfare. According to an expert on conflict resolution Bishnu Raj Upreti:[1]

The CPN(M) were very successful in polarizing the Nepali people...by dichotomizing identities such as 'oppressor-oppressed,' 'ruler-ruled', 'poor-rich' landlord-landless' and 'patriot-non patriot'. In this way they deepened (and created new) political, social, cultural and economic cleavages' Their dichotomies fueled the already developed feelings of injustice and frustration in the Nepalese people.

The Maoists justified their revolution by arguing that it reflected the country's objective conditions as well as their own subjective preparations of expanding the movement fast with coercion, brutality and violence. Nepal's difficult geography marked by high mountains, deep valleys interspersed with heavy forests and scattered settlements offered them an excellent habitat for the guerilla warfare. The poorly manned security outposts in isolated mountains and valleys were easy targets for nocturnal raids, causing heavy casualties that forced the government to withdraw security units from many rural pockets. The countryside, devoid of security presence, became an easy playground for the indoctrinated youth sold on utopia. The terror tactic unleashed by them forced the local community to accept their diktat without question, as any defiance of their order or denial to pay extortion was met by physical annihilation or mutilation on charges of abetting the enemy camp. Their atrocities did not spare even the old and the infirm; insensitivity was a tool of intimidation. To demoralize the security forces, their family members were often harassed and bullied.

The Maoist war had ideological support from radical communist groups outside the country. The CPN (Maoists) were among the founding members of the Revolutionary International Movement (RIM) with which they maintained constant contact and gained knowledge about the insurgency experiences in Peru, the Philippines, Turkey and Iran. They maintained close strategic links with other Maoist parties of the SAARC region such as People's War Group (PWG) and the Maoist Communist Centre (MCC). They also considered the economic, political, social, cultural and geographical conditions of the South Asian region as ideally suited for the Maoist revolution. To coordinate the revolutionary processes in these countries, they created a regional alliance with other parties in the form of Confederation of Communist and Maoist Parties of

South Asia (CCOMPOSA). Prachanda, the Maoist supremo, declared Nepal's People's War to be a part of the grand international proletariat movement with the objective of contributing to the attainment of the communist goal of 'ending all forms of human exploitation'. This was in keeping with the Leninist theory of the fusion of national liberation movements with the international proletarian movement.[2]

Cost of conflict

The insurgency inflicted heavy loss to the country in physical, socio-economic and political terms. In terms of human cost, a total of 17,880 human lives perished during the period of armed conflict. The number of violence victims in the form of the physically handicapped and displaced population was even larger. The displacement of 22,863 families of 79,571 persons occurred due to the Maoist violence and terror, torture, extortion and intimidation, and also due to the counter strategy by security forces to contain the Maoists. Furthermore, a total of 8,935 people were rendered disabled, 9,000 women were widowed, 1,530 persons disappeared and 3,142 were abducted.[3] There was an exodus of a large number of youth to foreign lands, including India, to escape forced conscription by the rebels and to search for jobs.

There was large scale destruction of development infrastructure including roads and bridges, telephone towers, power stations and transmission lines, banks, schools, police posts, offices and other government buildings. A total of 14,438 individual properties were damaged. School buildings topped the list of public properties destroyed with 2,149 units, followed by 2,072 village development committee offices, 1,047 local government offices, 986 government offices at district headquarters, 130 DDCs and municipalities and 101 suspension bridges.[4] The loss not only troubled the collective lives of the people but also added an enormous burden to the state. The Asian Development Bank estimated in 2006 that $129.6 million worth of physical infrastructure was damaged during the conflict/civil war period.[5] It created a real socio-political and economic chaos in the country. Disruptions in economic activities caused by strikes, blockades, shutdowns and extortions drove up business costs and discouraged private investment, contributing to an economic slowdown. Some important export-oriented industries, joint ventures and multi-national companies such as Colgate Palmolive, Jyoti Spinning Mill and Surya Nepal's textile factory in Biratnagar were shut down while many others struggled to stay afloat, creating setback to the export front that led to declining export/GDP ratio. There was a steady decline in tourist arrivals from a peak of about half a million in 1999 to 338,000 in 2003.

The productive capacity of the country was depleted and resource allocation distorted, setting in motion a vicious cycle of poverty and conflict. The conflict intensified in the late 90s, negatively affecting the expansion of health, education and other socio-economic facilities in rural areas. Growth of primary schools and health units declined drastically. Over 7,000 private schools were closed and 3,000 teachers were displaced from public schools. School children were abducted en masse for indoctrination and conscription. Immunization of children in the conflict areas also registered a steep decline. Extension of drinking water facilities declined sharply. Construction of roads was also adversely affected. The most poignant fact was that the incidence of the damage and loss was highest in those remote rural areas which were already impoverished, backward and devoid of basic public services.

The development expenditure which hovered at around ten percent of GDP before the conflict steadily declined to around six in 2004. This decay in development expenditure reduced consumption and investment, leading to lower growth rates; furthermore, it was accompanied by increasing recurrent cost, particularly due to a rise in security expenditure as a result of the escalating Maoist violence. The security expenditure doubled from 1.3 percent to three percent of GDP during the same period.[6] The combined police and army spending that never exceeded ten percent of the annual budget in previous years reached twenty percent with the escalating armed warfare. Additional security demand was met through extra-budgetary spending, especially after 2002/3, which represented about 20 percent of the security expenditure. In addition, hardware and technical assistance were received from countries like India, USA and UK as part of counter-terrorism measures under bilateral assistance. During the insurgency, the total size of the Nepal army and police increased by around eighty percent along with increasing sophistication in their arsenal and facilities. This was in response to the phenomenal growth and expansion of the Maoist military strength as reflected in their daring combat operations against the security forces.

Due to data limitations and methodological challenges, the precise quantification of the cost of the war in financial terms is difficult. Estimates vary:

according to DFID, the cost of the war was between 8–10 percent of GDP; the Nepal Peace Campaign (2004) estimated the cost at about $66.2 billion between 1996 and 2003.[7] The economy that registered an average decadal growth rate of 5.2 percent between 1985 and 1994 slowed to 4.1 percent between 1995 and 2004. In particular, the non-agricultural growth declined from seven to three percent per annum during the conflict years.[8] The World Bank estimates that if the GDP had continued to grow at the same rate attained in 1991-2000, the aggregate loss between 2000 and 2003 would amount to $3.0 billion.[9] Using the Harrod-Domar growth model to show the effect of increased defense spending on economic growth from 1996 to 2006, a study shows that the opportunity cost of the conflict (in terms of lost output) was about three percent of Nepal's current GDP. In addition to this, the indirect cost of conflict comprised of lost tourism revenue, disruption in trade and commerce, and a significant toll on children.[10]

Failed peace attempts

The Maoist insurgency was not taken seriously in the beginning in view of their poor popular support. Their mother party, the United Front, had won only nine out of 205 seats in the House of Representatives in the parliamentary election of 1991; this too was only possible after forming an electoral alliance with other communist parties. The United Front was itself divided, after one faction opted to remain in the parliamentary politics. However, as the insurgency started gathering intensity (resulting in human casualties, loss of public and private properties and affecting the economy and social lives), the police started two security operations code-named Operation Romeo and Kilo Sierra 2 in the Maoist-affected districts to counter Maoist activities adopting an offensive coercive security strategy. These operations proved counterproductive as they antagonized the local population. Reports of arbitrary arrests, harassment and mistreatment of innocent people started coming out. Extra-judicial killings were also recorded at some places.

As the insurgency was reaching its peak, the infamous Palace Massacre took place on June 1, 2001, killing eight members of the royal family including the King Birendra and Queen Aishwarya. Allegedly murdered by the Crown Prince, this episode disgraced the institution of monarchy and delegitimized the enthronement of the late King's brother, Gyanendra, from the start. Soon after this, in July 2001, the Maoist army attacked a police post in Holleri in

Rolpa, killing thirty-one policemen and abducting sixty-nine hostages. The incident was the turning point that led to Prime Minister Girija Prasad Koirala's resignation complaining of noncooperation in countering the Maoist offence by Nepal Army which owed its de facto loyalty to the king.

The peace talks with the Maoists began during the premiership of Sher Bahadur Deuba who came to power after Koirala's resignation. To facilitate the peace talks, a ceasefire was declared together with the release of many Maoist leaders and withdrawal of court cases against them. Several Maoist leaders and cadres came over ground holding public meetings and rallies, even displaying arms in some places. Using the opportunity to expand their organizational network, they walked away from peace talks abruptly and started launching attacks against the security forces in places like Dang, Surkhet and Syangja.

The attack on the army garrison in Dang was particularly daring as it killed more than two dozen security personnel and a large arsenal of weapons including LMGs, SMGs, SLRs, rocket launchers, mortars and a cache of other arms and ammunition were looted. The government had no choice but to declare a state of emergency on 26 November 2001 for a period of six months, and to brand the CPN(M) a terrorist organization. The emergency was later further extended for three months. As the state of emergency was extended by the Prime Minister without consulting his party Nepali Congress, he was asked by the party to furnish an explanation for the decision. But to everybody's surprise, Deuba recommended the dissolution of the House of Representatives on the midnight of 22 May 2002, announcing the date of mid-term general elections on 11 November.

This author was the Finance Minister then. I and two other cabinet colleagues, the Education Minister Amod Prashad Upadhyaya and the Minister for Women, Children and Social Services, Rajendra Kharel, resigned immediately the next morning protesting the Prime Minister's unilateral midnight action without consulting the party and his cabinet colleagues and the instant announcement by the king under suspicious circumstances. This decision, in fact, was suspected to have been instigated by the king.[11] We warned that this action could be a prelude to autocracy, as the likelihood of holding the election in November was dim because of the worsening security situation, which had prompted the government just a few days back to extend the period of emergency. The government had also failed to hold elections even for local bodies. As widely expected, the decision to hold elections on the scheduled date was withdrawn, giving an alibi for the monarch to sack the Deuba government for 'incompetence' in holding the scheduled elections. The King then assumed powers himself through a few hand-picked nominees. Thus, Nepal entered a new phase of political development after the royal takeover of 4 October 2002.

Obviously, the royal takeover was facilitated by the untimely dissolution of the House of Representatives. The absence of an elected legislature, a state of emergency with the suspension of fundamental rights and the precarious security situation created an enabling condition for the royal takeover of power. The peace initiative was resumed under the premiership of Lokendra Bahadur Chand handpicked by the King on 11 October. As a precondition for the peace talks, the court cases and the international red corner notices against the Maoists were withdrawn. However, the talks failed again when the government refused the key demand to abrogate the constitution, form an interim government under their leadership and hold elections for the constituent assembly. The Maoists were not ready to renounce violence by laying down arms and decommissioning their army and militia.

It is to be noted that when the Maoists were sitting for peace talks, their international ideologues were opposing it on the ground that the revolutionaries never sit for talks, because it dilutes the revolutionary fervor and that a real class struggle would not end in a negotiated settlement, leaving no clear winner or a loser. They considered the pacifist ways out of armed conflicts and peace negotiation as an anti-insurgency tool invented by the imperialists.[12] However, the Maoists defended their action on tactical grounds to advance the cause of the revolution towards ultimate victory, citing historical instances of Brest-Litovsk Treaty of 1918 under Lenin and the Chungking Negotiations under Mao-Tse Tung in 1938. By using peace negotiations as a tool, they were successful in getting many of their detainees released and court cases withdrawn. They came over-ground, expanded their organization and mobilized huge amounts of money through extortions. It has been estimated that their organizational strength increased severalfold during the two cease-fire periods. It now appears that they never meant to negotiate for peace in good faith.

Peace process again

The sequence of royal takeover that started in October 2002 reached its culmination on 1st February 2005, when King Gyanendra sacked his third handpicked prime minister and assumed direct control of the country's administration by announcing a new cabinet under his own chairmanship. Despite his promise to restore multiparty democracy and peace within three years after implementing effective reforms, his subsequent actions had all the elements of an indefensible coup that mimicked what his father had waged in 1960. A state of emergency was declared suspending fundamental rights, political leaders were put under house arrest or detained, internal and external communications cut off and press and media came under heavy censorship. A series of ordinances were brought in to tighten the royal grip over all walks of life. It is to be noted that the image of Nepal's monarchy had suffered heavily after the palace massacre of 2001. The royal action of October 2002 and the latest action of direct rule invited heavy criticism and hostile reaction both internally and from the international community.

In the aftermath of this political development, a new political climate emerged and the crisis deepened. The authoritarian and absolutist rule of the king motivated political parties to unite. The direct conflict between the State and the Maoists until then gave way to a triangular power conflict between the monarch, the constitutional political parties and the rebel Maoists. The political parties representing ninety percent of the seats in the dissolved parliament joined hands and formed a Seven Party Alliance (SPA) to collectively fight for a common cause against the royal action. Almost all sections of the society including civil society, trade unions, media and professional organizations came out openly against the royal rule. The popular forces that traditionally considered the institution of monarchy as a necessity for political stability and national unity started having second thoughts. The largest political party Nepali Congress which had espoused the cause of constitutional monarchy since its birth removed it from the party statute in its eleventh national convention. A broad consensus emerged in the alliance for a reform agenda favoring restructuring of the state power to make it equitable and inclusive.

Against this backdrop, the Maoists sensed an unprecedented opportunity to align with other political forces to jointly oppose the monarchy. They revised their earlier agenda of 'New Democratic Revolution' in favor of 'Bourgeois Democratic Revolution' to free the Nepali society from feudal order. They urged other political parties to rally behind a common minimum program of 'Democratic Republic'. Their new theme was a two-way revolution starting with a multi-party democratic republic and then a peaceful transformation of the state. The political parties also considered the new developments as conducive to enter into dialogue with CPN(M) to restore peace and democracy. Two major party leaders—Nepali Congress President Girija Prasad Koirala and CPN(UML) leader Madhav Kumar Nepal—were authorized by their respective parties to open dialogue with the Maoists. As a gesture of confidence, the Maoists announced unilateral ceasefire to create an atmosphere for launching a movement: the political parties had refused to start joint action until the Maoists renounced violence and accepted to join peaceful multiparty politics. After a few behind-the-scene parleys in India where the Maoist leaders were sheltered, the seven-party alliance (SPA) and CPN(M) signed in New Delhi the twelve-point memorandum of understanding, which led the country towards a negotiated peace. It is believed that the government of India was instrumental in facilitating and mediating the negotiation between the two sides.

The MoU declared the autocratic monarchy as the principal obstacle on the path to peace, democracy and progress, and committed themselves to exert all forces against it to establish 'full' democracy. The Maoist expressed their commitment to multiparty democracy and peaceful democratic values. Both sides agreed to undertake self-evaluation of their past mistakes and promised not to repeat them. An election to the Constituent Assembly under international supervision that would decide the future political set up was considered the ultimate basis for the lasting peace. They also agreed on the need for an all-powerful interim government to hold elections. The MOU also agreed to place the armed forces of the CPN(M) and the Nepal Army under international supervision of the UN or other reliable international bodies until the holding of the CA election.

The new deal and the accompanying ceasefire enabled the agitating political forces to reach out to the countryside after a long gap without fear of the Maoist violence to reestablish contact and mobilize their cadres for agitation against the royal rule. The SPA, particularly on the strength of the Nepali Congress and CPN(UML), successfully demonstrated their mass support by organizing huge rallies and mass meetings throughout the country that culminated in a massive public uprising popularly known as the *Jana Andolan 2* from 6th to 24th April 2006, forcing the King to succumb to the agitating parties. The outcome was the royal announcement to restore the dissolved House of Representatives and accept the people as the ultimate source of sovereignty in keeping with the roadmap presented by the SPA.

Interim Constitution, CPA and elections

A new interim government was announced with Girija Prasad Koirala as Prime Minister. To enable their participation in the restored House of Representatives (HOR), the CPN(M) was offered thirty-three percent of seats by fiat. The restored parliament stripped the King of his power as the Supreme Commander of the Armed Forces and suspended his role as the head of state. A power-sharing arrangement was also negotiated with the Maoists. Subsequently, on 21 November 2006, the new government and the CPN(M) signed a Comprehensive Peace Agreement (CPA) formally announcing the end of the civil war. The pact, among other things, included the provisions for stripping the King of his political rights and nationalization of royal property, scrapping of the Maoist parallel administration, termination of military action and army mobilization, rehabilitation and integration of Maoist army combatants, formation of commissions for peace and rehabilitation, transitional justice and state restructuring.

The CPA paved the way for Maoist participation in the interim government. As part of the CPA, the Agreement on Monitoring of the Management of the Arms and Armies (AMMA) was also signed, keeping, in particular, the Maoist combatants in temporary cantonments, and confining Nepal Army within their barracks. Requested by the Government of Nepal, the UN Mission in Nepal (UNMIN) was established to work on the verification process of Maoist combatants. A new Interim Constitution was promulgated, but it met with violent protests by the Madhesh-based parties for its failure to address their demand for a commitment to a federal structure. The constitution was later amended to address this.

The much-awaited election for the Constituent Assembly (CA) took place in April 2008, in which the CPN(M) emerged as the largest party, but short of a majority. The newly elected CA passed a resolution on the very first day of its sitting on 28 May 2008 abolishing the institution of monarchy that had reigned in modern Nepal since 1769. The country was declared a Federal Democratic Republic. King Gyanendra became an ordinary citizen overnight. Contrary to wide speculation of a possible resistance by the king, the outgoing king announced his decision to cooperate and left the palace in a dignified manner. Not a single bullet was fired as Nepal made the momentous leap from a traditional monarchy to a modern republic.

On 18 August 2008, Pushpa Kamal Dahal Prachanda, Chairman of CPN(M), was sworn in as Prime Minister of a coalition government, joining hands with CPN (UML). The government did not last long as it came into conflict with the President over its decision to take full control of the armed forces by sacking the Army Chief of Staff Rukmangad Katuwal, replacing him with a pliable general who would have been subservient to their mission of capturing state power through a cunning process of integration of rebel forces into Nepal Army.

Prachanda tendered his resignation on 4 May 2009, following the President's refusal to accept the controversial cabinet decision. Madhav Kumar Nepal of UML, who formed a coalition with Nepali Congress and other parties, succeeded him. The Maoists attempted to overthrow this government by launching an indefinite Nepal Bandh, centered in Kathmandu, without success. This period also witnessed further cabinet turnover, with three consecutive Prime Ministers including Jhalanath Khanal (UML), Baburam Bhattarai (M) and Khilaraj Regmi who as chief justice headed the subsequent interim cabinet with the mandate to hold an election for the second CA in 2013.

The first CA, 2008-2012, was not able to agree on the content of the constitution in a period of four years. This was after two extensions, since the expiry of its original mandate of two years due to lack of consensus among major parties on contentious issues including the criteria for federalization and the form of governance. This failure triggered the election of second CA in 2013. Nepali Congress emerged as the largest party after the election; subsequently, its Chairman Sushil Koirala became the Prime Minister of the coalition government in collaboration with CPN(UML). It was during his premiership that the constitution drafting was completed and formally promulgated. The distinctive features of the constitution, in view of their importance, will be discussed separately in the next chapter. The second CA period was not free from a power struggle among the political parties, as evidenced in frequent changes in government. This period saw four Prime Ministers in four years. Koirala was succeeded respectively by K.P. Sharma Oli, Pushpa Kamal Dahal and Sher Bahadur Deuba. These coalitions were a result of frequent changes in alignments and realignments between the three main political parties. The general election of November 2017 catapulted the unified strength of the UML and Maoists to power with the strong parliamentary majority under the leadership of Oli. The two parties had unified into a single party under the name the Nepal Communist Party just prior to the election, in order to influence the election outcome.

Management of arms and armies

The most sensitive components of the CPA were the issues of integration and rehabilitation of the Maoist combatants and transitional justice. Following the agreement to invite the United Nations to monitor the arms and armies, the United Nations Mission in Nepal (UNMIN) was established on 23 January 2007 initially for one year but subsequently extended until January 15, 2011. The UNMIN was mandated to verify the combatants registered in the camps and to monitor the management of arms, armies and activities of the cantonments. They were also mandated to monitor the activities of the Nepal Army. A high-level Special Committee for Supervision, Integration and Rehabilitation of Maoist Army Combatants (SC) representing major political parties headed by the Prime Minister was constituted in 2008 for overall policy direction and supervision of the task. This author was one of the members of the SC representing the Nepali Congress.[13] A Joint Monitoring Coordination Committee (JMCC) was set up under it to coordinate the implementation of the CPA provision AMMA. The JMCC was chaired by the UNMIN chief with membership from both Nepal Army and the Maoist Army.

Claiming themselves to be former Maoist army combatants, a total of 31,252 persons had registered for verification. Out of this 19,602 were verified as meeting the agreed criteria and eligible for integration and rehabilitation of which around twenty percent were women. Approximately 4,000 were verified as late recruits after CPA or as minors, and 8,640 did not appear for verification. The under-age and those not meeting the criteria were subsequently discharged from the camps. UNMIN also registered and stored 3,475 weapons of the Maoists, and 2,855 weapons of the Nepal Army at *Chhauni* barrack for monitoring. The combatants were deployed in seven temporary cantonments and twenty-one satellite cantonments.

The peace process gathered momentum after the departure of UNMIN in January 2011, when the challenging task of monitoring the cantoned arms and armies were taken over by the SC and its secretariat. Even in the midst of confusion and contradiction between major parties and stakeholders on the issue of integration and rehabilitation of combatants, a seven-point agreement was signed on 1 November 2012 through national consensus. This settled all contentious issues including the number of combatants to be integrated into the army, norms and modalities for integration, rank determination and cash amount for voluntary retirement.

Following the SC decision in November 2011, the former combatants were given three options for their reintegration: induction into the national army, rehabilitation or a remunerated voluntary retirement. As a result of fresh updating of verified combatants and their regrouping into various options, it was found that out of 17,052 combatants who participated in the process, 7,323 opted for voluntary retirement, 9,723 for integration and only six for rehabilitation. Ninety-four combatants who were verified in 2007 were reported dead, while 2,456 were missing. The voluntary retirement package consisted of a cash grant to each ex-combatant by the government between Rs. 5,00,000 to 7,00,000 in three categories based on their rank.

It is interesting to note that only six ex-combatants opted for rehabilitation, an option favored by the government and the donor community, as this option involved technical training and some cash arrangement and soft loan to start a business for sustainable livelihood. Five of them completed electrical training and one opted for another technical training. With regard to the 9,723 individuals opting for army integration, the SC fixed a maximum ceiling of 6,500. After further categorization and regrouping, 3,223 ex-combatants were verified for army integration and had to further meet the academic and physical norms required for officers and general categories. After passing all these phases, 1,444 ex-combatants were integrated into the Nepal Army, seventy-one as officers and 1,351 in the non-officer general category. A total of 3,475 verified weapons were handed over to the Nepal army on the day when formal integration started. Of the handed-over weapons, 2,850 were found looted earlier during insurgency from the Nepal army.

A unique aspect of the management of ex-guerillas in Nepal's peace process is the decision to pay cash incentives for voluntary retirement which was disliked by the donor community fearing the risk of cash misuse. In the absence of reliable data, it is difficult to say what the retirees are doing currently in society. Some of them have become political workers by joining their parent party. A preliminary assessment showed that the retirees used their cash mostly in the purchase of land, the building of houses, household expenses, children's education and to start small businesses. A significant portion of them, around twelve to fifteen percent are estimated to have left the country seeking better opportunities abroad, a phenomenon that is in keeping with the growing trend of rural youth migration from the countryside. Based on interviews with the ex-combatants by the media and other civil organizations, it appears that most of them have reintegrated successfully. There are also few reported cases of misusing the money in unproductive and unsustainable ways through purchasing luxury items.

The total cost of the management of arms and armies was estimated at Rs. 19.7 billion. As the donor community was reluctant to pay cash money for voluntary retirement, the entire cost of the package was paid by the Nepal government.

UNMIN's controversial role

The peace process in Nepal was driven by internal forces, with engagement and participation of multiple actors including international institutions. The principal factor for its success, however, was the dominant role played by internal political forces in the process through consensus building. The UN involvement was requested in June 2006 by the new government after the political change with the mandate for creating an atmosphere for free and fair elections and observation, monitoring the code of conduct during the ceasefire, management of arms and armies on both sides and monitoring of NA to ensure it stayed within barracks and that weapons were not used against any side.

Despite the generally positive contribution by UNMIN since its formal establishment, part of its conduct in the context of the election process and monitoring of arms and armies was heavily criticized. The general expectation of impartiality by a UN body was sadly belied. First, UNMIN failed to restrain the widespread pre-election threat and intimidation by Maoist cadres against candidates of other political parties. Following the installation of the Maoist-led government after the election, unlawful criminal activities in the Maoist cantonments and outside by the Maoist combatants were reported in the media. To public dismay, UNMIN failed to monitor and control them. The cantonments were freely used by the Maoist leaders for indoctrination and political training.

Secondly, the number of combatants—19,602—verified by UNMIN came under question after an infamous videotape of the speech by Prachanda in the *Shaktikhor* camp before the 2008 elections was leaked. Addressing the Maoist cadres, he proudly revealed the way he had shrewdly outmaneuvered UNMIN into accepting several times more combatants compared to the approximately

7,000 militia that they actually had. It may be noted that the Maoist party exaggerated the number of combatants through fresh recruitment towards the end of 2006 with promises of salary payments and promises of integration into the security forces. UNMIN kept silent on this and included these late recruits in their verification process. On the other hand, the UN maintained that the new recruitments by Nepal army to fill up the vacant posts was a violation of the CPA and AMMA (which had restricted additional recruitment). This position was rejected by all non-Maoist parties, and eventually by the Supreme Court ruling, which said that recruitments to fill up vacant positions without raising numerical strength of the army cannot be regarded as additional recruitment.

The UN's biased role in favor of the Maoists was evident on many other occasions. They were quick in pointing out any minor act of violation of the CPA and the code of conduct by the Nepal army, but gave the benefit of the doubt in case of violation by the Maoists. While the UN highlighted time and again the inadequate facilities for the ex-combatants in the Maoist camps, they remained silent and did nothing to alleviate the humanitarian sufferings of the internally displaced Maoist victims. At the UN Secretary-General Ban Ki-Moon's meeting with parliamentarians during his visit to Nepal in October 2008, I had drawn his attention to these issues.

The UNMIN's continued treatment of the temporary cantonments of the Maoist combatants at par with the barracks of Nepal also came under heavy criticism. Although AMMA had referred to 'two sides' or 'parties to conflict' to denote Nepal government and CPN(M) and also Nepali Army and the Maoist combatants, Article 6 of the CPA had declared the end of armed war and Article 10.5 had stipulated that the concept of two sides would cease to exist after the establishment of the interim Legislature-Parliament—which had been duly constituted in January 2007 of which the CPN(M) was a part. Furthermore, on August 27, 2010, in a meeting called by Prime Minister Madhav Kumar Nepal, leaders of seventeen parties representing an overwhelming parliamentary majority had unanimously recommended that Nepal Army should not be subject to UNMIN monitoring and not be treated at par with the Maoist combatants. This was because the NA was governed by the provisions of the Interim Constitution and relevant laws of the land, which was not the case in respect of Maoist combatants lodged in temporary cantonments awaiting integration and rehabilitation.[14]

The prejudiced nature of UNMIN in performing their role in Nepal's peace process was clearly reflected in their reports which also dragged the high office of UN Secretary-General into controversy. I myself wrote an open letter to Ian Martin, the UNMIN Chief and Special Representative of the UN Secretary-General drawing attention to the biased nature of the report they submitted on 24 October 2008 to the Security Council. I again wrote another letter to Ian Martin's successor, Karin Landgren, reacting to the Security Council news report on the 6119th meeting that contained a paragraph on Nepal based on UNMIN's report of May 5, 2009, which reflected its institutional bias. Nepal's then Permanent Representative to the UN, Madhu Raman Acharya, also fired a salvo at the Secretary-General's report of 26 October 2009 for making references which implied parity of Maoist fighters with Nepal Army. The report suggested the need for national unity government for the timely promulgation of the new constitution and integration and rehabilitation of the Maoist combatants, at a time when the country was under the coalition government of non-Maoist parties. Ironically, the UN had remained silent on the need for a national unity government, when the Maoist led the majority government. In an article published in Kathmandu Post, a senior journalist and civil society leader Kanak Mani Dixit alleged: 'Seemingly even-handed, the report subtly distorted picture of our peace process, papering over intransigence of the Maoists as a primary roadblock.'[15] Furthermore, regretting the prejudiced nature of the report from an institution known for its independence, impartiality and integrity of the highest order, I published an article entitled 'Questioning UN's Impartiality' in the media, excerpts of which read:

> *What is intriguing is the UN's silence at the Maoist failure to show their commitment to basic UN values such as rule of law, pluralism, universally accepted human rights, and non-violence which remain the foundation of CPA. The prolonged parliamentary obstruction, daily incidents of murder and violent actions, continued occupation of public and private property, and repeated threats of capturing the state power through street agitation and blatant violation of the letter and spirit of the peace process...Even in the face of irrefutable evidence and violent actions on ground, the UN and the international community have not spoken up. They seem to be in an appeasement mode. Even more disturbing is the naïve approach at times of romanticizing the rebel actions in the third world and rationalization of the same, however unacceptable it may be.*

The next UNMIN report of September 2010 invited further controversy. The report of the Secretary-General to the Security Council (S 2010/453) recommended further extension of UNMIN's mandate. Four former foreign ministers including K.P. Sharma Oli of CPN (UML), Chakra Prasad Bastola and myself from the Nepali Congress, and Prakash Chandra Lohani from the Rastriya Prajatantra Party wrote a joint letter to the Secretary-General raising objections to the report. We particularly objected to the tone and content of the report that treated the Nepal Army at par with the rebel forces, and the Nepal government with the Maoist party. The letter also questioned the UNMIN recommendation to gloss over the UNMIN mandate bypassing the then caretaker government of Madhav Nepal—thereby questioning the legitimacy of the outgoing transition government that was legally constituted. The SG was also asked to retract the objectionable paragraphs of the report and also to look into their legality and appropriateness.

At the same time, a *note verbale* (PMN/UNMIN 281/2010) was issued and circulated by the then UN Permanent Representative of Nepal, Ambassador Gyan Chandra Acharya, to all members of the Security Council pointing out the inaccurate and biased parts in the text of the Secretary-General's report sourced from UNMIN Chief and RSG Karin Landgren. It also referred to public complaints in Nepal about how the UNMIN had failed to play an impartial and effective role expected by the people. 20 specific instances of inaccurate and imbalanced reporting and actions by UNMIN were listed, tarnishing the UN's high reputation and damaging historically warm relations with Nepal.[16] Ultimately, the Nepal government in consultation with concerned parties including (CPN/M) agreed to extend UNMIN's office in Nepal by four months until January 15, 2011. Following the departure of UNMIN on this date, its function was taken over by the SC and its secretariat, when the peace process received momentum towards the settlement through internal consensus as described above. The process of rehabilitation/integration of the Maoist combatants proceeded smoothly without the presence of the UNMIN.

Transitional Justice

The Comprehensive Peace Agreement signed on 21 November 2006 committed to establishing the truth about the conduct of the Maoist war to ensure justice and reparation to the victims of conflict. To that end, the CPA provisioned to establish two transitional justice mechanisms, namely a Truth and Reconciliation Commission (TRC) and a Commission for Investigation on Enforced Disappeared Persons (CIEDP). This was further incorporated in the constitution of 2015 and followed up by necessary legislations on property confiscation and enforced displacements. It is to be noted that the international humanitarian law regime including international human rights law (IHRL) and international humanitarian law (IHL) are applicable for the period of armed conflicts. Acts such as murder, torture and rape are treated as crimes against humanity. Certain crimes, notably those against humanity, genocide, trafficking, piracy, slavery, torture and forced disappearances are considered international crimes for which concerned nations are under obligation to investigate the truth and prosecute suspected perpetrators and to compensate the victims. The perpetrators of such crimes may not benefit from amnesty or pardon.

After passing the necessary legislation to implement the constitutional provision and CPA commitment, the government constituted the TRC and CIEDP in 2015 with a two-year mandate to investigate the war-era crimes and to provide justice to victims. The mandate includes the delivery of justice and provision for reparation for the victims of serious human right violations including violent killings, abduction, torture and assault, sexual violence, incapacitation and enforced disappearances.

It has been reported that approximately 60,000 complaints have been registered in TRC and nearly 3,000 cases in CIEDP. Despite tenure extension of the two commissions, there has been no tangible progress in providing transitional justice to conflict victims due to legal shortcomings and administrative hurdles. The victims complain of lack of justice delivery because of the atmosphere of impunity prevailing in the country. The commission members themselves had also expressed reservation about the prevailing Act which they did not consider friendly to the human rights of victims. They had advised its reformation and amendment to be consistent with international standards. The main reservation pertains to the provision of amnesty in the legislation even for perpetrators of extreme cases of human rights violation, which could aggravate the climate of impunity in the country.

On April 17, the five rapporteurs of the UN Human Rights Commission for Human Rights wrote a strong letter to the government of Nepal expressing concern over the transitional justice process in Nepal. They pointed out lack of impartiality and transparency in the selection process of the new leadership of the two transitional justice commissions, to succeed after the expiry of the extended term of the incumbent leadership on 14 April 2019. They also urged to amend the Transitional Justice Act immediately in line with international standard in consultation with the conflict victims, victim families, civil society and National Human Right Commission. Other international rights bodies including Amnesty International, International Commission of Jurists, Human Rights Watch and Trial International, have also appealed the government along similar lines recently, expressing concern about inaction in addressing the conflict-era human rights violations. It is unfortunate that even after twelve years of the Comprehensive Peace Agreement, transitional justice that constituted one of its three main components (including constitution making and integration and rehabilitation of the Maoists combatants) has made little headway, as the war-era victims still await justice.

Concluding remarks

The Maoist conflict inflicted heavy economic cost to the nation, together with millions of death and other casualties, disruption of social and economic lives, destruction of physical assets and infrastructure, leading to derailment of development and slowing down of economic growth. The peace process that failed in early attempts got a new lease of life after the Royal takeover in 2005 that brought the constitutional parties and the rebels closer leading to the signing of twelve-point Memorandum of Understanding in November 2005 with a common agenda to fight against the absolutist monarchy. The peaceful mass uprising following this agreement forced the king to accept the sovereign power of the people restoring the House of Representatives, which further resulted in the signing of the Comprehensive Peace Agreement on 21 November 2006.

The country passed through a long period of political transition since the signing of the CPA in 2006. The most positive side of the peace process in Nepal is that it was predominantly home-grown, assisted at a technical level by the international community, particularly the United Nations whose role was not without controversy. The role played by India was important in the initial stage of the process, particularly in facilitating dialogue between SPA and the Maoist leaders sheltered in India that culminated in the signing of the historic twelve-point agreement. The support of other development partners, external community, particularly some OECD countries, was in creating an atmosphere to encourage the peace process and support its implementation with some advisory and financial assistance through such mechanism as the Nepal Peace Trust Fund.

The notable outcome of the peace deal is the mainstreaming in the constitutional plural politics of the CPN(M) that fought a violent civil war with disastrous impact for over a decade with the aim of establishing a Stalinist one-party communist rule. Another significant aspect of Nepal's peace process is the successful integration and rehabilitation of rebel combatants, a contentious subject in a post-conflict situation. The success is mainly attributed to constant dialogue and negotiation between the main political forces on sensitive and controversial issues. The new constitution representing the most significant component of the peace deal is committed to addressing the fault lines and structural weaknesses of the Nepali society the Maoists had tried to exploit to sell their vision of a communist utopia. The main features of the new federal constitution and its implementation challenges are discussed in the next chapter. A rough calculation of the financial cost of the completed parts of the peace process, namely the constitution-making through the two elected constituent assemblies, the management of erstwhile Maoist combatants and preliminary relief to the conflict-affected families reached over Rs. 166 billion by November 2018.[17]

There is still one unfinished task of completing the transitional justice component of the CPA: there has been a prolonged delay in ensuring justice to the victims of conflict who suffered the most from the atrocities perpetrated by the warring sides.

Notes

1. Upreti, Bisnu Raj (2009). Nepal's Armed Conflict and Trajectory to Peace. In Upreti, Topperwien and Heiniger (Eds.). *Peace Process and Federalism in Nepal: Experience, Reflections and Learning*, (p. 28). South Asia Regional Coordinator Office of NCCR North-South.
2. *A World to Win*. (May 28,2001).
3. Nepal Institute of Policy Studies. (2013). *Nepal Peace Process : A Brief overview, in Policy Paper*, Issue 1, Volume 8. Ministry of Peace and Reconstruction. Retrieved from http//www.rahat.gop.npuploads/4330 File Ashad1.pd.
4. Ibid.
5. Quoted in ADB, DFID and ILO (2009). *Country Diagnostic Studies: Nepal: Critical Development Constraints*, (p. 31). Mandaluyong City, Manila.
6. Ra, Sungsup and Singh, Bipul (2005). *Measuring the Economic Cost of Conflict: the Effect of Declining Development Expenditure on Nepal's Economic Growth*. Asian Development Bank.
7. Ibid. (p. 3).

8. For details see Mahat, R. S. (2005). *In Defence of Democracy*, (p. 326-327).
9. Quoted in ADB, DFID and ILO. (p. 46).
10. Pradhan, Gyan Nepal's Civil War and its Economic Costs. *Journal of international and Global Studies.* Retrieved from *https://www.lindenwood.edu/resources.*
11. This suspicion was vindicated after the publication of the book *Maile Dekheko Durbar*, (pp. 306-7) by King Gyanendra's military secretary Bibek Kumar Shah who was one of the players behind the scene in the Narayanhiti Palace secretariat in those days. In his memoirs, he says that the king had advised the Prime Minister to recommend the House dissolution. Deuba had gone to the palace on 22 May night with a blank letter pad; the palace secretariat drafted the recommendation letter at 10PM, in which the PM put the signature. The King formally accepted it and announced the dissolution at 11PM.
12. Borga, Luis Arce (2003). *Criticisms of Peace Negotiation*. Brussels.
13. The members of the SC chaired by the Prime Minister comprised of this author and Minendra Rijal from NC, Bhim Rawal and Ishwor Pokhrel from NCP/UML, Barshaman Pun and Janardan Sharma from NCP/M, and Jitendra Dev and J.P. Gupta from Madheshi Front.
14. Gautam, Kul Chandra (2015). *Lost in Transition: Rebuilding Nepal from the Maoist Mayhem and Mega earthquake*, (p. 238). Nepa-laya: Kathmandu.
15. Dixit, Kanak Mani (2009, November 3). A response to Secretary-General. In *The Kathmandu Post.*
16. Gautam, K. C. Ibid. Chapter 9.
17. *My Republica.* (2018, November 21).

Chapter Five

Writing the Constitution

The present constitution of Nepal was promulgated on September 20, 2015, replacing the interim constitution of 2007. This is the seventh written constitution in the history of Nepal. The first constitution called Baidhanik Kanoon (Constitutional Law) was announced on 26 January 1948 by Rana Prime Minister Padma Shamsher. Despite its announcement, the constitution giving limited rights to the people could not be implemented because of resistance from other powerful members of the Rana oligarchy. The end of the Rana regime in 1951 saw the promulgation of the Nepal Interim Government Act by King Tribhuvan in consultation with the new cabinet. The Act restored the authority of the king and introduced some democratic reforms and institutions including the provisions of fundamental rights of the citizens, and constitutional bodies like the Supreme Court and the Public Service Commission.

The third constitution was the Constitution of the Kingdom of Nepal 1959 that introduced a plural parliamentary democracy. However, in it, the king assumed powers to dissolve the parliament, which he duly abused by staging a royal coup against the first popularly elected government of Nepal led by BP Koirala. In 1962, he issued a new constitution introducing the Partyless Panchayat polity that vested powerful executive authority in the king. This constitution was brought to an end following the popular uprising of 1990. After a hiatus of over thirty years, another democratic constitution was announced in November 1990 that restored democratic rights of the people, and instituted a multi-party parliamentary democracy, limiting the role of the monarchy to constitutional status.

The Interim Constitution of 2007 was an interim political arrangement agreed between the Seven Party Alliance (SPA) and the CPN(Maoist) as part of the Comprehensive Peace Agreement as elaborated in the previous chapter.

We, the sovereign people

The most distinctive aspect of the latest constitution of Nepal is that it has been drafted by the elected representatives of the people. All previous constitutions, except the Interim Constitution of 2007 preceding this, were promulgated by the king. The Nepali people had been demanding a constitution written by the elected constituent assembly for over seventy years: its formulation by themselves was considered to be the sovereign right of the people. Although the Constituent Assembly agenda reached its peak after the Maoist conflict and the 2006 uprising against the monarch, its origin can be traced to the birth of the Nepali Congress. The Nepali Congress manifesto of 1949 asserted that the government shall have to be run by the people according to the constitution prepared by their elected representatives. This plea for the rule of law was one of the main agenda of the 1950 revolution. Following its success, King Tribhuvan addressed the nation promising a constitution prepared by elected representatives of the people. During the post-Rana transition period, BP Koirala was the prominent advocate for the constitution by people's elected assembly. He argued that when laws are legislated by people's representatives, the same argument naturally applies with respect to the constitution, which is the basic law of the land. The principal rationale behind the constitution by the people is to recognize that people are the ultimate source of national sovereignty and therefore legislating the supreme law governing the nation falls within their sovereign right.

However, much water flowed down the Bagmati river during the interim period until 1959 that was marked by division and fragmentation among and within parties giving an opportunity for the monarch to manipulate the situation in his favor. Furthermore, King Mahendra who succeeded King Tribhuvan in 1955 was not committed to democracy in the same manner that his father was. Aspiring to carve a larger political role for himself, the shrewd and ambitious king postponed elections to buy time and consolidate power. Sensing the new king's autocratic ambition, Nepali Congress together with National Congress and Praja Parishad formed the United Front and launched *satyagraha* demanding an early election. Ultimately the King announced the election for parliament instead of the constituent assembly. Given the risk of losing the opportunity to seek a popular mandate in the country's first parliamentary election, the Nepali Congress and other parties accepted the election as a step towards institutionalizing representative democracy.

The long-standing Nepali aspiration for the nation's supreme legal charter through the elected constituent assembly (CA) was finally met in 2015. The drafting proved to be a long-drawn struggle along an intractable path of finding a compromise among various forces with antagonistic philosophies and agenda. The elected assembly was composed of radical Maoists and liberal democrats, federalists and anti-federalists, nationalists and sub-nationalists championing the cause of ethnicity-based provinces. The first CA elected in May 2008 had the mandate to complete the constitution in two years. Because of disagreement among political parties on various contentious issues, including the nature of federalism and the form of government, the term was extended twice until 28 May 2012. Because of the CA's failure to complete the constitution drafting by then and the Supreme Court judgement against further extension of its term, the election for the new CA was held on 19 November 2013. The Nepali Congress emerged as the largest party from the election, following which a coalition government took office under the Premiership of Sushil Koirala, the President of the Nepali Congress.

The second CA completed the constitution-making on 16 September 2015 and it was formally announced by President Ram Baran Yadav on 20 September 2015. The devastating earthquake that struck the country in April 2015 had brought urgency to complete the drafting of the constitution by resolving contentious issues, and rallying the country for reconstruction after the disaster, the biggest since 1934.

The constitution which institutionalized Nepal's transition from a constitutional monarchy to a republic, and from a unitary to a federal form of governance has 308 articles, thirty-five parts and nine schedules. Signifying the authorship of the constitution by the people of Nepal themselves, the preamble of the constitution begins with these words:[1]

> *We, the Sovereign People of Nepal, internalizing the people's sovereign right and right to autonomy and self-rule, while preserving national freedom, sovereignty, territorial integrity, independence, national unity and dignity...*

The preamble made a commitment to ensure economic equality, prosperity and social justice by eliminating all forms of discrimination based on class, caste, geography, language, religion and gender. The preamble also dedicated itself to the goal of socialism based on democratic norms and values including a competitive plural democracy, individual liberty, fundamental human rights, adult franchise, periodic elections, press freedom, independent judiciary and the rule of law.

The preamble, thus, makes it amply clear that the socialist goal is to be pursued through democratic means. The constitution has declared the country as a sovereign, secular, inclusive, and socialism-oriented democratic republican state. It defines secularism as the preservation of religion and culture being practiced since ancient times, and the freedom to choose religious and cultural practices. The constitution has restructured the country into a federal republic, consisting of three tiers of government at the center, provinces and the local level. A bicameral parliamentary system has been adopted with two Houses, namely the House of Representatives and the National Assembly at the federal level. The House of Representative consists of 275 members, of which 165 (60 percent) are elected from the first-past-the-post Westminster-style electoral system and the remaining members from proportional representation based on the popular vote polled by the political parties treating the whole country as a single electoral constituency. The legislature at the provincial level is unicameral whose cumulative size across seven provinces is twice as large as the federal parliament. Here too, sixty percent of the members are elected on the basis of the first-past-the-post system and the remaining forty percent on the basis of proportional representation. The constitution has all other elements of a democratic constitution including an independent judiciary and several constitutional bodies.

Federalization

Federalization of the country with unitary history since its foundation two and a half centuries ago is the core and contentious feature of this constitution. Federalism was not the agenda of any major political party in Nepal, except that of Nepal Sadbhawana Party that had very limited electoral support even in Madhesh/Tarai, the region of their support base. It was also not the agenda of the CPN(Maoist) during the insurgency period. They stood for ethnic autonomous regions with the right to self-rule. The agenda of the SPA was inclusive democracy through state restructuring and reforms. The federal agenda was, however, raised by some groups, particularly the Madhesh-based parties and some ethnic groups, as the only means of state restructuring for inclusive democracy to properly reflect the diversity of the Nepali society in the state power structure. When the Interim Constitution was promulgated without a commitment to federalism on 27 August 2007, the Madhesh-based parties waged violent protests. The Madheshi community and some other ethnic groups considered federalism as a solution for their legitimate aspirations. As the issue became emotive and divisive after the successful 2006 popular uprising, the other political parties including the Nepali Congress and NCP(UML) ultimately acquiesced to the demand of declaring the country a Federal Democratic Republic with amendments in the interim constitution. The amended article 138 committed itself to federalism and inclusive governance by eliminating the centralized and unitary system of government with the objective of bringing an end to the discrimination of various kinds.

The announcement met with a mixed reaction of joy, despair, indifference and ambivalence. One school of thought tried to project federal system as the panacea to all ills of Nepali society, particularly relating to underdevelopment and regional disparities, over-centralization of political power, exclusion and discrimination. Some accepted it as a fait accompli, while others were skeptical saying it could turn into a siren song, leading to a road of disintegration. The worst fear was alluded by Shyam KC, one of Nepal's most prominent journalists. In an article in the Kathmandu Post, he cautioned about the risk of turning the country into another Yugoslavia: how in a short history of one hundred years, the Kingdom of Yugoslavia turned into the Democratic Republic, and then to Federal People's Republic, further to the Federal Socialist Republic and again to the Federal Republic of Yugoslavia. By the turn of the century, there is no trace of Yugoslavia, as the nation had vanished from the face of the earth, following the emergence of a number of ethnic nations after a series of bloody ethnic wars. Kul Chandra Gautam, a former UN Assistant Secretary-General also observed:[2]

> *Let us be clear that, unlike democracy, human rights, non-violence and pluralism, federalism is not a universal value or norm, but a political choice. So, support or opposition to it must not be treated as inherently progressive or regressive view, but a pragmatic and strategic political choice. Perfectly intelligent, reasonable and progressive thinkers can justifiably take a position in favor of federalism or against it, or different models of federalism.*

I also expressed my views on the subject in the media highlighting the challenges of the federal structure, while accepting the reality with suggestions to make it workable:[3]

> *The challenge before us is to guard the country against the risks of falling into divisive and destructive course or another form of autocracy in order that a smooth transition towards a peaceful, democratic, strong, united and prosperous Nepal with workable federal structure is ensured.......the question now is not whether it is suitable for Nepal or not. The road to federalism is fait accompli. The challenge is how to craft a system that meets the criteria of administrative convenience, economic rationality, and offers opportunities of political and cultural space for all communities without discrimination. The mosaic of diversity of this nation exists practically in every region which must be recognized and respected. The model should therefore address ethnic and regional aspirations, while strengthening racial harmony and national unity.*

Through 'disaggregation'

There are over two dozen federal countries in the world which have forty percent of the world's population. They include some of the largest and complex democracies like India, USA, Germany, Mexico and Brazil. There is no single model of federalism, as its historical evolution differs from country to country. A federal state is usually created through two modes, aggregation and disaggregation. In the first and more common model is the formation of a federation when more than one sovereign country with independent status agree to be united under one federal state through aggregation. The objective is to address issues of common concern like mutual defense and economic development. Most of the successful federal countries like the USA fall under this category of 'born federals. The other model is converting a unitary state into a federation by dividing the country into various provinces to share power. There are very few examples of such 'converted federals' in recent years through disaggregation, Belgium in the developed world and Ethiopia and Nigeria in the developing world.

After the national decision to go federal, questions emerged with regard to the basis of the country's division. Nepal is a country of ethnic, cultural and geographic diversity. Ethnic aspirations which had remained dormant for centuries under the centralized rule started finding expressions in various forms, peaceful and sometimes even violent. The ascendency of ethnic politics propelled some sections to demand provinces with ethnic identities. At the same time, the consideration of the economic sustainability of federating units while carving out provinces was equally important. The reality of Nepal's multi-ethnic and multi-linguistic character is reflected not just at the aggregate national level, but also in the prospective and proposed federating units. No viable province possessed exclusive ethnic or linguistic predominance. They have mixed populations with different mother tongues. Of the seventy-five districts in Nepal, only Chhetri community had majority population in nine districts; other major groups – Newar, Magar, Tharu, Tamang and Gurung had one district each with the majority population, grossly inadequate to make a viable federal unit.

A predominantly Hindu country with more than eighty percent Hindu population, the country declared itself secular to distance the statecraft from religion. The same logic was also used against aligning provinces with particular ethnicities or tribes. Furthermore, the ethnic state is contrary to the principle of inclusive polity. The demand for ethnic identity and aspirations of historically disadvantaged communities including Madhesis, Tharus, Muslims, Dalits and indigenous groups are real and need to be addressed. The solution was to address their concerns through appropriate statutory provisions including affirmative actions, 'special status regions' with autonomy and other measures providing necessary political, administrative and cultural space.

Despite vocal opposition by a small minority, particularly represented by United Front party, there was support for federalism among the major political parties after its announcement by the interim constitution through amendment. But the debate and controversy over its nature, number and territorial demarcation of provinces continued. This was the main reason for the failure of the first CA to complete the constitution. Even after the outcome of the second CA, the stalemate dragged on. In Kul Chandra Gautam's words, '*the federalism continued to be a lightning rod throughout Nepal's recent constitution-making process.*'[4] Ultimately, the CPN(Maoist) signed a sixteen-point agreement with Nepali Congress and CPN (UML) in June 2015 abandoning their stringent advocacy for ethnic identity-based federalism. The main reason for the policy shift seems to have been the result of second CA election, which relegated CPN(M) to the third position; other parties advocating stringent federalism including the Madhesh-based parties also fared badly in the election. The sixteen-point deal proposed an eight-province model, keeping on hold the actual demarcation which was to be done later by the Federal Commission. Naming the province was also postponed leaving it to be christened later by state assemblies.

Meanwhile, the Supreme Court issued an interim order that all issues of the constitution including the demarcation and naming of the provinces should be completed before the promulgation.

The interim order and increasing public pressure led the major parties to revise their position and come up with a six-province solution. But this led to an eruption of protests turning violent in some parts of the country, especially in the Karnali Zone and Surkhet, leading to loss of lives and injuries. Finally, there was a last-minute settlement on September 20, 2015, deciding upon seven provinces. Even this model that finally found place in the constitution was resented particularly by the Madhesi Janaadhikar Forum-Democratic and other Madhesh-based parties who had been demanding a separate Tharu province. The demarcation of the country into seven provinces was done by grouping together the existing districts, with the exception of Nawalparasi and Rukum districts which were split into two, each aligned with different provinces, and included in Schedule 4 of the new constitution. In terms of population, province 3 is the largest with 5.529 million people, while the smallest is Karnali province with 1.570 million people. Territory-wise, Karnali is the largest with 27,984 square kilometers, while the smallest is province 2 with 9,661 square km. All provinces except province 2 and 6 include north-south territories including plains, hills and mountains. Province 2 consists of only plains, and province 6 only hills and mountains. All provinces are multi-ethnic and multicultural.

Local empowerment

The imperative of decentralization at the local level through the transfer of authority has long been recognized in Nepal ever since the Panchayat days, although the actual implementation suffered then due to ambiguities in the demarcation of authority and highly centralized administrative structure of the government. After the advent of democratic rule in 1991, laws were enacted to specify the organizations, functions and authorities at the village, municipal and district levels. These bodies were empowered to formulate and pass annual programs and budget in their respective areas. The government employees deputed to these bodies were made accountable to the elected representatives at the local level. The legal basis was provided to form 'users committees' comprising of stakeholders' representatives to implement local projects. The revenue base of local bodies comprised of central level grants and collection of local taxes like land revenue and royalties from the extraction of natural resources.

The Local Self-Governance Act of 1999 was a landmark development that guaranteed fiscal and management authority of basic services with regard to schools, health posts, postal services, rural roads, small irrigation to local bodies. The law also empowered urban municipalities with wide-ranging functions in public utilities, social services and urban-related activities, and fiscal authority to raise various forms of taxes and fees.

It was widely feared that with the introduction of the federal system, the decentralized authority at the local level would come to an end as the power could shift to the provincial level. This would be against the fundamental democratic objective to bring governance closer to the people. Furthermore, the mandate of the second People's Movement was state restructuring against highly centralized governance with supremacy at the top. Local self-governance was considered necessary to safeguard the rights and sovereignty of the people for the sake of peace, sustainable development and resolution of conflicts. Therefore, while formulating the constitution it was decided that the local bodies should not be at the mercy of provincial government in managing their affairs, hence the need for constitutional guarantees of their functions and authority. The three tiers of governance including local government with comprehensive authority at the local level was codified against this background. Following the recommendation of the Local Body Restructuring Commission created as per the constitution, there exist at present a total of 753 local governments through merger, realignment and reconfiguration of approximately 3,900 Village Development Committees and municipalities. Of the 753 local governments, six are Metropolitan Cities, eleven Sub-metropolitan Cities, 276 Municipalities and 460 Rural Municipalities. At the district level, there exist seventy-seven district coordination committees whose function is limited to monitoring and coordinating the activities of the municipalities within the district and performing a bridging role with the provincial and federal governments.

The extensive power and functions entrusted at the local level is one of the most prominent features of the constitution, probably without parallel in other developing countries. The long list of their jurisdiction includes maintaining law and order with municipal police, delivery of basic health and sanitation, basic and secondary education, local development projects, licensing of radio stations, management of local markets, environment conservation, construction of local infrastructure, care of senior citizen and the disabled, agriculture and livestock, drinking water, small hydroelectricity and alternative energy, conservation of wasteland, wildlife and mines, preservation of language and culture, agricultural statistics, unemployment data and so on. The local government has also been bestowed with authority to legislate, impose local taxes including property and land tax, various fees, advertisement, entertainment and business taxes, and manage local courts and dispute settlement.

Inclusive representation

Inclusive governance and elimination of all types of discrimination were the principal motives behind the political change, subsequently enshrined in the preamble of the 2015 constitution. The constitution has incorporated various statutory provisions to empower the disadvantaged communities and create an equitable society reflecting the diversity and multicultural character of the country. Regarding the topmost positions of the nation, the President and Vice President, article 70 of the constitution states that election of the President and the Vice President has to be held so as to represent different gender and communities. The legislative wings at all three tiers will have a minimum of one third women representation. While electing the speaker or deputy speaker of the federal parliament and the provincial assemblies, the post of either speaker or deputy speaker should go to the woman. The constitutional provision mandating a minimum of one-third legislative representation of women makes Nepal's parliament one of the most gender inclusive in South Asia and other regions too, as shown by global data map of Inter-parliamentary Union and Women.

At the local level, women fill either the post of the mayor or deputy mayor, and provision has been made to ensure representation of women, Dalits and minorities in the executive and legislative mechanisms too. Another landmark feature of the constitution to ensure social inclusion is the reservation of a minimum of forty percent seats in the federal and provincial legislatures based on proportional representation of indigenous communities, Khas Arya, Madhesi, Dalits, Tharu and Muslims, communities from backward regions and minorities on the basis of population and geography. There is also a provision for compulsory representation of persons with disability. Statutory provision has been made for proportional representation of these clusters while filing candidacy for the election of legislative wings at the federal and provincial levels for proportional representation through closed list.

Establishment of different constitutional bodies to address the concerns and interest of the traditionally neglected communities is another distinct feature of the Constitution of Nepal 2015. Part 27 of the constitution provides for the formation of six separate national commissions: National Women Commission, National Dalit Commission, National Inclusion Commission, Indigenous Nationalities Commission, Madhesi Commission, Tharu Commission and Muslim Commission. Each Commission will have one chairman and four members appointed by the President on the recommendation of the Constitutional Council. The commissions are mandated to formulate policies and programs concerning the rights and interest of the concerned community, carry out research on legal and other reforms and forward to the government, monitor and review their implementation and compliance to relevant international agreements and treaties etc.

Fundamental rights

The fundamental rights and duties enshrined in part 3 of the constitution further reflect the spirit and letter of the preamble to put an end to all forms of discrimination with an objective to create an egalitarian society. The thirty-one fundamental rights from article 16 to 46 encompass political, social, economic, cultural and environmental rights, with hardly any parallel in the developing world. Part of these rights which are often found in other democracies include the right to live with dignity, freedom, equality, property, justice; and the right against torture, preventive detention, exploitation, untouchability and discrimination. The elaborate set of fundamental rights also includes the right to privacy, clean environment, education, social justice and the right to preserve and promote one's own language and culture.

Other ambitious provisions in the list include such economic rights as the right to basic health care from the state, right to food, right to employment, right to appropriate housing, right to free basic education and right to acquire education up to the secondary level in mother tongue etc. Similarly, the constitution guarantees various rights of women including safe motherhood and reproductive health, right of children to health care, nurturing, appropriate upbringing and overall personality development, rights of Dalits to free education up to higher level, rights of senior citizens, economically poor, physically incapacitated and helpless single women to special protection and social security and consumers' right for quality food and services. The constitution guarantees constitutional remedies for the enforcement of all these challenging rights with the enactment of necessary laws.

The constitution comprises of all the provisions for federal, decentralized, democratic, inclusive and progressive governance. The fundamental rights ensuring people's access to services and resources from the state, progressive provisions for women participation and the representation of traditionally neglected communities, together with democratic principles of the rule of law, independent judiciary, separation of power between main state organs with checks and balances makes it a rare document combining the democratic and progressive features. Clearly, the constitution represents a unique compromise between major political parties with conflicting backgrounds and philosophies. In the 601-member Assembly, 538 members supported the constitution, while sixty voted against. A few refrained from the voting process. The task now is to effectively implement the constitution in the face of demand for amendments, managerial complexities and fiscal challenges.

Opposition voices

The opposition to the constitution came mainly from the Madhesh-based parties and some splinter groups. The Madhesh-based Rastriya Janata Party continues to treat the Constitution Day of 19 September as 'Black Day' holding protest rallies, attended even by a provincial minister or two in Province 2. The opposition centers mainly on the demarcation of provincial boundaries and parliamentary representation. While the promulgation of the constitution was celebrated by the vast majority of the public and received warmly by the global community, there was agitation in some parts of Madhesh; the reaction of the immediate neighbor India, whose support would have mattered most, was frigid. The Madhesh agitation continued for four months, bolstered by a de facto trade and transit blockade from the Indian side leading to strangulation of the Nepali economy, as India accounts for two-thirds of external trade, and ninety percent of third country trade passes through India. There were also news reports in some foreign media distorting and misrepresenting the constitution with allegations of the document being elitist and non-inclusive favoring Hill Khas supremacy, ignoring the constitutional provisions of an elaborate set of socio-economic and cultural rights and proportional representation of forty percent parliamentary seats to redress the under-representation of traditionally deprived communities and other progressive provisions.

Another allegation against the constitution, that it did not accept population-based representation, is also untrue. Taking into account the specific character of demographic distribution in Nepal where hugely inaccessible and sparsely populated Himalayan districts coexist with densely populated Kathmandu valley and the Tarai-Madhesh region, the constitution provides for representation based on mainly population, with consideration of geography too, particularly for the eighteen Himalayan districts. If population had been the sole basis of representation, the 18 Himalayan districts would not have proper representation. The population density in these districts with rugged mountains with no transportation network is as low as 3–10 persons per square kilometer, where it takes months on foot to visit all settlements of one parliamentary constituency, as compared to around 500 persons per square kilometer in the central and eastern Madhesh. It is a common practice in all democracies including India and the USA to incorporate other aspects too besides population in parliamentary representation. If population had been made the sole factor in India, the Lok Sabha of India would have much larger representation from very populous northern states, while smaller states and union territories like Sikkim, Pondicherry, Andaman and Nicobar Islands, Lakshadweep, Mizoram and Nagaland would not have been represented as at present. It is also pertinent to mention that all mid-hill districts in Nepal despite difficult geography accepted population-based representation at par with the Tarai-Madhesh districts. Under the present constitutional arrangement, the Tarai-Madhesh region is estimated to garner 48 percent seats in the national legislature contrary to the misreporting by some commentators that it will be only one-third of the seats.

The other criticism was related to the delineation of federal provinces demanding two exclusive Madhesh provinces, or a merger of Morang and Sunsari districts in Province 2, and Kailali in Province 5 while excluding the hill districts. The existing alignment of Tarai with some hill districts in these two provinces was based on the complementarity of resource endowment, viability, economic and social interdependence. In my view, any change in the proposed alignment should be the prerogative of the people on the ground who are the ultimate stakeholders, rather than leaving the fate to behind-the-scenes machinations of a few political hands. It is the sovereign right of the people in the concerned districts to decide their future by aligning themselves with one province or the other. According to article 274 of the constitution, any alteration of the provincial boundary would require the endorsement of the concerned provincial assembly.

While the demand of the Madhesh-based parties for a constitutional amendment to address these and some other issues continues, the constitution implementation has now taken shape following the election of all three levels of legislature participated by all parties, and subsequent formation of governments. Murmurs continue to be heard from the traditional parties like the Rastriya Prajatantra Party, some sections of the Nepali Congress and various other groups on secularism in a country with a predominantly Hindu population. They demand a national referendum to settle the question. There is also opposition to the restrictive citizenship provision for children of Nepali women married to foreign nationals, in contrast to children of Nepali fathers irrespective of the mother's citizenship. In a democracy, such issues raised from different quarters are not unusual, which eventually will have to be settled through due process of law and constitution.

Management and fiscal side

The country now has a massive superstructure of multiple governments. There are now approximately 37,000 elected representatives with legislative authority at three levels, hundreds of ministers at the federal and provincial levels, and thousands of executive members at the local level. The constitution has also provisioned about a dozen constitutional commissions, something rare even in a federal setup. The need for constitutional bodies arises to ensure impartiality and independence without executive influence in sensitive matters like public auditing, general election, civil service recruitment and human rights. But the constitution has provisioned for multiple commissions even on matters which are solely the responsibilities of the executive to ensure fulfilment of constitutional obligations in favor of the disadvantaged and neglected minorities.

To enable these bodies to perform the duties and functions entrusted by the constitution will require administrative structures and human resources. As the new governance structure has resulted from state restructuring, the old headquarters and administrative centers have become redundant and are displaced, hence the imperative of building fresh physical infrastructure in new locations. Even after more than one and a half year of the formation of provincial legislatures and governments, majority of the seven provinces have failed to decide their names and locations for provincial capitals because of conflicting positions based on regional and ethnic considerations. Obviously, in view of the insufficient administrative capacity of the sub-national and local governments to perform their functions, the immediate priority should be on building institutional capacity with necessary manpower, financial arrangements and legal framework. The institution-building costs including wage bill, other administrative expenses and building physical infrastructure will be quite high. The annual recurrent budget of Nepal already accounts for more than 25 percent of GDP, which is likely to increase further. The World Bank estimates that the transitional cost of building a new architecture will be between three and four percent of annual GDP for a period of four years.

The present constitution of Nepal is different from earlier constitutions drafted by constitutional experts and jurists and promulgated by the king. Formulated by the popularly elected assembly, it naturally reflects popular aspirations. The aspirational elements have been reflected in various aspects of the constitution including the fundamental rights. Some of the provisions that represent moral responsibility of the government and generally included in the directive principles of the state policy in other democratic constitutions have been codified as fundamental rights in Nepal constitution enforceable in the court of law. The constitution is largely rights-based, ensuring maximum rights including those with economic and fiscal implications. The constitution also requires that necessary legal provisions for the enforcement of these fundamental rights should be enacted within three years of the commencement of the constitution. Due to delay in drafting the laws, there was a last-minute rush to present about seventeen fundamental rights bills in the parliament just about two weeks before the expiry of the deadline on 18 September 2018.

The legislative process was completed on a fast-track mode suspending the rules of procedure without much discussion and deliberations in the parliament and its committees. Eleven bills were passed hurriedly by the National Assembly in a single day on September 16 without any deliberation. There has been very little appraisal on the financial and other implications of these rights-related legislations which could create further difficulties while enforcing the laws in future. It may be recalled here that even the constitution was passed in 2015 on a fast-track mode with a behind-the-scenes agreement among main political leaders, without undergoing clause-wise deliberations in the Assembly. The price of short-cutting a legislative process without adequate consultation and feedback from the stakeholders will be felt during the implementation phase of the statute.

Fiscal federalism is a new and difficult subject for Nepal. Despite the constitutional provisions of separate economic rights and responsibilities for the three tiers, confusion has arisen in practice resulting in duplication and overlapping of authority. A phenomenon of competitive populism has begun to surface among provinces and local governments to inflate the size of budgets by raising tax and borrowing. There are public complaints and protests against a lack of transparency in expenditures and excessive taxes by local and provincial governments. There are reports of fees levied even on basic government services like registration of birth, marriage, migration and death, and taxes on livestock.

In some municipalities, property and business taxes have been raised multiple times. There are also reports from many places about taxes levied on intra-provincial and interprovincial movement of goods, services and vehicles in clear contravention to Article 236 of the constitution that prohibits any discrimination and obstruction through taxes and other means on the movement of goods and services between municipalities and provinces. A high-level committee constituted by the government to investigate the tax disputes and complaints concluded that there were cases of taxes levied by some provincial and local governments against constitutional provisions. It also admitted the lack of legal clarity and discrepancies between constitutional and legal provisions on tax provisions, and that the tax row also arose due to a sharp rise in tax rates and services fees without adequate discussions among stakeholders.

Disputes have arisen between national and sub-national governments on matters of taxes, resource allocation and transfer. It is natural that provincial and local level governments have limited volume of revenue and administrative capacity to match their broad set of functions and responsibilities, hence the need for fiscal transfer and other support from the center. There are complaints from the provincial and local governments about the federal government keeping most of the resources with itself, even as the bulk of the responsibilities are shouldered by the sub-national and local governments. The provincial chief ministers held a joint meeting in Pokhara on September 7, 2018, to formulate a common position on issues concerning them. They accused the central government of not delegating power and being apathetic towards the concerns of provincial governments that lacked necessary manpower and recruitment authority for security services. Their request for a joint meeting with the Prime Minister for the first time was reportedly denied on the suspicion that it was an attempt to gang up against the Prime Minister even though six of the seven chief ministers are from the same party.

Article 234 of the constitution has provisioned the Inter-State Council under the chairmanship of the Prime Minister 'to settle political disputes arising between the federation and the province and among the provinces.' The three meetings of the Council held at various occasions until the end of April 2019 have failed to make any headway in resolving the disputes between the federal and sub-national governments. There are reports of jurisdictional conflicts on various issues including security arrangements, recruitments of police and civilian employees etc, in the absence of timely promulgation of federal laws concerning concurrent list between the federal and provincial governments.

The provincial governments opposed the federal executive order issued on 28 October 2018 on deployment and transfer of police personnel. The executive order was issued, following the passing of a police bill by Province 2 Assembly, prior to the enactment of the related umbrella bill by the federal parliament. The Province 2 has also prepared a bill to set up a district administration office with responsibility for security, law and order matters in parallel to the Chief District Officer office of the federal government. The central government is generally accused of harboring an 'anti-federal' attitude and behavior by the provinces resulting in creating institutional and operational bottlenecks in constitution implementation.[5] On the other hand, there are reports of haphazard and reckless spending of taxpayer's money by provincial and local level governments in recurrent and non-productive expenditure including fruitless training programs and seminars, raising of perks and privileges, doling out various gifts and grants, and buying and renting luxury vehicles for elected representatives even at local levels.

The jurisdictional confusion and controversy on fiscal matters arose also because of the delay in setting up the National Fiscal and Natural Resources Commission. The constitution has provisioned its creation with the principal function of developing the norms and measures for distributing the fiscal resources from the federal consolidated fund vertically between the three tiers of government, horizontally among provincial and local governments. The body is also responsible for suggesting reform measures on revenue and expenditure for the three levels of government. Even after one year of government formation at all three tiers, thousands of development projects in various sectors approved and initiated by the previous government at the center are in disarray and left in the lurch because of the confusion over their ownership. The federal government abandoned them on the ground that they do not fall under the federal list. The sub-national or local governments have not taken them over in the absence of formal handover with adequate funding and execution mandate.

Concluding remarks

The 2015 constitution of Nepal is a milestone document that represents the culmination of long struggles for democratic rule and popular sovereignty, post-conflict transition and the peace process, the Palace Massacre that obliterated a legitimate monarchical lineage of the long past, and the devastating earthquake of 2015. It is a historic statute written by popularly elected peoples' representatives, committed to establishing a just and inclusive society with strong devolution of power with few parallels in the developing world.

The country is presently in the transitional phase of implementing the constitution and is faced with the birth pangs of a new polity of the federal republic. The constitution written by the elected representatives of the people naturally reflects popular aspirations. The high popular expectations created by constitutional provisions are accompanied by some unmet aspirations too. The transition to Nepal's federalism, away from a unitary centralized state, is naturally not a smooth affair. It is beset with challenges that call for due care, hard work, perseverance and a work culture and mindset different from the past. The main task at present is building of institutional capacity at the subnational and local levels to perform the tasks entrusted by the constitution, with supporting legislations, regulations and necessary manpower that are lacking at present.

There is also a challenge of making federalism financially sustainable in view of the high cost involved in managing the political and administrative superstructure of three layers of government. It may be pertinent to recall that the size of the civil service was cut down by twenty-five percent as part of administrative reform after the democratic political change of 1990 leading to the containment of regular expenditure. Now, under the new constitution, the size of bureaucracy is likely to go up by about forty percent. Driven mainly by the rising cost of this political and administrative superstructure, growing unproductive expenditure resulting from competitive populism at different levels of government, increasing non-contributory social security spending, the recurrent expenditure that already accounts for around two-thirds of the annual budget will further escalate with new public liabilities and obligations inherent in the constitution. All these factors are likely to result in heavy fiscal stress, unprecedented in Nepal's recent history of generally balanced budgets and sound macroeconomic management. There is, therefore, the imperative of better governance and fiscal leadership to make the federal constitution functional and financially sustainable, while accelerating the economic growth process so that additional resources are generated to fund all the promised constitutional mandates and liabilities.

Notes

1. Everest Law Associates and Legal Research Center. (2074 v.s.). *Nepalko Sambidhan, 2072, Pahilo Samsodhan* v.s. *2072, Magh 9*. Kathmandu.
2. Gautam, Kul Chandra (2016). *Lost in Transition Rebuilding Nepal from the Maoist Mayhem and Mega Earthquake*, (p. 300). Kathmandu.
3. Mahat, Ram Sharan (2009, August 17-18). The Challenges of Federalism. *Republica*, Kathmandu.
4. Gautam, K. C. Ibid.
5. After the end of the Council meeting on April 27, 2019 the Chief Minister Prithvi Subba Gurung of Gandaki Province is reported to have blamed the central leaders as guided by old mind-set and not internalizing the federal spirit in coordinating with the provincial governments. He remarked 'they are neither devolving power nor providing resources' (2019, April 28). *The Kathmandu Post.*

Chapter Six

Yam Between Two Boulders

Geo-strategically situated on the southern lap of the Himalayas between India and China -- the two of the world's largest nations -- Nepal is both a place of origin and confluence of two great religions, Hinduism and Buddhism. While a predominantly Hindu population is a common link between Nepal and India, Buddhism spread to Tibet and further to East Asia via Nepal. Lord Buddha, born in Lumbini in Nepal, mediated and achieved the highest state of spiritual enlightenment '*Nirvana*' in Bodhgaya, India. The intermingling of the Indo-Aryan and Tibeto-Burman civilizations has made Nepal a tolerant mix of more than a hundred ethnic communities with distinct languages or dialects through history, leading to the emergence of a national character that is uniquely rich and diverse.

Historical perspective

Nepal-India cultural and social relations date back to pre-historical times. There is evidence of connections between the two countries during the religious epochs of *Treta Yug* and *Dwapar Yug*, which represent the times of Hindu legends Lord Rama and Lord Krishna. There are sites in Nepal where the Indian Rishis are believed to have lived, mediated and written holy books and performed religious rites.[1] The extant international boundaries of Nepal are about two hundred years old, with one substantial addition of a swathe of territory (Naya Muluk) in the southwest in 1857.[2] But the history of Nepal as a mountain civilization goes back at least two millennia. There are accounts written by Chinese pilgrims who travelled to Nepal via the Himalayan passes in the seventh century. The most important milestone in Nepal-Tibet relationship was the marriage of Nepali princess Bhrikuti to the king of Tibet Songtsan Gampo in the seventh century. Bhrikuti, the daughter of Licchavi Emperor Anshuvarma, was a devout Buddhist who played a major role in promoting Buddhism in Tibet. As part of her dowry, she took with her to Tibet Newar craftsmen, Buddhist sculptures and scriptures. Princess Bhrikuti was considered Green Tara in Tibetan iconography, in recognition to her contribution in spreading Buddhism and Buddhist architecture in Tibet. Nepali craftsmen, under her direction, were responsible for building many monasteries, temples and palaces including the famous Jokhang Temple, considered the most sacred in Tibet at the heart of Lhasa. Trade of bronze, gold and silver idols of Tara and other deities formed a commercial cornerstone between the two countries.

In the modern territory of Nepal, there existed multiple kingdoms and principalities whose boundary extended to some parts of today's India and China. In western Nepal, there existed a powerful kingdom of Malla rulers, the Khas Empire whose boundary extended to some parts of the present western Tibet. There were at least eighteen Himalayan passes in the central Himalayas used for trade, religious and cultural interactions with Tibet. Of them, Kerung and Kuti passes were the most prominent routes because of the relatively low elevation of 13,000–14000 feet and proximity to Kathmandu valley which was the main entrepot between Tibet and South Asia. The altitude of other passes was more than 17,000 feet and invariably snowbound for several months of the year. From the emergence of Tibet in the seventh century to the opening of Gangtok route in 1902, Nepal was the main center of trans-Himalayan trade. Many ethnic Newar merchants of Kathmandu were permitted to do business with Tibet.

Conflicts occurred between the Malla rulers of Kathmandu and Shah rulers of Gorkha to control the Himalayan trade routes to Tibet because of their strategic and commercial importance. The expanding military power of the Gorkha kingdom under the farsighted political leadership of King Prithvi Narayan Shah eventually amalgamated all valley kingdoms, the *Chaubisi Rajya* of the Gandaki region, the Karnali basin, and Sen kingdoms of Makwanpur, Chaudandi and Bijayapur in the east and several Terai districts through a series of military conquests that laid the territorial foundation of modern Nepal. The national boundary underwent further expansion during the regency regime of Prithvi Narayan's second son, Bahadur Shah, when Nepali borders reached the Tista river of Sikkim in the East and Satlaz river of present-day Himachal Pradesh in northwest India.

The nation's projection and drive as a regional imperial power and an expansionist military strategy led to a costly clash with the British in 1814–16. In the aftermath of this Anglo-Nepal war, the country surrendered one-third of its newly acquired territory. Nepal also fought a war with Tibet in 1778 after Prithvi Narayan Shah's death because of the dispute arising over the circulation of Nepali coins in Tibet and the imposition of taxes on goods traded between India and Tibet through Nepal. The war ended in Nepal's favor, with Tibet agreeing to use coins on Nepali terms and conceding several commercial benefits to Nepal including the stationing of Nepal trade representative in Tibet and granting of a monopoly on trans-Himalayan trade to Nepal by closing alternative trade routes. But the treaty of Kerung signed in 1789 could not end the hostility; war further broke out in 1791 in which China intervened. It eventually led to Nepal-Tibet-China Treaty of 1792 under which Tibet came under greater control of China. Nepal had to give up important economic benefits from Tibet and was also required to pay a quinquennial tribute mission to China that continued until 1908.

Yam between two stones

The great warrior and statesman Prithvi Narayan Shah was not only the founder of modern Nepal but his understanding of contemporary foreign power dynamics of his time, strategic knowledge and foresight made him a wise founder of Nepal's external policy too. His oft-quoted remarks from *Dibya Upadesh* about Nepal's security vulnerability and limitations are as follows:

> *The kingdom is like a yam between two boulders. Maintain friendly relations with the Emperor of China. Great friendship should be maintained with the emperor beyond the Southern Seas (i.e., the British), but he is clever. He has kept India suppressed and is entrenching himself in the plains. One day the army will come. Do not engage in offensive acts. Fighting should be defensive.*

The dictum remains a reference point for Nepal's security policy even today. There was a failure to strictly adhere to this policy by latter successors by overstretching the military might for unrestrained expansionary and offensive endeavors with both the powers in south and north, which made the country pay dearly through the loss of territory, national pride and economic benefits. At a time when the British East India Company was rapidly colonizing the native kingdoms and principalities in India, Prithvi Narayan Shah naturally visualized the danger from their growing power. He followed the policy of keeping them in good humor but at a safe distance. Immediately after his enthronement, he visited Benaras to get first-hand information on the political and security situation of the subcontinent and explore technological know-how to manufacture ammunition. The objective was the creation of a unified and strong country to meet possible imperialist threats.

Suspicious of the motive of the British East India Company, he followed a protectionist trade policy. After the conquest of Kathmandu, he banished all Capuchin missionaries and foreign traders on suspicion of their being secret British agents, and prevented Europeans from entering the country. His expansion drive also moved eastward after the victory over Kathmandu to prevent the British from opening trade routes in the East in a bid to preserve Kathmandu's monopoly as an entrepôt for Indo-Tibet trade.

The interest of the British East India Company in Nepal was to expand the trans-Himalayan trade with Tibet for which it sent several missions since 1767.[3] Following reversals in the 1791 war with China, Nepal agreed to sign a commercial treaty with the British in 1792 in the hope of getting military assistance, laying the foundation for trade relation between the two countries for the first time. But as subsequent development did not serve Nepali expectation, the suspicious attitude towards the British continued. However, the British pursuit of commercial interests was unchanged. In 1801, taking advantage of the court feud, the British were successful in pressurizing Nepal to sign a treaty which, among others, provided stationing of a British residency mission in Kathmandu. Captain Knox was the first British Resident entrusted with the mandate of securing implementation of the 1792 treaty, assessing trade prospects with Nepal and Tibet and ascertaining the possibility of securing a chunk of timber-rich Tarai forests in exchange for cash or equivalent Company territory.

Alignment with Britain

After the restoration of political stability and consolidation of power following the Kot Massacre of 1846, Jung Bahadur Rana went to war with Tibet for the third time in 1855 to reassert dominance over Tibet and for commercial gains. The war ended with the signing of the 1856 treaty that regulated commercial relations between the two countries for almost a century. The treaty acknowledged the Chinese suzerainty over Tibet, provided for the trade fair in Kuti and Kerung every spring where the Tibetans could come and exchange with Nepali merchandise, stationing of a Nepali representative in Lhasa and annual tribute payments by Tibet to Nepal.

During the Rana regime that lasted for 104 years between 1846 and 1950, friendship with Britain remained the cornerstone of Nepal's foreign policy. The main objective was to maintain independence and territorial integrity in the face of fierce wind blowing strongly across the entire region that brought the entire subcontinent under foreign domination. Being friendly with the British was considered to be a necessary strategy by the Ranas to sustain their family rule. Impressed with the gallantry and martial qualities that the highlander Nepali forces demonstrated in the 1814-16 war, the British made overtures to enlisting Nepali youth in the British army. This long-standing British interest was served in 1885 under Rana Prime Minister Bir Shamsher when Britain was granted permission for unrestricted recruitment of Nepali youth in British Gorkha regiment in India. This practice, despite episodic bursts of controversy, continues to this day, albeit in small numbers.

Another notable aspect of the history of Nepal-Britain relationship is Nepal's contribution to the two World Wars. Fighting on the side of allied forces, the Nepali youth who left the country for combat and non-combat operations numbered approximately 200,000 in the First World War and 160,000 in the Second World War. The countryside of Nepal was stripped of the youth population during the period, and the loss of Nepali lives in the First World War in proportion to the population at that time, was higher than that of any other nation that participated in the war. Nepal also offered cash and large amounts of in-kind contribution (cardamom, tea, blankets and broad-gauge sleepers) to support the British. The British reciprocated Nepal's exemplary gesture by an unconditional annual cash grant of one million Indian rupees in perpetuity, which was further raised to two million after the Second World War. A new Anglo-Nepal Friendship Treaty was signed in 1923 that recognized Nepal's status as an independent nation, allaying the controversy regarding Nepal's independence. It also permitted the unrestricted duty-free import of overseas goods by Nepal through Indian territory.

Diversification drive

The end of the Second World War and India's independence from Britain in 1947 opened new international space for Nepal to expand and diversify external relations. The Rana regime realized the limitation of self-induced reliance on Britain and initiated diplomatic relations with USA, Burma and France. Attempts to gain UN membership was vetoed by the Soviet Union. The Rana regime, desperate for survival in its last days signed a Treaty of Peace and Friendship in 1950 with India that virtually brought the country under an Indian security umbrella. The Indian military mission arrived in 1952 to reorganize the Nepali army, and subsequently, Indian military mission was deployed along the Nepali border with China for military intelligence purpose. The mission ended only in 1970.

The dawn of democracy after the end of Rana oligarchy coincided with the emergence of newly independent nations and the onset of the Cold War that divided the world into two power blocks. The realization of the changing power dynamics by the new democratic rulers led to further rapid diversification of foreign relations including the upgradation of relation with the US to ambassadorial level and the establishment of diplomatic relations with China, Soviet Union, Germany, Switzerland and Japan in the 1950s. Projecting the strict non-alignment policy, the BP Koirala government diversified the foreign relations establishing diplomatic relations with seventeen countries including the state of Israel and Pakistan in a period of eighteen months of his government. For many decades, Nepal was the only country east of the Suez Canal to host the Israel embassy. The border delineation and demarcation with China were also successfully concluded during BP Koirala's premiership.

When BP Koirala was prime minister, an incident took place in Nepal's northern border near Kore Pass of Mustang district when Chinese troops fired at Nepali border guards killing one soldier and taking ten others hostage. BP Koirala denounced the Chinese action as an attack undermining Nepal's sovereignty and violation of border delimitation agreement concluded just a few months earlier, under which China and Nepal pledged not to deploy armed forces or patrols within twenty kilometers of the border. Reacting to this incident, Indian Prime Minister Nehru hinted at unilateral Indian military action, as any aggression against Nepal and Bhutan would be treated as aggression against India. Prime Minister Koirala immediately retorted to this statement by saying that Nepal is a fully sovereign country that would decide its own external and home policy based on its own judgement without ever referring to outside authorities. Not objecting to this statement, Nehru immediately remarked that there is no question of India taking unilateral action. The Chinese Prime Minister wrote to the Prime Minister of Nepal expressing deep regret and apology for the unfortunate and unexpected incident due to carelessness on the part of low-ranking Chinese troops, and also paid compensation for the losses incurred on the Nepali side. This episode speaks of the independent foreign policy assertively pursued by BP Koirala to the satisfaction of both neighbors. In his address to the fifteenth session of the UN General Assembly, he declared that United Nations can neither be a universal body nor can it reflect the political realities existing in the world until the People's Republic of China with 630 million population is given a rightful place in the Organization.[4]

Building on the modern foundations laid in the 1950s and the 1960s, the Panchayat regime continued to diversify Nepal's foreign forays. Nepal successfully promoted its vital interests in preserving its independence, territorial integrity, and reaping economic benefits pursuing a policy of friendship with all countries. Development assistance from bilateral and multilateral bodies were the major sources of infrastructure financing in the country as Nepal's own internal resource was meager. Nepal was also able to develop an independent identity by taking up impartial and independent position on a number of regional and international issues such as those relating to China, Vietnam, Israel and Palestine. The goodwill arising from this policy was reflected in the support extended by 120 countries from diverse backgrounds for Nepal's proposal floated by King Birendra in 1975 to be known as a Zone of Peace. India refused to support the proposal on the ground that the objective behind it was to extricate Nepal from the framework of the 1950 treaty.

The restoration of democracy in 1990 gave a further boost to Nepal's drive for expansion and diversification of international relations in a new era of globalization. The democratic credential of the new dispensation enhanced the country's external image contributing to further economic cooperation from bilateral and multilateral sources. At present, Nepal has diplomatic relations with 166 countries and more than two dozen residential missions. It is a member of all international multilateral organizations, regional bodies and has served twice in the Security Council. The most visible role in the UN has been its contribution to peacekeeping operations. Starting with a contingent of 571 army personnel sent for the peacekeeping mission in the Sinai desert of Egypt following the 1973 Arab-Israel War, Nepal's cumulative contribution has reached approximately 45,000 troops in UN peacekeeping operations across various conflict-ridden hotspots around the globe.

Promotion of national interest in its dealings and relations with the outside world is the fundamental objective of any country. Nepal has evolved a foreign policy preserving its image as an independent sovereign country living within the compulsions dictated by physical location, history, culture and external environment while advancing its economic interests. Loyalty to the British, together with the policy of isolationism in the past was instrumental in ensuring the survival of the country as an independent nation. The isolationism under the Ranas kept the country hermetically closed from external influence, thereby helping safeguard its independence, but at a tremendous economic cost. When it opened up fully to the world in 1950, it was distressingly poor and lagging.

A new world order emerged after the Second World War, characterized by de-colonization and brewing cold war rivalry between the two superpowers. The dawn of democracy after 1950 in the new global context saw fresh postulates and strategies of foreign policy to adjust to the changing international reality. Nepal's UN membership in 1955 provided a forum to play a role in the international arena unfettered by the limitations imposed by Nepal's location between two large Asian countries. Adherence to the principles and objectives of basic UN Charter became one of the basic features of foreign relations. Active engagement in the General Assembly and its various subsidiary bodies, two-term membership of the Security Council, ECOSOC and others, membership of all UN specialized agencies with development partnership and substantial contribution to UN peace-keeping forces contributed in enhancing Nepal's international image as a reliable global citizen. The UN has ranked the country as the fourth largest contributor to military and civilian components of peacekeeping operations. Nepal has taken an independent position on contentious global issues. At the same time, Nepal never wavered from its policy of recognizing the right of Palestine to become an independent state. It has called for Israeli withdrawal from territories occupied in the 1967 war.

Nepal is also one of the founding members of the Non-Alignment Movement, the genesis of which goes back to Nepal's participation in Afro-Asian Conference in Bandung in early 1955. The policy of non-alignment was a natural choice for Nepal given its geographical location and history. The principle of neutrality between the two major powers propounded by Prithvi Narayan Shah from the days of its foundation has stood the test of time; the country was able to preserve its independence in the face of major upheavals in the subcontinent. The Non-Alignment Movement was started amidst a polarized world of the Cold War period by countries which did not want to be identified with either block in their search for new relations across the world. The movement was often haunted by the shadow of the Cold War. US Secretary of the State John Foster Dulles called the movement 'immoral', while some other nations close to the Soviet Union tried to use the forum for anti-Western campaigns. In such a situation, Nepal joined a small group of member countries to prevent derailment of the movement from its fundamental tenets. Being an active participant in all summits, ministerial and other official level meetings, playing a balanced and moderate role helped enhance Nepal's reputation as a moderate peace-loving country. However, with the end of the Cold War, the breakup of the Soviet Union and the collapse of communist regimes in eastern Europe, the relevance of the Non-Alignment Movement has come under question leading to shrinkage of its activities.

Regionalism and power dynamics

From the time of the conception of the idea of regional cooperation among South Asian countries mooted in the late 1970s, Nepal has been its strong supporter. The enthusiasm resulted from the perception that regionalism mitigates the compulsion of overdependence on a single neighbor, providing broader space for economic and political relations. The concept of the South Asian Association for Economic Cooperation was floated initially by the President of Bangladesh in 1980. The Indian response was initially one of hesitation because of suspicion that it could be a forum for its smaller neighbors to gang up against the biggest country by regionalizing bilateral issues. Pakistan was even more apprehensive and showed little interest. Because of India's preponderance in the region, it was suspicious that the forum could result in creating a regional market for Indian products and be an 'Indian show' for all practical purposes. After persistent efforts at the diplomatic and political levels to mitigate fears of the two major neighbors, SAARC was formally launched in Dhaka in December 1985. In its three decades of history, SAARC adoption of conventions and passing of resolutions have covered a vast number of areas including combating terrorism, poverty alleviation, regional development fund, drug and human trafficking, South Asian Free Trade (SAFTA), regional power grid connection and others for regional cooperation. The concrete outcome in terms of economic integration, however, has been inadequate. SAARC remains the least integrated region of the world where intra-regional trade or investment is less than 5 percent, not different from pre-SAARC days. The deep-seated enmity between India and Pakistan and occasional hiccups between India and smaller neighbors have been the principal factor behind slow progress. Nepal joined another regional grouping BIMSTEC (Bay of Bengal Initiative for Multi-sectoral Technical and

Economic Cooperation) in 2004, that includes all SAARC member countries (excluding Pakistan, Maldives and Afghanistan) plus Myanmar and Thailand from Southeast Asia. Freedom from bilateral conflict, along with the inclusion of the fast-growing economy of Thailand was expected to generate greater trade and investment benefits. Nepal is also a participant of the South Asia Sub-regional Economic Cooperation (SASEC) that brings together Bangladesh, Bhutan, Maldives, Myanmar, Nepal and Sri-Lanka in a project-based partnership that aims to promote intraregional trade and open up trade opportunities through improved connectivity, modern customs administration and development of economic corridors across SASEC countries.

It is obvious that BIMSTEC and SASEC groupings are the outcomes of mainly Indian initiatives where the nation could play a dominant role in view of the size of their economy, a role obstructed by Pakistani ambivalence in SAARC. Its Look East policy which was subsequently renamed Act East policy is also reflected in the importance accorded to these regional bodies, at a time when China's ambitious Belt and Road Initiative attracts global attention. The BRI initiative involving trillions of dollars of investment aims to build a wide network of land and sea connectivity with major markets centers of the world, Asia, Africa, Eurasia, Middle East and Europe to boost trade ties. Nepal signed the Memorandum of Understanding with China for participation in OBOR with the objective of promoting transport connectivity, trade, finance and people.

Nepal was also one of the early supporters of the China-sponsored Asian Infrastructure Investment Bank (AIIB), a supplementary initiative of the BRI, because of its potential to become an additional investment source to fill the much-needed infrastructure gap. This author, as the Finance Minister of Nepal, had the privilege of representing the country in early meetings and become one of the twenty-one signatories of the MOU of the AIIB in 2014 in Beijing. The original membership of fifty-eight countries has now reached ninety-three from all continents, including Europe.

Geopolitics and the 'neighborhood effect'

A subplot of the landlocked nature of Nepal is that it is actually India-locked in view of the barrier imposed by high mountains along the northern border with China, an open border of 1,864 kilometers along the sprawling Indian subcontinent. The social, cultural and religious affinities between Nepal and India, together with the common ties of history, have resulted in a unique relationship without any parallel. This multi-layered and multi-dimensional interaction between the two countries manifests frequently in a love-hate relationship, which every few years tends to go through highs and lows in mutual fondness.

One often hears the Indian side complaining of Nepal's ingratitude as reflected in Nepal's refusal to remain within an Indian security domain as per the 1950 treaty, despite Indian support to democratic movements and various economic projects. The Indian complaints are often related to the neutral position taken by Nepal during the 1962 Indo-China war despite the 1950 treaty, the perceived use of Nepali territory for anti-Indian activities by Pakistan's intelligence agency ISI and Nepal's decisions on various crucial internal and external matters without consulting India. But at the same time, Nepal's national psyche is resentful of the big-brotherly and often interventionist attitude of India, as reflected in the latest trade and transit blockade in 2015 after the promulgation of the constitution, supporting the movement of Madhes-based parties protesting the 2015 constitution passed overwhelmingly by the Constituent Assembly.

One important subject of mutual interest between the two countries relates to the use of water resources. This subject has been elaborated in a separate chapter of this book. The general complaints in Nepal relate to the failure to realize the benefits provided in the agreement of Kosi and Gandak agreements, and the annual inundation of vast tracts of Nepali territory along the border during monsoons caused by construction of embankments on the Indian side. There also exist a few cases of territorial dispute along the border, particularly related to Kalapani/Lipulek in western Nepal and Sustha in mid-Terai which have rendered the task of scientific delineation and demarcation of borders between the two countries still incomplete.

The British had crafted a policy of 'Himalayan frontier' placing Nepal within the Indian security perimeter. This security and strategic perception was also reflected in India's external policy after independence. One of the clauses of the 1950 peace and friendship treaty requires the two sides to inform each other in case of frictions with other neighbors affecting the relation between the two countries. The follow-up letter of exchange in 1965 mentioned that neither government shall tolerate any threat to the security of the other by a foreign aggressor. It also said that any arms and ammunition imported from third countries and passing through Indian territory will require the agreement of the

Indian government. The treaty also agreed to grant national treatment to each country's citizens in matters of residence, employment, ownership of property and participation in trade, commerce and human movement. Although the treaty still remains on paper, some of the provisions like 'equal national treatment' to each other's citizens are not operational for practical reasons. Work permits were introduced in Nepal to all foreign employees including Indians, fearing a high influx of people from the populous neighboring states of India. After repeated urging from Nepal to amend the 'unequal treaty', the two governments formed in 2016 a high-level Eminent Persons Group (EPG) on Nepal-India relations with a mandate, among others, to take a fresh look at the treaty and suggest measures to expand ties between the two countries. The completed EPG report is yet to be formally received for consideration by both governments.

Nepal's relation with the other neighbor China is more straight-forward and uncomplicated. Its historical relation was mainly with Tibet because of the long distance from Beijing. After Tibet became part of China, the traditional ties continue with the recognition of Tibet as an autonomous region of China. Unlike with India, the barriers of geography, culture, ethnicity and language have led to limited interactions between the two countries. Nepal never wavered from the 'One China' policy and its legitimate claim for permanent membership in the Security Council. The border demarcation with China initiated during the Prime Ministership of BP Koirala was successfully completed in 1962. The main political interest of China in its relation with Nepal is to prevent Nepali soil from being used for anti-China activities by Tibetan activists. They suspect such anti-Chinese activities instigated by foreign forces. The Chinese interest in Nepal grew further when bloody protests erupted in the Tibetan plateau on the eve of Beijing Olympic Games in 2008. Demonstrations were also held in Kathmandu by Tibetan refugees. The main Chinese political interest in Nepal remains to ensure it through diplomatic efforts as a buffer zone to check the perceived Western infiltration to destabilize the region and to harm China. China has traditionally kept itself aloof from internal political upheavals in Nepal, treating it as Nepal's internal matter. In recent years, however, matching its growing global clout, China has begun to take a deeper interest in Nepal's internal political developments and maneuverings.

Nepal has proven its goodwill by putting down the subversive activities in Tibet with support from Tibetan Khampas based in Nepal. It was found the Tibetan Khampas based in Nepal, armed with sophisticated arms and ammunition, communications system and logistics were aiding the subversive activities of Khampas in eastern Tibet fighting against Chinese rule. The Nepal government mobilized the Nepal army in a successful massive operation to flush out the Khampas from Nepal in the early 1970s. China's policy in Nepal has always been pro-establishment based on the five principles of Panchasheel, and non-interference in Nepal's domestic politics, and in return, it expects Nepal's support on issues such as Tibet and Taiwan concerning its national interest. Particularly, during the monarchial rule of the Panchayat days, Nepali regime successfully used the China card in countering Indian influences in Nepali politics. Nepal purchased military hardware including anti-aircraft guns, medium-range SSM, and AK 47 among others in 1989 causing Indian resentment, arguing that this was against the spirit of 1950 treaty.[5]

In recent years, Nepal has sought to benefit more from China's rise, reflected in economic aid, military hardware and logistic support, people-to-people exchanges, and humanitarian assistance. The country has availed of grant aid to strengthen army capacity to deal with natural calamities and for purchasing equipment for Nepal's UN peacekeeping forces in conflict-affected areas. The volume of trade between the two countries and Chinese investment in Nepal have increased significantly in recent years. The participation in BRI and Nepal's AIIB membership has further enhanced economic relations. Furthermore, during Prime Minister KP Oli's China visit in 2016, transit and transport agreements were signed to extend transit facilities via Chinese territory for Nepal's external trade, with the aim of reducing Nepal's total dependency on the Indian seaports for Nepal's trade with third countries. In a protocol finalized in September 2018 and signed in April 2019, China has agreed to grant access to Nepal to use four of its seaports including Tianjin, Shenzhen, Lianyungang and Zhanjiang and three dry ports for trading with third countries. A strategic railway link between the two countries through Tibet as part of the Nepal-China Multi-Dimensional Connectivity Networks is also under negotiation. It was also incorporated in the joint communique of the second conference of Belt and Road Initiative held in April 2019. The detailed project report including feasibility studies and financial modality is yet to be prepared and finalized.[6] It may also be mentioned here that one of the outcomes of Prime Minister Oli's India visit in 2018, was the Indian offer to extend Indian railway from Raxaul to Kathmandu which was interpreted as a response to the proposed extension of Tibetan railway from Shigatse to the Nepali border.

Reactions and reality

Some of these developments appear to have alarmed hawks in the Indian think tank orbit. This has often been interpreted as a policy shift towards China, away from Nepal's traditional Indo-centric foreign policy. Even normal acts in Nepal related to external relations are generally construed in terms of pro or anti India or China.

The long open border used by millions for cross border movement, deep social matrimonial ties, the common pantheon of Hindu gods, the similarities in language and culture leading to a shared Bollywood experience, millions of citizens from both countries absorbed in each other's economies and continued recruitment of Nepali citizens in the regular Army since the British days are some aspects of this unique relationship between the two neighbors. In economic terms, India accounts for two-third of Nepal's external trade and some 90 percent of transit traffic passes through Indian territory.

India represents one prominent source of development assistance and foreign investment. Furthermore, the historic role played by India in helping Nepali democratic struggles of 1950, 1990 and the peace process of 2006 following the Maoist insurgency that culminated in the country's transformation to a federal democratic republic are political aspects of the relation, which contributed to the establishment of ties between political leaders of the two countries at various levels. Both countries have adopted a liberal parliamentary democracy with respect for human rights and pluralism.

Promotion of the national interest is the primary objective of foreign relations of any sovereign country. The paramount considerations behind Nepal's national interest remain peace, stability and economic development while preserving territorial integrity and independence of the country. Foreign relations in the modern world is largely guided by economic factors. It is mainly this consideration that has contributed to the expansion of economic ties with China in recent years, which is not a zero-sum game. It is not at the expense of India or any other country. It is in the national interest to seek flexibility and leverage with policy options vis-a-vis India, without contesting or questioning its regional domination, given its paramount size in South Asia. Nepal naturally sought diversification of transit routes because of the risk arising from the sole dependence to India. The price paid for declared and undeclared economic blockades by India in the past brought about innumerable suffering to the Nepali populace, in addition to a heavy negative impact on the economy. It was the trade blockade/obstruction following the promulgation of Nepal's constitution in September 2015 that prompted Nepal to seek alternative transit routes via China.

The growing economic influence of China across continents is a reality that is generally acknowledged globally. South Asia is no exception to this. China's volume of trade with South Asia has reached $127 billion in 2017. Of this, bilateral trade with India amounted to $84.4 billion, with 19 percent growth over the 2016 figure, despite bilateral tension in the year caused by the Dokhlam fracas. India suffered a trade deficit of more than $52 billion, because of the low export volume of $16.3 billion compared to import of $68.1 billion. Bangladesh has a $15 billion deficit with China in the total annual trade volume of around $16 billion. In the fiscal year 2017/18, Nepal's total foreign trade amounted to $12.15 billion where India accounted for 65 percent, and China 12 percent. Total import from India amounted to nearly $7.43 billion against the export of less than $428 million, compared to $1.44 billion from China against the export of only around $23 million. Nepal's trade deficit in the year amounted to $7 billion with India and $1.21 billion with China.

On foreign direct investment, China is emerging as the top source in Bangladesh, Pakistan and Sri-Lanka. Chinese investment in India amounted to $2.8 billion in the last five years between 2013 and 2018, although constituting only around 3 percent of total FDI inflow.[7] India still tops the total foreign direct investment in Nepal. The total FDI as of mid-July 2016 amounted to Rs. 27.3 billion from India, compared to Rs. 10.8 billion from China. Since 2017, the flow of FDI commitments from China has gone up surpassing other countries including India. Chinese investment is increasing mainly in sectors like hydropower, cement and tourism. In the first ten months of the fiscal year 2017/18, Chinese investment commitment was equivalent to Rs. 29.8 billion, more than three times the size committed by Indian companies in the same period. Tourist arrivals from China has also registered a phenomenal growth, but still a little short of Indian flows. On development assistance, India disbursed $59.3 million in 2016/17, compared to $41.2 million from China. In 2017/18 disbursements from India and China were respectively $56.7 million and $58.7 million.[8]

Concluding remarks

Historically, the end of the British rule in India and the demise of Rana oligarchy in Nepal contributed to expanding Nepal's relations with the outside world. The expanding bilateral and multilateral relations with the global community helped the country develop not only a distinct personality of its own but also diversify its political and economic relations. Even in the midst of the country's expanding contacts with the international community, the relation with the two neighbors remains dominant, reinforced by their status as emerging global economic powers. Nepal has benefitted from its economic relations with both neighbors; the potential contribution from their rising economic clout to Nepal's economic future is, however, much higher. This can be aided by joint investments in Nepal's hard infrastructure as well as burgeoning investments, tourism, and trade in both goods and services. The World Investment Report of UNCTAD reports that FDI outflow from China in 2017 was $125 billion and from India, it was $15 billion. Nepal has a preferential trading arrangement with both countries which offers huge markets if we build the capacity to export valuable products at competitive prices.

The famous dictum 'yam between two boulders' is generally treated as the reference point of Nepal's geo-strategic setting even today. It emphasized the policy of preserving the territorial integrity and national independence by maintaining good neighborly relations with two giant powers. The promotion of economic interest represents another imperative in the modern world. To preserve and promote the national interest, it is necessary to prioritize rational policies on the foundation built in the past, balancing and responding to their legitimate interests and not offending their sensibilities. There is also a need to remain independent of the perceived competition and at times of adversity posed by occasional tensions between the two nations.

Nepal's multiple transport connections with India and proposed new transport corridors with the Tibetan region of China will ease the movement of cargo. The Tatopani-Khasa since 1965 and Rasuwagadi-Kerung in recent years are the only road transport routes with Tibet until now. In the near future, new corridors are being opened up from Hilsa in the West to Kimathanka in the east, in addition to the newly proposed railway links. The three-country land link will convert the traditional constraints posed by the country's landlocked state into an opportunity to expand trade. To seize the opportunity, the country will have to attract investment from both countries and others to produce exportable products based on the country's comparative advantage. For this, an appropriate investment climate needs to be created. In addition, Nepal's strategic location has the potential of becoming a transit link for Chinese companies manufacturing goods for India and Indian companies manufacturing goods for China.

Nepal's entrepôt glory of the past could take the modern form of an attractive transit point if part of this trade could pass through Nepal. The economic sustainability of the proposed Lhasa-Kathmandu and Raxaul-Kathmandu railway links between Lhasa and Kathmandu can be economically justified only in the context of this transit link for which a tripartite agreement will be necessary. China also sees Nepal as a gateway to trade with South Asia, particularly India and Bangladesh, that could be facilitated by railway connection. Addressing the Fourth China Tibet Tourism and Cultural Expo in Lhasa on September 7, 2015, the Chairman of the Tibetan Autonomous Region Qi Jhala said that the objective of the Tibetan railway extension via Nepal up to the borders of India is to penetrate the South Asian market, particularly the populous Indian states of Uttar Pradesh and Bihar and to Bangladesh.

Tourism is another area holding great opportunity. Thousands of Indian pilgrims visit the Hindu-Buddhist holy pilgrimage of Mount Kailas and Mansarovar Lake using Nepal as a transit. The number will increase many-fold with improved connectivity. Similarly, attracting a fraction of four million tourists who visit Tibet annually mainly from mainland China could give a big push to Nepal's tourism industry. The priority on transit and tourism would enhance the country's ability to play a bridge between more than the two and a half billion people of the two neighbors. As one commentator put it succinctly, '*this would certainly be preferable to the rote rendition of traditional Nepali political equidistance voice by every Nepali Prime Minister on a visit to Beijing. Nepal needs to view its two massive neighbors not from the perspective of politics, but rather through the lens of economics.*'[9]

In addition to managing the relation between the two powerful neighbors in view of the geopolitical setting and their growing importance in the global economic scene, the country will have to adjust its foreign policy in response to the imperatives of the character of the global community. The traditional connotation of physical security against a foreign threat is becoming less relevant. The increase in internal turmoil, socio-economic destabilization and externally inspired domestic upheavals are new threats that point to the imperative of revising traditional approaches and modalities. The character of economic diplomacy has undergone a transformation. There is a need to make it more advanced in response to the increasingly complex process of painstaking and sophisticated negotiations in trade, investment and technology transfer with various actors including bilateral, multilateral and transnational corporations. Negotiating with non-state actors is equally important. This requires strengthened institutional capacity of policymaking and implementing agencies including the Ministry of Foreign Affairs and other bodies. They all have to be equipped with advanced management systems and well-trained manpower fully conversant with the state-of-art knowledge and techniques of negotiation on the concerned subjects.

Notes

1. Details in Acharya, Madhu Raman (2019). *Nepal World View,* Volume I, Chapter 1. Adroit Publishers: New Delhi.
2. Four modern districts of Banke, Bardiya, Kailali and Kanchanpur were returned to Nepal in recognition of the services of 9,000 Nepali troops led by Rana Prime Minister Jung Bahadur Rana to quell the Sepoy Mutiny at Lucknow.
3. For details, see Mahat, Ram S. (2005), op. cit (pp. 5-8).
4. Extract from BP Koirala's speech to the 15th session of the UN General Assembly, quoted in Bhattarai, Dinesh (Ed.) (2017). *Nepal's Foreign Policy: From Expediancy to Pragmatism,* (p. 26-27). Jananayak B P Koirala Memorial Trust: Kathmandu.
5. For details on Nepal-China relation in military cooperation, see Bhattarai, Kamal Dev (2019, May 17-23). A Brief History of Nepal China Defense Ties. In *The Annapurna Express.*
6. The construction of railway link from Kerung to Kathmandu, the most talked-about priority of the Oli government is not likely to commence until the completion of 500-kilometer Shigatse- Kerung link on the Chinese side by 2025. According to the reports prepared by the Chinese side, the extension of link from Kerung to Kathmandu, once started, would require another nine years for completion. See *The Kathmandu Post.* (2019, April 29).
7. Lama, Mahendra P. (2018, November 14). With Eyes Wide Open. In *The Kathmandu Post.*
8. Ministry of Finance. (December 2018). *Development Cooperation Report*: 2017/18.
9. Sakya, Sujeev (2009, May 1). *The Opportunity of the Yam.* Retrieved from https://sujeevshakya.com/2009/05/the-opportunity-of-the-yam/

Chapter Seven

Unleashing Hydropower

Much has been said and written about Nepal's enormous energy potentials. The wide panorama of the Himalayan snow peaks and the heavy monsoons are a gift of nature to Nepal in the form of abundant water resources. They hold immense prospects for huge energy generation, irrigation, drinking water, and supplementary benefits including flood control and navigability. Most rivers in Nepal originate from glaciers, while monsoon precipitation augments seasonal flows. Rainfall between June and September accounts for 75 percent of the total annual downpour. In addition to the snow-fed waters and rainwater in different catchment areas, utilization of groundwater is possible for different purposes to meet human needs using different structures and technologies depending on the location and purpose.

Power generation from water resource offers several advantages compared to those from other sources. Hydro energy is a renewable and sustainable source without input cost, low operation and maintenance expenses and zero carbon emission. No consumption of water is involved while producing power. The other benefits of hydro energy include its greater production efficiency compared to other sources, and flexibility in capacity response to variation in energy demand, and the possibility of multi-purpose use and management of water for irrigation and flood control with regulated water. Although the contribution of hydropower to total global power production is only 17 percent, its share in renewable power generation is 70 percent. Among the more than 150 countries producing hydropower globally, Nepal's relative advantage to produce hydropower in an economically feasible manner is considered one of the best. The gradient of the country's location, ranging from sixty meters above the sea level in the south to 8,848 meters in the northern Himalayas within a distance of less than 200 kilometers is best-suited for power generation.

Endowment and utilization

The Himalayan, Mahabharat and the Churia mountain ranges span Nepal's distinctive horizontal shape. The Himalayan basin feeds Sapta Koshi, Gandaki, Karnali and Mahakali rivers from its snowmelt and glaciers during the dry season. The second group includes the Bagmati, West Seti, Mechi, Kankai, Kamala and Babai, which originate in the mid-mountains and derive their water from rainfall. The third category originates in the southern slopes of the Mahabharat and the Churia hills with nominal flow used only for irrigation. The total number of rivers under these large and small river systems adds up to around 6,000 covering a distance of 45,000 km. Surface water is estimated to occupy 2.7 percent of the country's territory.[1]

The total mean runoff of these river systems from Nepal is estimated to be 5,038.8 cubic meter per second (cumec), comprising 4014.85 cumecs from the Himalayan rivers, 565.94 cumecs from Mahabharat rivers and 456 cumecs from lowland rivers originating in the Churia hills.[2] The total annual runoff from the major river basins, supplemented by smaller rivers in the lower mountains and foothills is estimated to be 207 billion cumecs, while the runoff from the Nepali territory only is 159 billion cumecs, the balance originating from Tibet and the Indian catchment area. About 80 to 85 percent of the annual surface runoff occurs during the monsoon. Further assessment of the groundwater potential indicates the availability of 13.2 billion cumecs as replenishable and economically exploitable.

The energy potential from Nepali rivers was estimated for the first time in 1967 by Dr Hari Man Shrestha as part of his PhD thesis at Moscow University. His pioneering work concluded that Nepal's waters possessed the theoretical potential of producing 83,000 megawatts of electricity. This has been an officially accepted estimate for policy-making and power development. But recently, this figure has been updated based on modern advancement in computer technology that offers benefits in the fields of water resources and power estimation. A new estimate using GIS and models based on hydro-meteorological data of the Department of Hydrology and Meteorology reveals that the total power potential and corresponding energy capacity of Nepal on a run-of-the-river basis at Q40 percent (flow exceedance) and 80 percent efficiency level is 53,836 MW and 346,538 GWh respectively.[3] The estimates of power and energy potential of the Narayani, Saptakoshi, Karnali river basins are 17,800, 17,008, 15,661 megawatts, and 113,373, 108,817, 102,324 gigawatt-hours, respectively. The potential of the Mahakali river on a run-of-the-river (ROR) basis is estimated at 2,262 MW of electricity and 14,981 GWh of energy annually. The electricity and energy potential of other water sources in Nepal would be 1,105 MW and 7,043 GWh respectively.[4]

Of this theoretical potential, 45,000 MW is estimated to be economically feasible from identified projects. The irrigation potential of Nepal is to cover six million hectares of land. The water flowing from Nepal contributes to 40 percent of total flow and 71 percent of the dry season water flow of the Ganga basin, the lifeline of 250 million people across northern India.

Hydropower generation in Nepal started with the commissioning of 500 KW Pharping power plant during the regime of Rana Prime Minister Chandra Shamsher in 1911, the year not very far from the time when the first usable light bulb was invented by Thomas Alva Edition in 1879, and eleven years after the first Indian hydropower plant was established in Darjeeling. China's first hydropower project was started in 1912, one year after Nepal. It took another twenty-four years to build the next hydropower plant in Sundarijal producing 640 KW in 1935. Before the start of the First Five Year Plan in 1956, the total installed power capacity in Nepal was 6,380 KW, including some diesel plants.

The potential use of this great natural asset has been limited so far in Nepal's development. There is an annual withdrawal of only around five billion cumecs for human use out of the more than 200 billion cumecs of annual water run-off. Out of the total 2.64 million hectares agricultural land in Nepal, only 1.77 million is estimated to be irrigable, because of difficult terrain and other factors of access to the regular water resource. The total irrigated land area from various sources including surface irrigation, groundwater, farmers' traditional methods and new technology stood at 1.43 million hectares as of mid-March 2018.[5] Only 40 percent of the total agricultural land has access to some form of irrigation facility throughout the year. While approximately 88 percent of the total population has access to basic drinking water, potable water meeting modern sanitary requirements is available to only 19 percent of the total population. According to the latest estimates, more than 90 percent of the population has access to electricity of which about two-third is provided by grid connections, the rest is dependent on micro schemes, off-grid connections and alternative sources including solar power, mainly in the rural areas. Due to inadequate power generation relative to demand, even grid-connection does not assure a reliable and uninterrupted supply.

Demand-supply mismatch

The total power generation as of mid-April 2018 stood at 1,073 MW, of which 1016 MW was from hydropower, representing just around 2 percent of the country's techno-economic potential; 54 MW was obtained from thermal plants and three MW from solar plants. The total energy demand in the year 2017-18 was 1508 MW.[6] One important aspect of Nepal's power scenario is the seasonal mismatch between demand and supply. The power demand reaches its peak during the dry season when total power production goes down to less than 600 MW. The energy demand during dry season reaches 19,872 gigawatt-hours against the total supply of 17,172 gigawatt-hours of which 9,024 is imported, resulting in a deficit of 2,700 gigawatt-hours.

Estimates for the current year 2018-19 show that the dry season total power supply including imported power will be 1,470 MW, against the demand of 1,842 MW, resulting in a deficit of 372 MW, the corresponding energy deficit will be 2.9 million megawatt-hours. On the other hand, the wet season supply including imported power for the year will be 2,283 MW against the demand of 1842 MW, generating a surplus of 441 MW with the corresponding energy surplus 0f 1.67 MWh. It is estimated that the dry season deficit will reach 1,287 MW and the wet season surplus to 670 MW, by the year 2022/23.[7]

The electricity generation in the months of December 2018 and January 2019 went down severely due to a sharp drop in water level in river basins where most hydro projects are located. On January 25, 2019, electricity generation stood at as low as 525 MW which could not meet even half of the country's power needs. The situation forced the NEA to raise power import from India to 565 MW to meet the peak hour demand.[8] The demand-supply mismatch marked by a high deficit in the dry season is attributed to power generation primarily by run-of-the-river projects. The only storage plant existing presently are the two Kulekhani projects with the total installed capacity of 92 MW. Hence, there is an imperative to develop more storage projects to meet the peak load demand and address the problem of deficit in dry season and energy spill in the wet season.

The underdeveloped state of hydropower generation makes the country largely reliant on traditional and other imported sources to meet energy needs.

The traditional sources, particularly fuelwood, agriculture waste and livestock dungs meet 69 percent of the energy requirements. Of the remaining 31 percent, electricity accounts for less than 4 percent; petroleum products, coal and alternative renewable energy sources such as solar, wind, biogas and micro-hydro account for the rest. Ironically, even the 4 percent energy supply from electricity is not wholly from the domestic production. To meet the power deficit and minimize load-shedding, the rest of the supply is met by importing power from India. Nepal spends around 22 billion rupees for importing power and other electrical equipment like diesel generators and inverters from India annually. Even with increasing power imports from India in recent years, the country suffers from frequent power shortages, power cuts and lack of electrification in many rural areas. The country faced power cuts of up to fourteen hours daily until two years back, resulting in huge economic losses, affecting industrial production and services sector and discouraging investment. The problem of load-shedding and power cuts has largely eased recently because of increased power supply commissioning of some small projects, imports from India and reduction in transmission losses.

Investment status

Traditionally, investment in hydropower was considered to be a field of public sector natural monopoly. As of 1991, total electricity generation in the country was a meagre 220 MW from government projects, almost all of them supported by foreign assistance. The liberalization policy started in the early nineties together with various legislations including the Electricity Act and Foreign Investment and Technology Transfer Act opened the field to domestic and foreign private investment. The introduction of a policy of power purchase agreement in foreign exchange enticed foreign direct investment under joint venture, starting with Khimti (60 MW), Bhotekosi (45 MW), followed by Upper Madi (25 MW), Indrawati (7.5 MW) and Upper Marshyangdi (50 MW) with a the total installed capacity of 187 MW with the investment of $337 million. A few other foreign investment projects under construction include Upper Trishuli 1 (216 MW), Rasuwa Bhotekosi (120 MW), Kabeli A (37.5) and Lower Solu (82 MW) with the investments nearing US$1 billion. This is in addition to the two multi-billion dollar projects Upper Karnali (900 MW) and Arun 3 (840 MW) awarded to two Indian companies following global competitive biddings. A few other projects completed entirely with domestic private investment are Madkhu Khola (13 MW), Mai Khola (22 MW), Thapa Khola (13 MW), Mailung (6 MW), Lower Modi (10 MW), Aankhu Khola (10 MW), Upper Madi (25MW), Hewa Khola A (15 MW), Indrawati 3 (7.5 MW) and a large number of small projects.

The projects completed in the public sector include Kaligandaki (144 MW), Middle Marshyngdi (70 MW), Marshyangdi 69MW), Kulekhani (60 MW), Kulekhani 2 (32 MW), Chamelia (30 MW), Chilime (22 MW), Gandak (15 MW), Trishuli (24 MW), Devighat (15 MW), Modikhola (14.8 MW), Jhimruk (12 MW), Aandhikhola (9.40 MW), Sunkosi (10 MW), Puwa Khola (6.2 MW) and a few other small projects. Other major projects under construction in the public sector include Upper Tamakosi (456 MW), Tanahu (140 MW), Rasuwagadhi (111MW), Trishuli 3A (60 MW), and Kulekhani 3 (14 MW).

Out of the total power generation of 1,073 MW, electricity produced by independent power producers currently stands at 511 MW, the rest is generated by the Nepal Electricity Authority and its subsidiaries in the public sector. A total of 172 power projects for which licenses have been issued for generating 4,642 MW are at different stages of construction, while applications for thirty-six well studied other projects for producing 3,466 MW of additional electricity are under consideration for production licenses. Similarly, survey licenses have been issued to 302 projects with an estimated capacity of 15,887 MW. NEA has signed power purchase agreements with private promoters to purchase 4,132 MW electricity from 244 projects including the already completed seventy-three projects with the installed capacity of 511 MW.[9]

As for the status of power transmission lines, the existing capacity comprises of two 400/220 kV transmission lines (Dhalkebar-Muzaffarpur and Khimti-Dhalkebar) with the length of 153 km, 32 lines of 132 Kv with the length of 2871 km, and 16 high voltage 66 KV transmission lines with the length of 514 km. Other high voltage transmission lines under construction include two 400 Kv (Hetauda-Dhalkebar-Inaruwa and Khimti-Bahrabise-Kathmandu) lines with 740 circuit km length, 10 lines of 220 kV transmission with 1199 km length and 20 lines of 132 kV with 1477 km circuit length covering different parts of the country. There are ninety-three other planned and proposed transmission lines including Cross-Border, and along the North-South basins and the Mid-Hills. These add up to a total circuit length of about 7,000 km of high voltage transmission lines of various capacities.[10] All the existing transmission lines and those under-construction are in the public sector.

Regional and bilateral cooperation

Even after utilizing water to meet Nepal's irrigation requirement, there will be enough water remaining to irrigate downstream land beyond its southern border. The mountainous topography of the country provides possibilities of building high dams to store immense quantities of water for multiple uses, including power generation, irrigation, and regulated water. The regulated water flow can result in augmenting the down-stream flow to ensure irrigation water in the dry season while mitigating flood damage in the plains caused by high monsoon rain each year.

The per capita energy consumption in South Asia comprising of one-fourth of the world population is 707 kwh, one of the lowest in the world. This figure is about one-fourth of the world average, while per capita generation is about one eighth.[11] As a fast-growing region of the world, its energy demand is rising commensurately. But due to inadequate power supply despite high energy imports, most countries suffer from energy outages affecting productive activities, social development and investment climate. The region accounts for about 7 percent of the world commercial energy consumption, excluding the use of non-commercial energy sources such as firewood, animal and agriculture waste and residue and other biomass. The commercial energy is largely dominated by coal, gas and petroleum products. The contribution of hydropower is about 17 percent. In India coal accounts for more than 50 percent of the commercial energy, while Bangladesh relies on gas for about 70 percent. In terms of electricity generation, fossil fuel contributes 71 percent of power supply in India, the share of hydro-electricity being 16 percent and the rest coming from other non-traditional sources, including wind, solar and nuclear plants. In Bangladesh, fossil fuel accounts for 98 percent of power generation, hydroelectricity contributes a mere 2 percent. Hydropower is the predominant source of power supply only for Bhutan and Nepal with the contributions of 99 and 92 percent respectively. In Pakistan, fossil fuel contributes 68 percent and hydropower accounts for 28 percent of electricity generation.[12]

South Asia is currently a fast-growing region of the world, particularly because of India's asymmetric size and momentum. The demands for commercial energy driven by rising incomes of a growing population, urbanization and economic growth cannot be met under the existing setting. The import bill of petroleum products is shooting up resulting in a wide trade deficit. It may also be mentioned that the reliance on imported non-renewable fossil fuel needs to be reduced from the perspective of economic sustainability too. Countries heavily dependent on fossil fuel are susceptible to frequent oil price shocks leading to macro-economic instability. Substituting imported oil with domestic renewable energy will improve our vulnerable balance of payments.

Considering the complementarity and synergy of the resource endowments among the countries of the eastern part of South Asia—Nepal, Bhutan, India and Bangladesh—the imperative of sub-regional cooperation becomes obvious to optimize the resource mix. Nepal, Bhutan and north-eastern part of India have the potential to generate 120,000 MW of hydropower. Bangladesh has a huge gas potential of 650 billion cubic meters. India has a well-developed coal industry and an estimated 315 billion tons of coal reserves, one of the largest in the world, that can meet the baseload power demand in the region. The hydropower of Nepal and Bhutan, and the gas available in Bangladesh can meet the peak load demand. Increased cooperation among these countries could be the most effective way of meeting the energy deficit of a growing region. After the development of the power projects presently in the pipeline, Nepal could export wet season surplus to meet the high demand in India that is not met by internal production. On the other hand, Nepal can import thermal power from India during the winter dry season when hydropower production is low.

The environmental problem caused by the rising temperature from the green house gas emitted by the burning of fossil energy sources including coal, gas and oil has been a matter of great concern in the modern world. Coal, which is the primary source of commercial energy in India, is of poor quality with low calorific value and high ash content that cause high atmospheric pollution. Rising temperature is melting icebergs in the Arctic and the Himalayas. The Himalayan glaciers of our region, which is the home of the largest concentration of ice after the polar caps, are receding faster than the icebergs in other parts of the world. This phenomenon is attributed mainly to the high carbon emission resulting from fast-paced industrial growth in India and China. Studies show that temperature in the Himalayas is warming faster than the global average in the last four decades. The consequence of this phenomenon of climate change is manifested in frequent droughts, crop failure, landslides, flooding and other natural calamities.

Against this backdrop, the imperative of exploring and exploiting clean energy sources cannot be exaggerated. The Hindukush-Himalayan region with the catchment area of more than 2.5 million square miles has enormous potential of producing clean energy that can fuel industrialization, solve energy problems, raise agricultural productivity and improve quality of life of the people. Nepal's untapped power potential from the commercially viable projects in four major basins and southern rivers is capable of producing over 45 GW. Nepal's power need in the foreseeable future will be just a minuscule portion of this potential, which offers a lucrative opportunity for the country to benefit from power export. Furthermore, one-third of the identified projects in Nepal have the possibility of being developed with a storage reservoir for multipurpose use including power, irrigation, flood control and inland navigation. The reservoir projects will have the capacity of holding 77 billion cubic meters of wet season monsoon water, about forty percent of the total run-off flowing from Nepal. The power produced from the reservoir projects can meet the peak hour power needs at a premium price.

Nepal's hydro potential can be an important source of meeting power needs not only of Nepal, India and Bangladesh, but also be a source of clean energy for sustainable growth contributing to boosting business activity, creating jobs, eradicating poverty and ensuring food security and environmental protection. Recognizing the need to promote sustainable growth without compromising the needs of future generations, the UN Secretary-General launched Sustainable Energy for All (SE4ALL) in 2011 with the objectives of universal access to energy, doubling the rate of improvement in energy efficiency and doubling the share of renewable energy in the global energy mix. Subsequently, Affordable and Clean Energy has been listed as one of the seventeen Sustainable Development Goals passed by UN General Assembly in 2015. It may also be relevant to mention here the potential opportunities for countries like Nepal from the Clean Development Mechanism (CDM)[13] developed by the Kyoto Protocol.

There is increasing realization on the part of political leadership in South Asia to expedite cooperation at regional and sub-regional levels through power trade. After series of attempts starting from 2004 in the Islamabad Summit that mooted the concept of energy ring, followed by Dhaka Declaration for the establishment of SAARC Energy Centre, and further work progress in Colombo 2008 and Male 2011 summits, the SAARC Framework Agreement for Energy Cooperation was signed in Kathmandu Summit of 2014. Subsequently, Nepal and India signed an agreement for electric power trade, cross-border transmission, interconnection and grid connectivity on 24 October 2014. The interlinkages of power and gas grids at regional and sub-regional levels would contribute to stabilizing the power system as a whole, bring operational efficiency and optimize the use of various available energy sources. Regional cooperation is a genuine positive-sum game where all players stand to gain. In December 2018, the two countries also agreed to set up an energy banking scheme to facilitate export of surplus power to the other when production exceeds demand and import back when there is deficit, thus preventing the waste of surplus energy of Nepal expected during the wet season in the near future and ensure benefit from the seasonal complementarities of power balance between the two countries.

Power trade status

Despite its immense potential, regional energy trade in South Asia is less than 5 percent of total trade within the region, confined largely to bilateral exchanges, particularly between India and Bhutan. Of the approximately 1,500 MW power generation from hydro projects of Chhukha, Kurichu and Tala in Bhutan , over 84 percent is exported to India, earning an annual revenue of $203 million, representing 47 percent of the national revenue. A number of other hydro projects are under planning and development to produce another 10,000 MW of electricity, mainly for export to India. The power exchange between Nepal and India started in 1971, but the level of exchange remains modest and largely limited to one way traffic from India. Nepal imported 1369.89 GWh from India through twenty interconnection points at various voltage levels against its nominal export of 3.21 GWh in 2015.[14] Nepal currently imports around 500 MW of power from India through various cross-border transmission lines. The shortage is acute in the dry winter months due to a fall in water level in most rivers. Most of the hydro projects in Nepal, except Kulekhani 1 and 2, are run-of-the-river projects generating power in full capacity when the water level goes up during the monsoon season. The main transmission lines through which power trade takes place are 132 KV Kushaha-Kataiya, Raxaul-Parwanipur, Tanakpur-Mahendranagar, Ramnagar-Gandak, 400 KV Dhalkenar-Mujaffarpur and Butawal-Gorakhpur planned for upgradation to 400. KV.

Driven by the immense potential to the mutual advantage of both countries, Nepal-India power cooperation has been a priority subject for discussion at official, non-official, and academic levels in both countries. The success story of Bhutan in powering its economic growth with the development of hydropower can be an inspiring model. Bhutan's per capita income in PPP terms rose from $475 in 1980 to $7,860 in 2015. The sooner Nepal unleashes its hydropower potential, the earlier it can reap economic benefits.[15] The urgent need to develop hydro energy is also necessary in view of the mounting trade deficit with India, which currently stands at more than $8 billion, as this is the only sector that has the known potential to partially offset the deficit. To facilitate the take-off of this sector calls for institutional, policy and governance reforms and capital investment in infrastructure and generation projects.

Meanwhile, Nepal is also entering into dialogue with China and Bangladesh for cooperation in the energy sector. Nepal and Bangladesh signed a power cooperation agreement in Kathmandu on August 11, 2018, to pave the way for exporting Nepal's surplus power to Bangladesh. The power export will have to be transmitted via the Indian grid. Bangladesh has expressed interest to invest in Nepal's hydro projects for import and has signed MoU with India's Vidyut Vipyar Nigam (NVVN) for transmission of 300 to 500 MW electricity generated in Nepal's Upper Karnali Project through the Indian power grid. During the Asia Economic Summit in October 2016, the commerce ministers of Nepal and Bangladesh agreed on the sidelines of the event to build two hydropower plants Sunkosi 2 and 3 with the total capacity of 1600 MW; the power generated is to be evacuated to Bangladesh via India through the BBIN economic corridor. A Dialogue Mechanism on Energy Cooperation has also been started with China to facilitate long-term planning and cooperation for the development of trans-boundary transmission line and development of hydro and solar energy. The first meeting of which was held on 27 September 2018 at Secretary level in Kathmandu. Meanwhile, the Nepal Government is seeking Chinese investment for various power generation and transmission projects.[16]

Mega multi-purpose projects

Most of the identified large-scale storage projects in Nepal for future development have the potential of generating multi-purpose benefits including the capture of monsoon floods and augmentation of river flow in dry season for irrigation. These are externalities creating downstream benefits to India and Bangladesh. In the absence of storage, river regulation and watershed management in the upland mountain areas, the lowland river deltas and coastal areas in India and Bangladesh will suffer from low irrigation and high level of monsoon floods and soil salinity. This makes it necessary to capture and internalize the externalities to ensure viability and consequent bankability of the project in the private sector too. Development of projects based entirely on the internal cost-benefit analysis could lead to a suboptimal return, in view of reduced benefit, but cost remains the same.

The mega projects like the Karnali Chisapani, Koshi High Dam and Pancheshwor generating multiple benefits identified long time ago are yet to materialize because of the controversy on cost and benefit-sharing and the atmosphere of suspicion and mistrust. The Indo-Nepal treaty on water resources started in 1920 that involved the exchange of territories to enable the construction of Sarada barrage on the Mahakali river at the technically feasible Nepali land. Subsequently, after India's independence from British rule, Kosi and Gandak agreements were signed respectively in 1954 and 1959 which later on became controversial because of the unequal distribution of benefits, a reality acknowledged subsequently even by the Indian side. The Koshi project irrigates 969,100 hectares of land in the Indian state of Bihar and only 91,100 hectares in Nepal. The Gandak irrigates 1,850,320 hectares in the Indian states of UP and Bihar, but only 46,900 hectares in Nepal mostly at the tail end of the canal. A further complaint from the Nepali side relates to the shortfall in receiving even limited irrigation and power benefits agreed in the treaties. These two treaties are mainly responsible for creating an atmosphere of distrust and suspicion with implications for subsequent developments of slow progress in materializing the immense potential for bilateral cooperation in the sector.

The Karnali Chisapani multipurpose project was first identified and studied by Japan's Nippon Koei. Its original estimate of 1,800 MW was subsequently revised to 3,600 MW by Australia's Snowy Mountain in 1968 and a further feasibility study was done by Norway's Nor Consult in 1976 with World Bank support. The project was conceived as a win-win project for India and Nepal, and the World Bank was considered a possible investor. In 1981, UNDP started a project supporting the Nepal government in training 250 engineers in India's Roorkee University for five years to create necessary manpower for the project construction. In 1989, the Himalayan Power Consultant, a consortium of Canadian and American consultants finalized another feasibility report upgrading the Karnali/Chisapani project to 10,800 MW at the cost of US$4.9 billion. The estimated irrigation benefit from the project was to be 0.19 million hectares for Nepal, while the total command land area of India to benefit would be more than three million hectares, as the lean season flow of the river would increase four-fold after the dam construction. Some reservation was expressed by India on the 24 volumes of this study report in 1990, particularly pertaining to the benefit assessment of 81 percent power, 18.9 percent irrigation and 0.1 percent flood control, arguing that only power benefit must be accounted for, as other benefits were negligible. The project languished until 2004 when the secretary-level discussions between the two countries led to reactivating the Karnali Coordination Committee to examine the possibility of implementing the project.[17]

The Pancheshwor Multipurpose Project, which is part of the Mahakali Treaty between Nepal and India, is another multipurpose mega project whose implementation has suffered considerable delay due to differing interpretations of some treaty provisions, including those with implication on benefit sharing. The project with the capacity to produce 6,480 MW electricity, irrigating 93,000 hectares of land in Nepal and 1.6 million hectares in India and flood control benefits to both countries having a 315-meter rockfill dam was signed amidst high enthusiasm, ratified by more than two-third parliamentary support in 1996. The project on the stretch of Mahakali Border River provided 'equal entitlement in the utilization of waters without prejudice to their respective consumptive water of the Mahakali river.' The detailed project report, assessing the energy, irrigation and flood control benefits within six months of signing the project has not yet been completed due to technical differences in position relating to preexisting use of water in the Sarada barrage, the location of the reregulating dam (Poornagiri or Rupaligadh) and origin of the Mahakali river. The Indian side is laying extra claim on the pre-existing water use in the lower Sarada dam, while Nepal is demanding 50 percent of the water, based on the principle of equal sharing. The Nepali side has expressed some reservations on the draft detailed project report prepared by the Indian Company WAPCOS. According to a news report, India has expressed its readiness to bear nearly 65 percent of the project cost of the project, in view of additional irrigation and flood control benefits to the Indian side, as the project provisions the project cost to be borne by the two countries in proportion to the benefits accrued.[18]

Saptakoshi High Dam is another multipurpose project proposed at the bilateral level aimed primarily at flood control in south-east Nepal and northern Bihar of India and power generation. One extra benefit from the project could be Nepal's access to the seaport in Calcutta through 165 kilometers long navigation canal. The proposal for a high dam in the Saptakoshi of Nepal has a long history, going as far back as the later part of the nineteenth century, because of the flood damage caused by the river to the huge landmass of Bihar. Koshi is nicknamed as the 'sorrow of Bihar' in India. After several efforts, the agreement was reached in 1954 to construct 25.91 meters high Koshi Barrage which was completed in 1965. The project brought some relief, but its limited capacity was inadequate to solve the problem and reap the potential benefit. The devastating flood of 2008 caused erosion of the embankments and displaced as many as 65,000 families. Furthermore, the project's life is coming to an end very soon, hence the pressure from both sides to devise an alternative. India has now proposed a 289-meter high dam with the capacity to generate 3,300 MW power and irrigate 300,000 hectares of land in Nepal and the Indian state of Bihar, in addition to flood control benefit and facilitating river navigation. The dam proposed at Chatara faces strong opposition from environmentalists and people living upstream, as the project will submerge large parts of fertile valley and villages in the eastern hill districts. Nepal has therefore planned the Sunkoshi Diversion project to build a dam upstream to divert water through tunnel to irrigate around 122,000 hectares of parched land of the five districts in the central Tarai, which will also contribute to control flood and sedimentation problem in the Saptakoshi river. After initial hesitation from the Indian side, the evaluation of technical aspects of both projects has been an agenda of bilateral discussion between the two countries.

Other issues and constraints

Availability of financial resources remains the principal constraint for Nepal's hydro development. Traditionally, limited investment in power development came from the public sector, assisted by development assistance from multilateral and bilateral sources. The bilateral sources are mainly India, Japan, Germany, Norway and the USA, while the World Bank, Asian Development Bank and European Investment Bank represent the main multilateral sources. In recent years, private sector investment is also rising especially in small and medium scale projects. The key to attract private investment in hydropower is the ability to produce power in a cost-effective manner in order that power can be sold at an affordable price domestically and in a price competitive manner for export in the neighboring countries. The risk perception could affect the investment flow. Higher the risk perception, the higher will be the expected returns on investment. To attract private investment in hydro energy, the private sector and public sector will have to work together for risk management relating to market, foreign exchange, government policy and production. To minimize the political risk resulting from unstable politics, a non-partisan consensus building among major political parties with the enactment of necessary legislation and regulations is necessary.

The frequent change in government and partisan approach to development assistance and foreign private investment in Nepal as reflected in some projects create political risks which have hindered potential external investment in Nepal's hydropower sector. The cancellation of a billion-dollar project Arun 3 in 1994, at the last moment—after financial closing with a liberal grant and soft loan from development partners including the World Bank, the Asian Development Bank and other bilateral development partners—represents a historic case in point. The World Bank's subsidiary IDA, which was the promoter and principal financier of this project, refrained from assisting hydropower generation projects for more than two decades after the cancellation of Arun 3. After nearly two decades, this project together with Upper Karnali were offered for private investment through international competitive bidding. Following a thorough appraisal of the bidding proposals and preparation of model Project Development Agreement, two Indian firms GMR and Satlaz Vidyut Nigam were finally awarded the contracts because of their attractive offers. It was a hard time convincing all coalition partners in the government before signing PDAs with selected companies, as both of them happened to be Indian. As per the PDA, the Upper Karnali Project is expected to generate 900 MW out of which 12 percent of cost-free energy and another 29 percent cost-free ownership of the project will go to the government. Even after awarding the contracts, there are instances of some political groups outside the mainstream politics obstructing project implementation with terrorist activities.

The politicking is evident from the fact that opposition to the Indian investment in the project was based on the argument that the Nepal government should build the project with its own resources. This point of view ignored the fact that the project was awarded after appraisal of proposals received following invitation for international bidding to develop the project on BOOT model on a public-private partnership basis. Ironically, there are other cases such as the Budhigandaki 1200 MW reservoir hydro project where the NCP government in September 2018 initiated to award an EPCF contract without competitive bidding to a Chinese company, Gezhouba Group Corporation, with a questionable past record in Nepal. This was despite the decision of the previous governments to build the project with internal resources for which 5 percent additional tax was levied on petroleum products to mobilize required investment capital. Under the EPCF model, the company will be solely responsible for engineering, procurement, construction and arranging funds for the project, to be paid back by the government. Naturally, this will result in high costs of the project adding debt liability to future government.

Excessive politicization and bureaucratic red-tape in decision making represent major factors behind slow progress in exploiting Nepal's hydro resources. It took more than eight years since the issuance of survey license for the 216 MW joint- venture Upper Trishuli 1 with a majority share of Korean South East Power Company to get the generation license following formal agreement on the PDA and the power purchase agreement. The dollar-denominated PPA in FDI funded projects became a contentious issue, because of the huge losses incurred by NEA due to exchange rate depreciation of Nepali currency, particularly with respect to Khimti and Bhotekosi, the two initial projects with FDI whose PPA was signed in dollars for the entire concession period. Eventually, the government announced a PPA policy in dollars only for a period of ten years or until the loan payback period of the project for only the portion of foreign loans.

It is natural for investors to be assured of a minimum rate of return with the assured market and necessary infrastructure for power transmission and distribution, particularly in large projects involving heavy investment. This is one reason which has hampered the execution of large projects. After receiving survey license for 650 MW Tamakoshi 3 Hydro project in 2007, Stat Kraft of Norway spent about a billion rupees in conducting surveys, technical updates and environment impact assessment. But it abandoned the project midway before signing PDA, because of its concern over finding a potential buyer in view of soured relation with India, after the imposition of undeclared trade blockade in 2015. The company had earlier planned power sale to India based on the Power Trade Agreement signed by the two countries. Similarly, China Three Georges Corporation (CTGC) withdrew from the 750 MW West Seti Dam Project in Doti. The construction license of the project was awarded earlier in the mid-eighties to Australia's Snowy Mountain Engineering Corporation but was terminated in 2011 because of its failure to cobble together financiers. Subsequently, the memorandum of understanding was signed in 2012 with

CTGC to execute the project. But after six years, CTGC pulled out of the project calling it financially unfeasible because of steep rehabilitation and resettlement costs. In the last-ditch attempt to save the project, Nepal government agreed to scale down the project capacity to 600 MW from 750 MW for the same contract and extend the dollar PPA from ten years as agreed before to twelve years. This did not help to alter the Chinese position, which further stated that it would be technically difficult and very expensive to transfer power from this project located in remote Far-West to the main demand centers.

As the development of power projects including production, transmission and distribution involves more than one ministry and department and requires the support of local communities in the project areas, close inter-agency coordination within the government and local community involvement is necessary to facilitate timely project execution. Experience shows that prolonged delay in meeting other requirements such as receiving the environment impact assessment, permission to cut trees for road access and transmission lines from different government bodies and problems relating to land acquisition have hindered timely project completion, in addition to obstructions from local communities. The completion of the World Bank-assisted high priority Khimti-Dhalkebar 220 KV transmission line project was delayed by about six years due to repeated obstructions by the local people in Sindhuli. Reservoir hydro projects face even more difficulties in view of the requirement of land compensation, rehabilitation and resettlement of the displaced families.

The time and cost overruns of hydro infrastructure projects have become a normal phenomenon particularly in the public sector resulting from the management problems like the ones mentioned above, plus other inefficiencies and leakages. Even the total cost of Upper Tamakoshi Hydro that made satisfactory progress in the initial stage has been estimated to reach Rs. 69 billion including interest on the loan from the original estimate of Rs. 35.29 billion, with the construction delay of four years.[19] Chamelia hydro project represents the extreme case of cost overrun where the production cost of power per megawatt went up to four-fold. The cost of Kulekhani 3 has more than doubled, while the Upper Trisuli A project cost has gone up from $89 million to $125 million with five years extension. One of the reasons behind the cost overrun is the exchange rate depreciation of the Nepali rupee against the dollar and the euro, resulting largely due to delays in project implementation.

Concluding remarks

The history of modern civilization over the last three centuries since the invention of the steam engine is largely influenced by the race for energy. The advancement of the energy revolution with the discovery of new energy sources and methods of their use has accelerated the pace of the industrial revolution. Oil and gas remained the new sources of energy in the twentieth century that contributed to post-war recovery. The rising temperature caused by excessive use of fossil fuel resulting in the melting of the polar and Himalayan glaciers with adverse consequences on the livelihood of the people has created conditions to intensify the search for clean and sustainable energy sources.

Against this backdrop, the enormous potential of Nepal's hydropower can not only serve our domestic needs and but also act as a lynchpin for accelerating economic growth and transformation by exporting clean renewable energy to neighboring countries. Unfortunately, the internal power generation at present fails to meet even the limited domestic demand with the per capita consumption of 245 KWh, very low by Asian standards. In the next few years, with the completion of various projects under construction, the country will be generating energy for export too, although due to seasonal demand-supply mismatch, there may be a need for power exchange to make up for dry season shortfall in internal production for some more years. Nepal's large hydro energy supply potential in the face of mounting energy demand, the generation mix with complementarities and synergy between countries create an appropriate condition for bi-lateral, regional and sub-regional cooperation for power trade.

The mega identified projects in Nepal are of multi-purpose reservoir nature capturing monsoon flows which will augment the lean season river flow creating irrigation and flood control benefits downstream, largely in India. Therefore, it is necessary to internalize these externalities spreading the cost over the downstream benefits for equitable sharing to make the projects economically viable and affordable. Furthermore, hydropower will find it difficult to compete with dirty coal and petroleum fired power unless the off-spin benefits are evaluated and priced. Proper regional and sub-regional understanding and cooperation is, therefore, a prerequisite for optimizing the utilization of Nepal's water resources.

Nepal's potential to be a clean energy powerhouse of the region for sustainable economic growth and bring economic prosperity to the people is therefore dependent on a strong commitment at the national, bilateral and regional levels. The country is also receiving goodwill and support from the international community and development partners. The achievement so far has, however, been modest mainly due to internal management problems which are attributed to unstable politics. They have consequent repercussions in policymaking, governance and external relations leading to loss of precious opportunities in the past. The initiation of the liberalized investment regime in the 1990s, together with institutional reforms created a favorable environment for private investment, but unstable politics and a long period of insurgency hindered the potential outcome. With the settlement of political problems after the promulgation of the new federal constitution and subsequent elections, there is now a need to focus full attention to tap the country's water resource potential in an optimal manner.

The external environment is also favorable with the signing of 2014 SAARC framework agreement on electric grid connectivity to ensure power trading within the region. Nepal's potential for hydropower development will largely depend on its exportability to the Indian market, for which the off-take market assurance of surplus power is required. This will be the basic framework of power cooperation with India. In addition to the Indian market, a power trade agreement has been signed with Bangladesh. With India providing land access for Nepal-Bangladesh power trade, the prospective power market has expanded. Bilateral talks have started for power cooperation with China also, but the extent of its potential is yet to be ascertained. Now the priority should be to attract domestic and foreign investment in power generation and transmission in the sector.

Nepal has lost a precious opportunity in the past to produce cheap hydro energy when the investment cost of hydropower plants was low. Bhutan took advantage of this opportunity by entering into timely agreements with India; its installed capacity at present is much higher than that of Nepal and the country earns almost half of its annual revenue from power export. This factor contributed to making Bhutan the highest-income country in South Asia in per capita terms. The investment cost of hydro projects has now gone up to around US$1.5 million per megawatt. Furthermore, apart from cheaper coal-based energy, solar energy is fast emerging as a cheap source, which is renewable and sustainable. The cost of electricity from solar photovoltaic is reported to be just one-fourth of what it was nine years ago and is expected to fall further.

Launching an ambitious plan to expand solar energy, India is fast emerging as a front runner in developing solar power in the fight against climate change, and has started to displace coal as an energy source. The World Bank is supporting $625 million to support the program of a Grid-connected Rooftop Solar Project for financing the installation of at least 400 MW of grid-connected rooftop solar photovoltaic units by 2022 across India.

It is also high time for Nepal to seriously consider the development of energy-intensive industries such as the urea fertilizer plant injecting high power input of domestic value addition in the final product and creating employment opportunities in domestic industry. This will not only reduce our dependence on fertilizer import but also offer domestic market to surplus power which often faces difficulty to find a buyer at the right price in the monopsonist market. The government can use the current fertilizer subsidy amount to subsidize the domestic production of fertilizer to make it affordable to farmers. Industries like cement and carbide are other potential energy-intensive industries that can also use Nepal's huge deposit of limestone cement and carbide. In recent years, the country has seen reasonable growth of the cement industry, which will be one major user of the country's hydropower. There is a significant need to encourage more of such industries. Opportunities also exist for hydropower to replace fossil fuel and other traditional energy sources in daily lives, for purposes including daily cooking and the means of transport that presently remain the major users of imported fossil energy.

Overall, there is an urgency to develop Nepal's hydro energy, as the delay is likely to make it less competitive, given the declining cost of other renewable energy sources resulting from advancement in technology. This calls for improved management efficiency, timely decision making, investment-friendly climate and quality execution of projects to raise investment efficiency. Negotiation with India on water rights and benefit-sharing and with other countries and foreign investors also require consensus-building among political parties keeping in mind the national interest and international practices to reduce risks of policy shifts with changes in government.

Notes

1. Dixit, Ajay (1995). Resource Endowment and Associated Uncertainty of Water Resources. In B. B. Thapa and B. B. Pradhan (Eds.). *Water Resources Development: Nepalese Perspective*, (p. 2). Konark Publications: Delhi.

2. Ibid. (p. 30).
3. Jha, Raghunath (July 2010). Total Run-of River Type Hydropower Potential of Nepal in Hydro Nepal. *Journal of Water, Energy and Environment,* Issue 7. Kathmandu.
4. Jha, R. Ibid.
5. Ministry of Finance. *Economic Survey 2017/18.*
6. Ibid.
7. National Planning Commission. (2017). *Bughigandaki Jalasayayukta Ayojana: Laganiko Khaka Tayar Parna Gathit Samitiko Pratibedan*, (p. 8).
8. In *The Kathmandu Post.* (2019, January 27).
9. Government of Nepal, Energy and Irrigation Ministry. (2075 v.s., Baisakh 25). *White Paper on the status and future programme for energy and irrigation.*
10. Government of Nepal, Energy and Irrigation Ministry. Ibid.
11. Lama, Mahendra P. (2010, December 17-19). *Political Economy of Energy Cooperation in South Asia.* South Asia Economic Summit: Kathmandu.
12. SAARC Energy Centre. (November 2015). *Optimum Power Mix for Sustainable Power Sector in South* Asia. Islamabad.
13. This mechanism under Kyoto Protocol allows the industrialized countries with the green house reduction targets to invest in emission reduction projects in developing countries. Under the scheme, projects that have reduced greenhouse gas emission will be awarded CERs (Certified Emission Reductions) that can be traded with countries and institutions not meeting CO2 emission targets.
14. Adhikary, Devendra (2016, April 26). Power Trade with India: Long Way to Go. In *The Rising Nepal.*
15. Nepal Energy Forum. (2017, May 22). Powering India-Nepal Ties: Analysis. www.nepalenergyforum.com
16. Nepal presented for possible Chinese assistance a number of hydro projects including Nalgadh Storage, Kimathanka Arun, Phulkot Karnali and Tamor Storage and various 400 KV power transmission projects. In *The Kathmandu Post.* (2018, September 27).
17. Pun, Sant Bahadur (2006). Water Resources in Nepal Conflict Resolution and Sustainable Peace. In *Foreign Policy and Development Issues,* Volume 2, (p. 87). Kathmandu.
18. *The Economic Times.* (2017, September 13).
19. *The Kathmandu Post.* (2019, June 6).

Chapter Eight

Coping with Disaster

Nepal's vulnerability to disasters, both natural and human-induced, is well known. Studies show that more than 80 percent of the country's population is vulnerable to floods, landslides, fires, cold wave, droughts, earthquakes and glacial lake outbursts floods. In 2018, the Home Ministry estimated that 1,454 lives were claimed by disasters, and a loss of about Rs. 10 billion was incurred.[1] The country's rugged and fragile geophysical structure, geomorphology, complex geology, unplanned settlement of increasing population, variable climatic condition, active tectonic processes and poor economic state account for the country's high susceptibility to such hazards. In terms of relative vulnerability, Nepal ranks 4th highest to climate change and 11th in earthquakes. Among twenty-one cities around the globe that lie in seismically hazardous zones, Kathmandu is said to bear the highest risk.[2]

Earthquake 2015

Nepal's geographical location between the Indian and the Eurasian tectonic plates makes it particularly vulnerable to seismic activities. The latest major earthquake to strike Nepal was on 25 April 2015 at 11.56 am. The epicenter was at Barpak of Gorkha. The quake lasted for 50 seconds and was originally recorded to be of magnitude 7.5 Mw by the US Geological Survey before it was upgraded at 7.8 Mw (or 8.1 Ms). The second earthquake of 6.6 Mw occurred on 12 May, followed by hundreds of aftershocks throughout the next twelve months. Reportedly, the earthquake was caused by the sudden thrust of the Indian plate along the fault lines diving underneath the Eurasian plate. The earthquake is said to have relieved compressional pressure between the Eurasian tectonic plate and the Indian section of the Indo-Australian Plane which subducts the Eurasian plate.[3] It was the worst natural disaster in eighty-three years after the 1934 Nepal-Bihar earthquake which had claimed 10,000 people. The most recent large earthquake after 1934 occurred in 1988 with a magnitude of 6.9 Mw, killing 1,500 people in Eastern Nepal.

In these earthquakes of 2015, nearly 9,000 people lost their lives, and more than 22,000 were physically injured, including some fatalities in nearby parts of India, China and Bangladesh. A total of 8 million people across thirty-one of the then seventy-five districts were affected. More than 600,000 homes were destroyed and 288,000 damaged. The most severe impact of the disaster was felt in remote rural areas of the country which lacked basic social and physical infrastructure for immediate search, rescue and relief. The impact of the two major quakes and a series of aftershocks also resulted in massive destruction of schools, health centers, government buildings, water and power systems, temples, cultural heritage sites, roads and bridges.

The earthquakes also triggered landslides causing devastation in various parts of rural Nepal and densely populated settlements. Many historical and cultural monuments including world heritage sites were damaged and destroyed. The earthquakes also caused avalanches in the Mount Everest region causing deaths of nineteen climbers, while hundreds of others were stranded in the high mountains. In addition to its major impact in central and eastern Nepal, the earthquake was also felt in the Gangetic plains of India, north-western Bangladesh, the southern part of the Tibetan plateau and western Bhutan.

Internal and external response

Two hours after the earthquake, an immediate meeting of the Central Disaster Relief Committee (CDRC) was held, chaired by the Home Minister Bamdev Gautam (who was also acting Prime Minister then), as per the mandate of Disaster Relief Act 1982. It recommended the government to declare a state of emergency in the severely affected fourteen districts. The CDRC is entrusted by the Act with the responsibility to coordinate and oversee rescue. The CDRC also formed the Central Command Post headed by the Home Secretary for operational functions. The state of emergency required an immediate mobilization of the army, other security forces and public institutions for rescue and relief operations.

The government called on the international community for aid and assistance. It extended customs exemptions to relief goods and visa fee exemption to foreign nationals entering the country for search and rescue (SAR) and humanitarian assistance. A cabinet meeting chaired by Prime Minister Sushil Koirala on 30 April took several relief measures in quake-affected areas. A decision was taken to offer financial assistance of Rs. 100,000 to families which had lost one or more members and cremation cost of Rs. 40,000 for each person. Assistance of Rs. 25,000 was provided to repair partially damaged homes, Rs. 200,000 cash grant in instalments and subsidized bank loans to those who wanted to rebuild their homes on their own based on the quake-resistant low-cost housing models designed initially by the National Planning Commission. The government also decided to set up the National Reconstruction and Rehabilitation Fund with the initial target of collecting US$2 billion for which the government allocated seed money of $200 million. The government also decided to provide cash grants through hospitals, and later offer free-of-cost medical treatment to all quake-injured people. Temporary shelters were created at sixteen places in the valley and other quake-affected areas for the displaced population.

The UN responded to the appeal by forming the Nepal Earthquake 2015 Flash Appeal Fund. Many friendly nations including India, China and other neighboring countries, multilateral institutions, INGOs and humanitarian bodies started sending aid and rescue teams. In view of the lack of proper transportation network in most quake-affected areas, helicopter services from Nepal army, private sector and neighboring India were mobilized for search, rescue and relief operations. A total of 132,427 security personnel were mobilized for search and rescue operations. A total of 4050 persons from seventy-six SAR teams and 135 canines were mobilized from thirty-four countries. More than eighty-seven international medical teams were mobilized for treatment of the injured. A special team comprising of representatives from relevant ministries and security forces was created and deputed to coordinate and facilitate the international teams arriving in Nepal and manage the relief supplies.

The post-quake situation also witnessed an unprecedented outpouring of relief aid from various institutions and individuals within the country, and from Nepal's growing diaspora. Distribution of food items, water, clothing and blankets, tents and tarpaulin, soap, hygiene kits and kitchen utensils received from organizations from within and outside the country continued for several months in the quake-affected areas. In order to ensure distribution of relief aid in an equitable manner, the government also appealed to the donors and relief organizations to coordinate and contact with the District Disaster Relief Committees (DDRC) while distributing relief goods at the local level.[4]

Appeal from Baku

Prime Minister Sushil Koirala was on an official trip to Bandung, Indonesia, when the quake struck; he immediately returned home on 26 April cutting short his visit to deal with the crisis. Meanwhile, the 48th annual meeting of the Board of Governors of Asian Development Bank was scheduled on 3–5 May in Baku, the capital city of Azerbaijan, to be attended by delegations led by Finance Ministers of member countries. I, as the then Finance Minister, was not feeling comfortable to go abroad for the meeting at a time when the country was facing such a massive agonizing calamity. A foreign visit by the Minister at such an hour was certain to be perceived negatively by the press. The need for all high officials to remain in the country was also obvious. On the other hand, there was the prospect to use the ADB forum attended by finance ministers of the member countries to appeal and mobilize support for post-earthquake relief and reconstruction. Sensing the uncertainty about my participation, the ADB Country Director for Nepal brought a special message from the ADB President urging me to attend the meeting to brief the international community about the Nepal situation and appeal for help. Briefing the cabinet about the dilemma I was feeling, I left it to the cabinet to take the decision on the matter. The cabinet made a positive decision for me to attend the meeting in Baku with the expectation to use the forum for international appeal.

The ADB annual meeting in Baku proved to be the first beneficial act in mobilizing international solidarity and support for relief, rehabilitation and reconstruction for the earthquake-hit Nepal.[5] Taking extra interest about the country, ADB president Takehito Nakao arranged a special meeting entitled Partnership with Nepal co-chaired by me and the ADB President to brief the meeting about the disaster and appeal for international support. In addition, I had the privilege of addressing four other meetings including the plenary session, two panel sessions and press conferences. I also chaired the SAARC Finance Ministers meeting. On the sideline I seized the opportunity of holding meetings with finance ministers of other friendly countries including Japan's Deputy Prime Minister and Finance Minister Taro Aso who also offered to co-host an international conference to mobilize support for post-earthquake reconstruction. The closing statement by President Nakao at the Annual Meeting included a paragraph on Nepal:[6]

> *I would like to convey once again our deepest condolences and sympathies to the Government and people of Nepal for the tragic loss of life and damage to properties caused by the 25 April earthquake. Many of you joined the "Partnership with Nepal" meeting that Minister Mahat and I co-chaired on 3 May, despite the short*

notice. Minister Mahat and I were encouraged by the strong support being extended by all partners. The international community should continue to provide priority needs for relief and recovery. After relief and recovery operations, we will discuss with the Government what is needed for reconstruction and rehabilitation, and work with the development partners to finance these needs. We welcome Japan's offer to organize with ADB and other partners a conference to support the reconstruction.

Encouraged by the positive outcome of the Baku annual meeting of the Asian Development Bank and outpouring of international solidarity and aid for the search, rescue and relief in the immediate aftermath of the earthquake, we started preparatory work to hold an international conference to mobilize further external resources particularly for the next phase of rebuilding and reconstruction. We intended to hold the conference as early as possible when the painful memory of the massive calamity and destruction was fresh, as any delay could divert global attention to disaster events elsewhere in the world. For this, consultation was started with relevant parties including the ambassadors and local donor representatives. Despite generally positive response on the matter, the suggestion was to hold the meeting in other donor capitals at a later date in view of the precarious security situation in Nepal due to frequent earthquake aftershocks, which was thought to deter high-level participation.

The Japanese government which had expressed interest to co-host the meeting also suggested holding the meeting in the late August or September, offering Tokyo as a possible venue. The Government of India sent messages offering to host the forum in New Delhi. Based on internal discussions within the government, we proposed to hold the meeting in Kathmandu itself with the objective to show the leaders and delegates of the world community with their own eyes the tragic devastation the country was facing. Furthermore, at a time when the economy was in doldrums following the disaster, the proposed event was expected to contribute towards the revival of tourist flow and business confidence in the country. Several consultations and official meetings were held at the Ministry of Finance with the local donor representatives expressing the government intention about the proposed conference. We urged them to ensure high-level participation in the proposed conference. In the last such local donor meeting, I announced the government's decision to hold the International Conference for National Reconstruction (ICNR) on 25 June 2018, exactly two months after the earthquake for which invitations were being sent. Responding to some skepticism about the adequate preparatory work, particularly the documentation required for the event, I assured them that they would be fully completed about a week prior to the event in order that the participating organizations could go through them before the meet.

Post Disaster Needs Assessment

As part of the preparatory work, the National Planning Commission under the overall leadership of its Vice-Chairman Govind Raj Pokharel was assigned with the task of preparing the Post-Earthquake Needs Assessment (PDNA) which would also outline the future strategy for reconstruction for presentation in the proposed international conference for national reconstruction. As promised to the development partners, the report was prepared in a timely fashion a week before the ICNR. Prepared by a core NPC team in collaboration with other relevant technical ministries and forty bilateral and multilateral development partners, the first volume of the report was released on 15 June. Together with the NPC, the core coordination group for the PDNA comprised of representatives from European Union, UNDP, World Bank, ADB and Japan. Prepared against a tight deadline of about three weeks, the report involved an intensive and rigorous exercise of twenty-three sector teams and 250 experts from the government and development partners. In preparing the report, broader consultations were also held with a wide range of stakeholders including the members of parliament, civil society, private sector, technical agencies and academia.

Among the main components of PDNA report included an assessment of the damage of physical assets of public and private sectors, losses in production of goods and services, effects on governance and decision-making process and increased risks and vulnerabilities. Damage assessment was done for major sectors including social, infrastructure, productive, and cross-cutting sectors including twenty-three themes/subsectors. The social sector comprised of housing and human settlements, education, health, nutrition and cultural heritage. Electricity, communication, community infrastructure, transport and water and sanitation were parts of the infrastructure sector. The productive sector included agriculture, irrigation, industry, commerce, tourism and finance. Governance, disaster risk reduction, environment and forestry were parts of the cross-cutting sector. The total loss and damage caused by the disaster was estimated at Rs. 607 billion equivalent to approximately US$7 billion.[7] Of that amount Rs. 517 billion (76 percent of the total disaster effects) represented the value of destroyed physical assets, while the remaining Rs. 189 billion or 24 percent of the total effect represented losses and higher costs of production of goods and services arising from the disaster. These estimates were based on the aggregation of data and information collected across social and other economic sectors and checked to avoid duplication of numbers.

Table 8.1: Summary of Disaster Effects
(Rs in million)

Sectors	Disaster Effects (NPR million)			Distribution of Disaster Effects (NPR million)		Losses in Personal income (NPR million)
	Damage	Losses	Total	Private	Public	
Social Sectors	355,028	53,597	408,625	363,248	45,377	
Productive Sectors	58,074	120,046	178,121	158,079	20,043	17124
Infrastructure Sectors	52,460	14,323	66,783	17,281	49,502	
Cross-Cutting Issues	51,872	1,061	52,933	1,755	51,178	
Total	517,434	189,027	706,462	540,362	166,100	17124
Total in US$ million	$5,174	$1,890	$7,065	$5,404	$1,661	$171

Source: National Planning Commission, Nepal Earthquake 2015-Post Disaster Needs Assessment, Kathmandu 2015.

As revealed by the data presented in table 8.1, the hardest-hit sector was the social sector comprising mainly of housing, accounting for 58 percent of the total loss and damage, followed by productive sector (25 percent), infrastructure (10 percent) and cross-cutting sector (7 percent). The estimated value of the total damage and losses was equivalent to one-third of the GDP in the fiscal year 2013/14, and more than 100 percent of the gross capital formation for that year. The loss and damage in the private sector was more than three times in comparison to the public sector, which is mainly attributed to the destruction of housing and production in the private sector.

The report also showed that the hardest-hit areas by the earthquake, with the exception of Kathmandu valley, were essentially poor, rural districts in Central and Western regions. Even in the relatively prosperous areas like Kathmandu, poor and vulnerable households were particularly affected. According to the World Bank simulations, additional 2.5 to 3.5 percent of the Nepali population largely from the hills and mountains, equivalent to 700,000 people were likely pushed into poverty in 2015/16 following the earthquake. Additionally, the deterioration of water and sanitation services, disruption of schools and health services and an increase in food insecurity worsened multidimensional poverty.

On the macroeconomic side, the report concluded that the earthquake would derail the higher growth trajectory experienced by the country after decades of political instability. The GDP growth was estimated to have been suppressed by over 1.5 percentage point, coming down to less than 3 percent from the earlier projection of 4.6 percent for 2015/16. On the fiscal side, there would be about 8 percent shortfall in annual revenue in 2013/14.

The report also offered suggestions about the pathways for the recovery program through multi-pronged strategy led by the government with the involvement and support of other sectors of the society and economy including the private sector, NGOs and development partners. A large number of activities for the implementation of the recovery and reconstruction in a short period of time required enormous preparation in institutional, financial and logistical terms. The suggestion was made to promote the principle of Build Back Better in recovery and reconstruction to contribute to resilience in the context of the vulnerability of the country to recurring natural disasters. While drawing upon lessons from good practices of other countries, the recovery program was developed and implemented in a uniquely Nepali way.

Conference for Reconstruction

The International Conference for National Reconstruction (ICNR) was held exactly two months after the devastating earthquake of April 25, 2015. The core objectives of the meeting were to appraise the post-earthquake situation of Nepal to the outside world, share international best practices and experiences for recovery and restoration, disseminate the findings of PDNA and seek financial and technical support from friendly countries and development partners for reconstruction

Contrary to initial skepticism about the scale of participation, the meeting was attended by fifty-eight delegations representing thirty-three countries and various multilateral organizations and INGOs with a total of more than 200 participants. It turned out to be probably the largest international high-level meeting ever held in Nepal. The heads of delegations included, among others, foreign ministers from India, China, Norway and Minister of State for Foreign Affairs of Japan, along with ministers from Bangladesh, Bhutan and Sri-Lanka, President of the Asian Development Bank, Vice President of the World Bank for South Asia, Under Secretary of the United Nations, and Development Commissioner from the European Union. They addressed the opening session of the ICNR which was inaugurated by Prime Minister Sushil Koirala. Foreign

Minister Mahendra Bahadur Pande delivered the welcome speech, and the theme address was delivered by me as Finance Minister. Video messages from UN Secretary-General Ban Ki-Moon, the World Bank President Jim Yong Kim, and the message from the US Secretary of State John Kerry were also presented.

The inaugural session was followed by various thematic and technical sessions. One session was devoted to the deliberations on the PDNA presented by Govind Raj Pokharel. There was a wide consensus among delegates about the quality of this document's credibility and inclusiveness to act as a foundation for the planning and implementation of the recovery and reconstruction phase. A presentation was made from the government side by the Finance secretary Suman Prasad Sharma about the concept and details of the planned National Reconstruction Authority as a new institutional mechanism to execute the reconstruction process quickly and efficiently with a span of five years.

One important recurring theme of the entire conference was the concept of Building Back Better (BBB) which represented a holistic approach to post-disaster recovery. This theme is globally applied across all sectors from infrastructure to health, education and finance. The aim of BBB in Nepal was its application in the major sectors like housing and education to create better post-disaster structures, plans and policies. It would be relevant to mention some suggested principles in which the BBB should be based. Relief activities should avoid damage to future recovery, and should learn from past mistakes. People affected by the disaster should be the drivers of growth, and be included in the decision making. Recovery of local economy and livelihood should be the central part of the reconstruction and recovery process, together with the recognition of diverse needs of different communities. To make the recovery program sustainable, communities must be allowed to use their own resources and capabilities wherever possible. Disaster assessment and reduction planning must take into account possible future hazards and risks. In other words, the rebuilding of more than a million destroyed houses and other physical assets should be done in a manner to withstand future shocks.

Building back better and enhancing disaster risk management and governance capacity also constitute themes of the Sendai Framework of Disaster Risk Reduction (2015-30) adopted in the UN World Conference in Sendai, Japan on March 18, 2015. The delegates from Japan presented in the ICNR a Nepal specific BBB strategy for disaster risk management in line with Sendai framework, particularly for the housing, education and governance sectors.

Disaster occurrence should lead to progress in policy and better governance: a major drive is necessary to improve the capacity of the state through policy reforms and legal frameworks, together with enhancing capacity building of the local community which can respond first at the time of crisis. The policy interventions for capacity building include community-level training, changing school curriculums, skills training, and communication and awareness campaigns.

Table 8.2: Pledges by Development Partners at ICNR 2015 (in US$)

SN	COUNTRY	GRANT (A)	SOFT LOAN (B)	TOTAL (A+B)
1	CHINA	766,927,000	0	766,927,000
2	INDIA	650,000,000	750,000,000	1,400,000,000
3	JAPAN	52,000,000	208,000,000	260,000,000
4	NORWAY	15,965,500	0	15,965,500
5	USA	130,000,000	0	130,000,000
6	ADB	0	600,000,000	600,000,000
7	WB	0	500,000,000	500,000,000
8	EU	111,890,000	0	111,890,000
9	EU(TA)	5,594,500	0	5,594,500
10	UK(DFID)	110,000,000	0	110,000,000
11	AUSTRIA	1,200,000	0	1,200,000
12	AUSTRALIA	4,635,300	0	4,635,300
13	CANADA	10,500,000	0	10,500,000
14	BANGLADESH	502,815	0	502,815
15	ROK	10,000,000	0	10,000,000
16	PAK	1,000,000	0	1,000,000
17	SWITZERLAND	25,000,000	0	25,000,000
18	SRI LANKA	2,500,000	0	2,500,000
19	SAUDI ARABIA	0	30,000,000	30,000,000
20	NETHERLANDS	26,000,000		26,000,000
21	SWEDEN	10,000,000		10,000,000
22	FINLAND	2,237,800		2,237,800
23	GERMANY	33,567,000		33,567,000
24	TURKEY	2,000,000		2,000,000
25	IMF	50,000,0000	50,000,000	50,000,0000
		1,971,519,915	2,138,000,000	4,109,519,915

*All currencies converted to US$ using Oanda.com on 26 June 2015

The act of seeking financial and technical support for the herculean task of recovery and reconstruction, which was the central objective of the ICNR, was conducted in a session chaired by me, in which pledges of support were made by development partners, friendly nations and INGOs in various forms and sizes ranging from financial support to humanitarian aid and foodstuff, capacity building, technical support in disaster management and skills training for rebuilding. The pledges of financial aid amounted to the grand total of US$4.1 billion including $1.97 billion in grants and the rest as a loan.[8] The source-wise break-down of this amount has been presented in table 8.2. As shown, in grant aid, China's pledge was the largest, followed by India, Japan, Norway, USA, EU and UK and others, while in terms of total pledge including loan, Indian commitment was the highest. Other major development partners that made substantial pledges of soft loans were ADB, the World Bank, Japan, Saudi Arabia and the European Union.

Note: In the case of India, $400 million from an existing commitment of loan of $1 billion was converted into grant; $250 million of the new commitment is a grant.

Viewed from all angles including the scale of participation, expression of solidarity, support and liberal pledges from the global community, the ICNR proved to be very successful. The size of financial assistance pledged by the international community on a single occasion was the largest ever in Nepal history. The government of Nepal also was commended by the delegates for organizing the conference of this scale in a very efficient and effective manner shortly after the disaster. Appreciation was also expressed for the swift rescue and relief actions of the government immediately after the quake by successfully mobilizing internal and external support. The rigor and the quality of the PDNA, and the swift design of the NRA through a presidential ordinance showed the best of Nepali competence and resilience to the world at a time of crisis.

Subsequent actions and progress

Following the ICNR, the Reconstruction and Rehabilitation Policy was prepared and approved in the second half of 2015, together with the enactment of formal legislation for the creation of National Reconstruction Authority (NRA) with the comprehensive and powerful mandate to plan and implement the recovery and reconstruction program. The main functions of NRA as laid down in the Act were: identification of priorities for reconstruction based on damage assessment, allocation of reconstruction funds to implementing ministries and agencies, approving plans, budget and programs, identification and acquisition of appropriate sites for reconstruction and relocation of affected communities, coordination and collaboration with key stakeholders to reconstruction, building implementation capacity together with skill training, monitoring to ensure safety and quality of reconstruction by using norms and standards and ensuring accountability and transparency through public hearings and reporting.

The broad objectives of NRA included reconstruction and restoration of partially and completely damaged residential, community and government buildings and heritage sites making them disaster-resistant, reconstruction of damaged cities and ancient villages, revitalization of productive sectors to create economic opportunities for livelihood, study and research on the science of earthquakes and its impact and post-disaster solution together with disaster risk reduction and resettlement of the affected communities in the appropriate sites.

The organizational structure of the NRA at the central level comprised of the Advisory Council at the top, the Steering Committee to approve annual plans, policies and the budget, the Executive Committee, District Coordination Committees, the Appellate Committee and Development Assistance and Facilitation Committee and various thematic groups. In addition, four ministries with a large volume of reconstruction work were initially equipped with central level project implementation units (CL-PIU). Later on, three CLPIU relating to housing, education/grant assistance and local development were brought directly under the NRA. The institutional arrangement at the local level in quake-affected districts comprised of NRA office and District Coordination Committee (DCC) to facilitate planning and reconstruction activities and ensure coordination between central and local bodies. The mechanism was also proposed at the municipal and village level for coordination with NGOs and civil society.

The NRA was formally established in December 2015. Since its establishment, numerous activities started as part of the recovery and reconstruction program. The Reconstruction and Rehabilitation Policy 2016 was prepared to provide a policy framework for steering rehabilitation and reconstruction. The organizational structure of NRA, implementation modality and approaches were finalized, together with guidelines for housing grant distribution, environmental impact assessment, land acquisition and registration, regulations for procurement and reconstruction and relationship with NGOs.

By March 27, 2016, the Central Bureau of Statistics completed the survey and documentation of 423,118 households. By mid-May 2016, the NRA developed the Post-Disaster Recovery Framework (PDRF) to further review the progress, and update the recovery objectives and strategies, financial requirements, guidelines for implementing the reconstruction and recovery activities, essentially based on the PDNA of June 2015, with some revision and updating. The PDRF was aligned with the 14th National Development Plan and the Sustainable Development Goals. The PDRF estimated that the total financial requirement for reconstruction, recovery and rehabilitation would be Rs. 938 billion. The key elements of reconstruction and rehabilitation policy were also defined. The standard approach for residential building is owner-driven construction supported by technical and financial government assistance to homeowners. Relocation of villages was discouraged except in unavoidable cases. Priority was given to vulnerable social groups in reconstruction programs with the engagement of the community, private sector, volunteers and diaspora. Disaster risk reduction was to be integrated with the principle of Build Back Better. Other policy guidelines were related to skills training, building codes and modes of cash subsidy for individual housing through the banking system.

The total budget allocated in the first three years after the earthquake amounted to Rs. 337.8 billion of which only Rs. 186.9 billion was spent. Internal sources contributed 64 percent of this actual spending, but represented only 30 percent of the budget allocation of 74 billion in 2014/15, 44 percent of the allocated amount of Rs. 113 billion in 2015/16 and 76 percent of Rs. 151 billion allocated in 2017/18. The main expenditure item in the total spending was the cash subsidy for private housing which accounted for 74 percent of the total. The government contributed 64 percent of this expenditure in private housing, the other sources were IDA, India, Japan, European Union and World Bank Trust Fund. Reconstruction and retrofitting of the destroyed and damaged private houses was the principal component of post-earthquake reconstruction. The government initially decided to grant Rs. 200,000 per eligible homeowner in instalments to assist housing reconstruction, which was raised to Rs. 300,000 in September 2016 because of the rising construction cost to be paid in three instalments based on construction progress in compliance with earthquake-resistant building codes designed by NRA. NRA had prepared thirty-four different design models for house-owners to choose from, while building residences. For partially damaged private residences, Rs. 100,000 was granted for repair and retrofitting in two equal instalments. To ensure availability of necessary skilled manpower and artisans including construction supervisors, masons, carpenters, electricians and plumbers for housing construction, 51,000 construction workers were trained. A total of 346 engineers, 521 sub-engineers and 575 assistant sub-engineers were mobilized to provide technical assistance at the local level for housing construction, progress monitoring and certification of grant payments in instalments.

By mid-April 2019, a total of 824,621 households were identified as being eligible for housing grants, including households added following the redress of complaints from quake-victims not included in previous beneficiary lists. Similarly, 64,367 households were identified as eligible for repair and retrofitting grants. By this date, the agreement has been signed for housing grant with 762,604 beneficiaries, of which the first instalment of Rs. 50 000 has been deposited in the bank accounts of 756, 408 families. Of this total, those who have received the second instalment of Rs. 150,000 numbered 564,944 beneficiaries and the recipient of all three instalments numbered 403,776 beneficiaries. According to NRA report, construction of 49 percent of the private houses has been completed, while the remaining subsidized houses are under construction in full swing. By this date, 382,200 houses have been completed. The task of rebuilding the rest is expected to be completed within two years.

Assisted by relevant technical departments of the government, NRA conducted a detailed geological study of 1,039 disaster risk-prone settlements, of which 272 human settlements were found necessary to be relocated. Provision was made to grant Rs. 200,000 to buy land to each household willing to resettle elsewhere on their own. A total of 1,848 such families were provided such grant, while the government arranged land to build houses for another 628 beneficiaries, as part of the development program for integrated settlements. The NRA approved the preliminary plan of developing twenty-nine integrated settlements.

Destruction and damage of cultural heritage, monuments of architectural value and historic settlements including some world heritage sites represented another important casualty of the 2015 earthquake. NRA decided to provide additional 50,000 subsidies for the reconstruction of each traditional individual house in the original design in historic settlements. A total of 753 cultural heritage sites were damaged, 133 completely and 620 partially. As of mid-February 2019, restoration of 224 sites was completed, while the reconstruction work is ongoing in 221 heritage sites. Restoration work has been particularly slow with respect to famous heritages like the Bhimsen Tower Dharahara, Ranipokhari, Kashtamandap, Gorkha Durbar and Nuwakot Sattale Durbar, despite the availability of liberal funding for the purpose from internal and external sources. To ensure necessary funding for the reconstruction and restoration of the precious national heritage sites, the national budget presented by me immediately after the earthquake for the fiscal year 2015/16 announced the levying of 1 percent additional service tax on telephone bills to finance the reconstruction and restoration of Dharahara and other heritage sites launching a campaign 'My Heritage, My Responsibility'. More than Rs. 2 billion has already been collected under this scheme. This and generous offers from other sources remain largely unutilized.

Destruction of the school buildings was the second major casualty after private houses. A total of 49,681classrooms of 7923 schools were completely destroyed by the earthquake. Therefore, after private houses, high priority was given to the reconstruction of school buildings by mobilizing internal resources and donor support from the Asian Development Bank, JICA, India, USAID and various NGOs. Reconstruction work has been completed with respect to 4,253 schools, while 2,131 school buildings are under reconstruction. The construction of the remaining 1,169 schools is yet to start. In total, reconstruction of 56 percent of the school buildings has been completed, and 28 percent under construction, while the construction of the remaining 15 percent is yet to start. More than two-thirds of the completed buildings were built by the school management committees, the remaining by NGOs and private contractors. The roles of school management committees, followed by NGOs have been prominent even for the school buildings under construction.

The progress in reconstruction has been partial with respect to government buildings and health centers. Of the total 483 quake-affected government buildings at central and district levels, 230 were completely destroyed and 253 partially damaged. Of them, reconstruction of 63 percent of the buildings has been completed, while that of 35 percent remains under construction. Repair and retrofitting of partially damaged buildings have been largely completed.

Rehabilitation of 207 government offices providing essential services has also been completed. Of the 1,197 health centers that were destroyed and damaged, 643 have been rehabilitated and retrofitted. Reconstruction and rehabilitation have been started for thirty-six of the seventy-five damaged roads. The Asian Development Bank has provided finance under the Earthquake Emergency Assistance Project for the reconstruction of seventeen roads in twelve districts with technical support from the Swiss, while the repair of other rural roads has also been initiated with government funding. In the drinking water sector, of the 3,212 damaged schemes, reconstruction of 791 has been completed, while 670 others are under consideration.

The other completed actions include skill training of 51,649 masons and carpenters, and short-term artisan training for 3,000 people to create necessary manpower for housing construction. The NRA has also launched training programs for livelihood and income generation in the districts hardest hit by the earthquake. A total of 202 NGOs have been granted permission to implement 292 projects, mostly in school construction, followed by housing, health centers, livelihood training, drinking water and sanitation.

Concluding remarks

The immediate aftermath of the massive earthquake was marked by an unprecedented response from within and outside the country. The search, rescue and relief work started with local volunteers who worked swiftly with security forces and international aid workers. The country witnessed a spontaneous outpouring of solidarity and support. The major challenge in extending rescue and relief in rural areas was the inaccessibility of road transport facility mainly because of destruction and damage caused by the earthquake. Efforts were made to restore the transportation routes and mitigate unsafe conditions internally by the government and private sector, and externally by development partners and the Nepali diaspora. Helicopters were used for rescue and relief operation in inaccessible mountain areas. This helped evacuate thousands of disabled and handicapped quake-victims to the nearest hospitals for medical treatment. Of the nearly 9,000 lives lost in the disaster, not a single death has been reported for lack of medical treatment. The ICNR held within two months of the earthquake also saw an unprecedented response from the international community with generous pledges to support reconstruction.

The disaster also created an opportunity for reconstruction under the theme Building Back Better drawing upon good practices of other countries through collaborative efforts with the international community. The disaster made a positive impact on the political situation inspiring the political parties and forces to unitedly cope not only with the calamity but to resolve long pending contentious issues in the country's constitution-making that led to its promulgation on September 20, 2015.

Following the swift and successful phase of search, rescue and relief operations that received appreciation from various quarters, the reconstruction work began with the establishment of NRA, backed by external pledges of financial and technical aid and internal resources. The reconstruction progress in the last three and a half years after the formation of NRA has been tepid as reflected in the slow progress of the rebuilding of individual houses, government buildings, cultural heritage sites, schools and other infrastructure. A significant portion of the affected families continue to live in temporary shelters, it is common to see damaged heritage buildings and sites such as the iconic Dharahara tower, Ranipokhari and historic central secretariat building of Singha Durbar still waiting for reconstruction and rehabilitation. This is attributed to several reasons.

The NRA became the victim of political wrangling and partisan squabbling. This caused delay and frequent change in executive management. The chief executive of the NRA was changed five times in the last three years, together with each change in government. Furthermore, a few months after the earthquake, the country suffered from an unofficial trade blockade from the Indian side causing disruption of supplies of goods including construction materials, which not only hampered the reconstruction program but paralyzed the whole economy. The political vacuum at the local level in the first two years due to the absence of local government was another constraint to drive the reconstruction process. The precise identification of the quake-victims eligible for cash subsidy continues to be problematic. There are allegations of unaffected households not meeting the eligibility criteria being listed in the beneficiary list due to political pressure while excluding some real victims. It may be noted that the total number of enrolled beneficiaries has now reached 812,161 from the initial estimate of nearly half a million based on the survey of the Central Bureau of Statistics. The NRA has yet to redress the appeals and grievances of thousands of other claimants. The job has now been handed over to concerned local governments elected in mid-2017.

The dismal performance is also evident in underspending of the allocated budget for reconstruction in the last three years. One often hears NRA complaints about inflexible administrative procedures and non-cooperation of ministries for the slow pace of rebuilding, as its proposal to bypass standard regulations to facilitate its performance failed to materialize. The poor follow-up action to negotiate and direct the US$4.1 billion pledged by the donors in rebuilding and reconstruction is also responsible for the slow pace. By mid-February 2019, the signed agreement amounted to Rs. 394 billion. There has been a general donor preference to use their aid money through international NGOs rather than the government mechanism. Of the Rs. 186 billion spent on reconstruction work by mid-November 2018, 67 percent has come from the donors. It has also been reported that part of the Rs. 100 billion soft loan pledged by India for reconstruction could not be received due to conditions attached to loans from the Export-Import Bank. The government is planning to utilize the amount in other projects and compensate reconstruction finance with its own resources.

Amid general disappointment and criticisms for the slow pace of recovery, the NRA planned to accelerate rebuilding individual homes by announcing deadlines to complete the building phases to remain eligible for the second and third instalment of subsidy grant. This has led to a spurt in home reconstruction in recent months. However, the increased construction cost due to rising demand for materials and labor after the earthquake has led to financial burden especially for the poorer and vulnerable groups whose access to low-interest loan promised by the government is limited. The only other option for families without other sources including remittance income is resorting to loan from informal sources.

The most positive development in the post-earthquake relief and rebuilding scenario is the increased spirit of volunteerism to support victims and affected people, bringing the people closer. The BBB principle has now been internalized by the government institutions with dissemination into other non-affected regions of the country also. The building codes have now been revised to strengthen the resilience aspect of infrastructures in pursuance of the BBB goal.

Notes

1. *Republica Daily*. (2019, January 9).
2. Maplecroft (2011), BCPR (2004). Quoted in Ministry of Home Affairs, Govt of Nepal. (December 2017). *Nepal Disaster Report 2017*.
3. Rafferty, J. P. *Nepal Earthquake of 2015*. Britannica.com

4. Ministry of Home Affairs. *Nepal Earthquake 2072: Situation Update as of 11 May 2015.*
5. The author's first interaction with the international community immediately after the 2015 earthquake in the ADB annual meeting in Baku to raise awareness among peers and press found mention in the first paragraph of the statement while announcing the award of Global and Asia-Pacific Finance Minister Year 2016. The award was conferred to me by the Banker Magazine of the Financial Times Group, London for the exemplary work done in the aftermath of the two disastrous earthquakes that hit Nepal in 2015 and in pushing for reforms to improve governance in the country's Ministry of Finance. (January 2016). *The Banker: Global Financial Intelligence since 1926.*
6. Extracts from the Closing Statement by ADB President Takehito Nakao at the 48th Annual Meeting of the Board of Governors , on 5 May 2015 in Baku, Azerbaijan.
7. National Planning Commission. (2015). *Nepal Earthquake 2015: Post-Disaster Needs Assessment.* Kathmandu.
8. Ministry of Finance. (2015, June 25). *International Conference on Nepal's Reconstruction: Towards a Resilient Nepal.* Kathmandu. Conference Report.

Chapter Nine

Rise of the Remittance Economy

The trans-border migration and movement of people is a familiar phenomenon in history. The prosperity of Europe and its transformation from an agricultural economy to a modern industrial economy is attributed to mass migration of labor from rural to urban areas. Similarly, the economic transformation and prosperity of North America was caused mainly by the migration of people, largely from Europe and Africa. That people tend to move to greener pastures with better economic opportunities is an established reality.

Economics of migration

We are living in a globalized world where free movement of factors of production is emphasized, although there are restrictions with respect to labor. Industrial goods are produced where the cost of production factors including labor is cheap and are sold where profit is maximized. Alternatively, countries endowed with cheap and surplus labor are used for low-cost production. Each year the developed economies of Europe and North America together receive approximately two million migrants, not because of their benevolence to poor countries but because for their regard to self-interest to raise productivity and competitiveness to maximize profit. Lester Carl Thurow, the former Dean of the Sloan School of Management at the Massachusetts Institute of Technology has spoken of the phenomenon of rising, moving and aging character of the demography of the modern world.[1] There is rising population in developing countries greater than the economy's absorptive capacity, which prompts the movement of surplus population to places with better economic prospects. On the other hand, there is a problem of the ageing of the population in developed countries where population growth is stagnating. These counties are in need of a young, productive and cheap labor force which can be supplied by poor developing counties with higher population growth.

Obviously, international migration is in the mutual economic interest of both receiving and sending countries that eventually contributes to global prosperity. Migration, however, is not just a North–South phenomenon. Within developing countries also, millions of people are moving from lagging to richer regions. Over the past decade, most of Nepal's labor has moved to developing nations like India, Malaysia and oil-rich Arab countries. Malaysia is a developing country on the verge of graduating to developed economy status, while India is a developing country. Nepal also receives labor from India, particularly for skills lacking here. Although migration is basically an economic phenomenon, it has wide socio-cultural ramifications.

According to the World Bank report, the officially recorded remittance flow to low and middle-income countries reached US$529 billion in 2018, up from $483 billion in 2017. The total global remittance including flows to high-income countries is estimated to have reached $689 billion in 2018 from $633 billion in 2017. India is the largest recipient with $78.6 billion, followed by China ($67.4 billion), Mexico ($35.7 billion), the Philippines ($33.8 billion), Egypt ($28.9 billion) and Nigeria ($24.3 billion). Remittance in South Asia amounted to $131 billion, compared to $117 billion in 2017. After India, Pakistan ($21.0 billion) and Bangladesh ($15.5 billion) are major receiving countries, followed by Nepal ($8.1 billion) and Sri-Lanka ($7.1billion). Given the relatively small size of the economy, the remittance inflow as a percentage of GDP in Nepal stood around 28 percent in 2018, the fifth-highest globally after Tonga (35%), Kyrgyz Republic (34%), Tajikistan (31%) and Haiti (30.7%). Its ratio in other countries of South Asia is relatively low, ranging between 8.1 percent in Sri-Lanka and 0.1 percent in the Maldives.[2]

Migration in history

Migration and remittance income are not the new phenomenon in Nepal. Arniko is probably the most famous early Nepali migrant, who in the 13th century moved to China to leave behind an indelible impression of Newari craft on Chinese architecture. As a mass phenomenon, outward migration from Nepal can be traced to the early 19th century. Population pressure and economic hardship due to oppressive land and labor policies in the countryside especially in the hills and mountains led the people to migrate to other areas within Nepal and abroad, particularly to India. Driven by trade relations with the North, there were also instances of some migration of labor and traders to Tibet. The famous epic of Nepali literature, *Muna Madan*, by the great Nepali poet Laxmi Prasad Devkota depicts the character of migrant Nepali youth represented by its central character *Madan* who undertook an agonizing and risky sojourn to Lhasa to make a fortune.

Impressed by the martial qualities exhibited by Nepali soldiers in various battles, particularly during the 1814–16 Anglo-Nepal war, the British started recruiting Nepali soldiers in their army. The Nepali soldiers who surrendered after defeat in the *Kumaon* and *Garhwal* region in 1816 were later invited to join the British army. Three regiments of Gurkha Rifles were created after formalizing the recruitment of Nepali soldiers. The subsequent policy of Nepal government did not allow direct Nepali recruitment into the British army until the treaty was signed by Rana Prime Minister Bir Shamsher in 1885 that paved the way for long-desired British interest to recruit Nepalis. Apart from the migration resulting from recruitment in the British Army, the British takeover of Assam in 1826 opened up opportunities for Nepali civilian migrants to work as laborers in tea plantations, land reclamation and lumbering. Subsequently, people started migrating permanently to Sikkim, Bengal, Assam, Bhutan and Burma. Darjeeling was a popular destination for Nepali migrants because of better income opportunities.[3] The tea plantations of Darjeeling expanded because of the steady supply of Nepali labor, as the British administration encouraged the settlement of Nepalis in the hills of Darjeeling and Shillong. To defend the Northeast, the British formed a strong force of Assam Rifles into which they recruited Gurkha soldiers which constituted about a third of the regiment.

The two World Wars were landmark events that led to a massive outflow of Nepali youth including Nepal army contingents fighting on the British side. It has been estimated that more than 200,000 Nepalis served during the First World War both as combatants and non-combatants. The countryside was then stripped of its youth. Nepal lost more people in the War in proportion to its population which was about five million at that time than any other country involved in the War. Nepal extended similar support to the British during the Second World War when approximately 160,000 Nepali soldiers and new recruits, in addition to the deployment of Nepalis in Gurkha regiments in India, are estimated to have played a vital role for the victory of the allied forces. In addition to the reputation of unparalleled ferociousness and bravery earned by the Nepalis under insurmountable adversity, the two world wars proved to be an important source of remittance income for the soldiers who returned home. The government, too, received an unconditional windfall of annual cash of Indian Rs. 1 million in perpetuity from the grateful British. This was doubled after the Second

World War. The total remittance brought about by the 200,000 soldiers who participated in the First World War was estimated to be around Rs. 250 million. The massive injection of this amount in the rural economy created disruption in the simple rural life based on the principle of self-sufficiency, with the influx of cheaper imported machine-made goods. Fifty percent of the increased annual gift was used for Nepal's development programs. Some of the projects financed by this cash gift during the Rana regime were the Bhimfedi-Amalekhgunj Road, the Amalekhgunj-Raxaul Railway and Matatirtha-Dhursingh Ropeway.

Nepali recruitment into the Indian and British army continued even after the end of the war and India's independence from Britain. Because of the high reputation and loyalty of the Gurkha army, both Britain and India wanted to continue the practice. As part of the British army, Gurkha soldiers served in Malay, Borneo, Belize and Cyprus and subsequently Hong Kong. From Nepal's perspective also, this was a good source of income and livelihood for the rural families whose members were serving in foreign armies. Joining the British and Indian army had been the preferred jobs for the Nepali rural youth belonging to specific ethnic groups. In addition to this, civilian job opportunities in India had started to attract migration of seasonal and permanent nature from the early days. According to the 1941 Indian census, 45 percent of foreign immigrants in India were Nepalis. The Nepal census of 1941 showed 87,722 Nepalis representing 1.4 percent of the population were reported to be away from home for six months or more. The number increased to 762,181 representing 3.24 percent of the population in 2001, of which 70 percent were from the hills and mountains and the rest 30 percent from Tarai.[4] Of the absentee population, around 80 to 90 percent had gone to India. Absentee population from Nepal living in India numbered 157,323 in 1952/54, increasing to 589,050 in 2001.[5]

India was the preferred destination for Nepali migrants in the past, because of proximity, porous and open border and similarities in culture and language, which made it easy to migrate from the Indian side also, particularly for the skilled job opportunities and business enterprises. The Treaty of Peace and Friendship of 1950 and various other trade treaties made it possible for Indian migration to Nepal for business and employment, particularly for skilled jobs and teaching. According to the Nepal census of 2001, the total number of India-born population of 583,599 constituted 96 percent of the total foreign-born population of 608,090, then living in Nepal. Interestingly, 589,050 Nepalis were living in India in the same year, indicating an identical flow of migrants between the two countries, their vast underlying population size notwithstanding.[6]

New job market and remittance surge

More attractive job markets opened up in East Asia, and the Middle East after the oil boom, but Nepal's restrictive passport policy and high travel cost were the major constraints for those willing to migrate in new destinations. The scenario changed following the transition to democratic rule in 1990. The democratic government liberalized access to foreign labor markets by decentralizing the application and issuance of passport authority through the district administration. This opened the floodgates of an exodus to new labor destinations including the Middle East, Malaysia, Japan, Korea, USA and Australia. The outbreak of Maoist insurgency and surging remittances from new destinations provided further incentives for migration of the youth seeking both job opportunity and safety. With a view to leverage the demand of Nepal's manpower in emerging economies, the government, in the budget speech by this author for the fiscal year 2055/56,[7] also announced a policy to start a dialogue with concerned governments of Gulf countries, East Asia and others for expansion of employment opportunities and protection of their labor interests. Policy measures were announced to launch training for required skills, ensure easy credit availability and repatriation of foreign earnings through banking channels. Promotion of foreign employment was also treated as part of the economic diplomacy pursued by the government, together with the promotion of FDI, development assistance and merchandise exports.

Consequently, migration of Nepali youth to new destinations registered a phenomenal surge with accompanying growth of remittance in foreign currency that played a vital role in contributing to poverty reduction and maintaining the balance of payment. The census data on absentee population residing outside Nepal which can be interpreted as the stock of migrants from the country shows its growth from 658,290 in 1981 to 762,181 in 2001 and 1,917,903 in 2011. The ratio of female absentees increased to 13 percent in 2011 from 11 percent in 2001. The fast-rising trend of manpower outflow is also reflected in the number of labor permits issued by the Department of Foreign Employment (DOFE) that increased from 3,605 in 1993/94 to 521,878 in 2013/14. A total of 3.5 million labor permits is reported to have been issued for Malaysia and the nations of Gulf Cooperation Council (GCC) during a period of ten years from 2008 to

2017. India and the Middle East are the major labor destinations accounting for more than 70 percent of Nepal's external migration, followed by ASEAN countries, Europe and North America.

According to the 2001 census, 70.2 percent of the migrant population were born in the hills and mountains and the remaining 29.8 in the Tarai. The ratio of Tarai migrants also increased with the opening of the new labor market in third countries. A 2009 survey revealed that 48 percent of migrant population originated in the Tarai, and 52 percent from hills and mountains, reflecting a general pattern of population density of the country.[8] According to the Migration Survey of Nepal 2009 by NIDS and the World Bank, a large proportion of remittance came from Qatar, Saudi Arabia, India, Malaysia and UAE, the other countries including Israel, UK and Japan. The survey also revealed that 43 percent of the total remittance went to the hills and mountains, and 57 percent to the Tarai.[9] The Nepal Living Standard Survey 2010/11 also shows that nearly two in three households in the Tarai receive remittances and the proportion for both the hills and mountains are roughly one in two households.[10]

A noticeable development in recent years is the emergence of the United States of America as one of the major sources, together with GCC countries, India and Malaysia. In the year 2016/17 and 2017/18, USA contributed the largest portion, i.e., 21.5 percent and 19.5 percent, respectively, of total remittance inflows into Nepal. The growing remittance inflow together with pension receipt over time since the fiscal year 1999/2000 is shown in table 9.2 below. The total remittance inflow increased from Rs. 36.8 billion in 1999/2000 to Rs. 755 billion in 2017/18, while pension receipts rose from Rs. 5.9 billion to Rs. 54.2 billion. The combined ratio of remittance and pension receipts rose from 11.3 to 26.7 percent of GDP during the period. Of the total remittance of Rs. 755 billion in 2017/18, the 19.5 percent that came from the USA, was followed by Saudi Arabia (13.6 percent), India (13.4), Qatar, (11.6 percent), Malaysia (10.7 percent), UAE (10.7 percent) and Japan (7.6 percent). Other countries contributing more than one percent of the total include South Korea, Bahrain and Kuwait. India and Britain represented the only source of pension receipts.

Economic impact

The real impact of the remittance income in the household economy particularly in reducing poverty has been shown by the reports of Nepal Living Standards

Survey conducted in 1995/96, 2003/4 and 2010/11. In 1995/96 the percentage of households below the poverty line was 42 percent, which declined to 31 percent in 2003/4 and further to 25 percent in 2010/11. More than 50 percent of this decline in poverty is estimated to have been contributed by remittances.[11] This is substantiated by data presented in table 9.1 below that shows the rising percentage of remittance recipient households from 23 percent in 1995/96 to 31.9 percent in 2003/4 to 55.8 percent in 2010/11, together with the increasing size of average annual remittance per household respectively from Rs. 15160, Rs. 34,698 to Rs. 80,439 that contributed to the rise in household income. The share of remittance as a percentage of the household income rose from 26.6 percent in 1995/96 to 35.4 percent in 2003/4, declined to 30.9 percent in 2010/11. The table also shows that nearly half, 44.7 percent, of the remittance income in 1995/96 was from within the country, which declined to 19.6 percent in 2010/11. The table also shows the declining share of remittance from India from 32.9 percent in 1995/96 to a mere 11.3 percent in 2010/11, while the contribution from other countries jumped from 22.4 percent to 69.1 percent during the period.

Table 9.1: Summary of Remittances Transfer and Household Income

	1		
Description	1995/96	2003/04	2010/11
Percent of all households receiving remittances	23.4	31.9	55.8
Nominal average amount of remittance per recipient household (Nrs.)	15,160	34,698	80,436
Share of total amount of remittances received by household			
From within Nepal	44.7	23.5	19.6
From India	32.9	23.2	11.3
From other countries	22.4	53.3	69.1
Share of remittances in total household income among recipients	26.6	35.4	30.9
Nominal per capita remittance received for all Nepal (Nrs.)	625	2,100	9,245
Nominal total amount of remittances received (million Nrs.)	12,957.8	46,365.5	259,088.5

Source: Nepal Living Standards Survey 2010/11: Statistical Report Volume Two, p. 80.

The data presented above shows the direct impact of remittances on household income. The real impact of this is reflected in multi-dimensional implications in the living conditions in terms of ownership of assets, investment in education and health, in addition to meeting immediate basic livelihood needs including food, clothing and other household expenses.

A recent survey in 2016 by the Nepal Rastra Bank[12] shows that 25.3 percent of the remittance income of households is spent on repayment of loan, 23.9 percent on food, clothing and other basic consumption, 9.7 percent in education and health, 3.5 percent in social expenses like marriage and others and 3 percent in household assets, while the remaining 28 percent is saved and 11 percent is invested. The survey shows that 66.6 percent of the households covered by the study save a portion of the remittance in one way or the other, while the other 33.4 percent spend on consumption and loan repayment. Banks and financial institutions are used by 64.5 percent of the saving households, others hold their savings with themselves or deposit in cooperatives. Most of the savings are intended for buying house and land, residential repair, investment in education or starting business enterprises. Thus, the earnings increasingly remitted to Nepal by the migrant population working abroad has made its impact on the reduction of multidimensional poverty measured in terms of consumption expenditure in multiple aspects of life including food, education, health, housing, and other assets and services like electricity, sanitation and drinking water associated with living standards. The 2018 study by the National Planning Commission and Oxford University shows that the headcount ratio of multidimensional poverty in Nepal has dropped sharply from 59 percent to 29 percent between 2006 and 2014. The remittance income is one principal factor contributing to this progress.

Some opine that despite the positive impact of remittances on the economy particularly in reducing poverty and raising living conditions of the people, it has not contributed in raising the productive capacity of the country because of its use mainly in consumption and other household expenditure. This notion is contested by the fact that the use of remittance in consumption, education, health services, and buying or repair of residences while preventing deprivation also enhances human productivity laying the foundation for future growth. The new philosophy of development as defined by Nobel laureate Amartya Sen means the widening of individual opportunities in life and multiplying freedom of individual choices rather than just producing goods. It may also be mentioned that it is the job of banks and financial institutions as financial intermediaries, to convert the household savings with them generated by remittance into investments, which depends on the market demand and the country's investment climate.

Table 9.2: Remittance and External Sector Indicators
(Rs in billion)

		1999/2000		2004/05		2009/10		2017/18	
		Amount	as % of GDP	Amount	as % of GDP	Amount	as % of GDP	Amount	as % of GDP
1	Remittance	36.8	9.7	65.5	11.1	231.7	19.4	755	25.1
2	Pension	5.9	1.6	12.5	2.1	25.9	2.2	54.2	1.8
	1+2	**42.7**	**11.3**	**78.0**	**13.2**	**257.6**	**21.6**	**809.2**	**26.9**
3	Exports	49.8	13.1	58.7	10.0	60.8	5.1	81.2	2.7
4	Imports	108.5	28.6	149.5	25.4	374.3	31.4	1242.8	41.3
5	Trade Balance	-58.7	-15.5	-90.8	-15.4	-313.5	-26.3	-1161.6	-38.6
6	CA Balance	-9.0	-2.4	11.5	2.0	-28.1	-2.4	-245.2	-8.2
7	BOP Position	14.4	3.8	5.7	1.0	-3.3	-0.3	0.96	0
8	Nominal GDP	379.5		589.4		1192.2		3007.2	

Source: Nepal Rastra Bank

The second conspicuous value of remittance inflow for Nepal is reflected in its contribution in maintaining a positive balance of payment when the country is suffering from chronic trade deficit. As revealed by the data in Table 9.2, the country's trade deficit increased from Rs. 15.5 billion in 1999/2000 to 1161.6 billion in 2017/18. The foreign exchange earnings from workers' remittance and pension has been the principal factor to reduce the current account deficit. As noted earlier, Nepal is among the top remittance-receiving countries globally relative to the size of the economy, and in per capita terms. Nepal's foreign exchange earnings from remittance income increased from 9.7 percent of GDP in 1999/2000 to 19.4 in 2008/09 and to 25.1 percent in 2017/18. The ratio of pension receipts as a share of GDP remains constant at around 2 percent of GDP. Thanks to remittance inflows, the country does not suffer from foreign exchange constraints despite the huge trade deficit, which has eased the nation's vulnerability to external shocks.

Remittances generate multiplier effects leading to income generation not necessarily confined to the remittance-receiving families, but also to different segments of the society. The foreign employment and remittance inflow have also given rise to the emergence of new business opportunities generating employment and income and contributing to government revenue. The passport fees of migrants and the VAT levied on passenger service charge also add to the state revenue. The annual fees and income tax paid by an increasing number of manpower recruitment and orientation agencies, money transfer, finance companies and banks are other sources of revenue attributed to foreign employment. The money spent in the process of going abroad and returning by the migrants to various other service providers such as training and medical institutes, travel agencies and airlines, photograph and photocopy shops, restaurants and hotels, local transport communications and insurance agencies have created plenty of enterprises and jobs. Remittance flow is the crucial factor behind Nepal's fast-growing service sector that remains the principal contributor to its economic growth.

The other benefits of foreign employment in non-monetary terms is the improvement of knowledge, skills, work ethic, professional discipline and other social assets learnt from the exposure to and experience in foreign countries. There are examples of many foreign returnees who have started small business enterprises such as restaurants, commercial farms, workshops, horticulture and livestock farming in Nepal, following the realization that putting in the same amount of hard work and discipline in one's own land could result in returns higher than the earnings abroad. One often comes across newspaper reports of such success stories that have transformed the lives of people in the countryside generating employment and creating demonstration effects for creative and innovative enterprises.

Problems and prospects

Increasing remittance inflows has been an important contributor to the economic wellbeing of the general population and macroeconomic stability of Nepal. One should also take note of the adverse impacts resulting from excessive labor outflow. The reduction of the young workforce from the country has constricted labor supply in farm and factories causing upward pressure on wages and production costs. On the positive side, the real wage increase resulting from labor outflow is one factor that contributed to poverty alleviation of the working population. The implication is that the erosion of competitive advantage of the economy weakens the export sector leading to a high trade deficit. At the same time, the sector is not free from problems stemming from the very start of the migration process. Migrant workers are subject to neglect and harassments both at home and destination countries. The failure of regulatory institutions to effectively check corruption and exploitation, and monitor the welfare of the migrant labor is mainly responsible for many of the difficulties arising in this sector.

There are cases and complaints of fraudulence and cheating of innocent people in the process of and after getting foreign employment. Because of poor oversight to more than 932 recruitment agencies and 733 registered agents operating in Nepal, more than 5,484 complaints have been registered at DOFE from 2014 to 2017 seeking prosecution of recruitment agencies and others, reimbursement and compensation.[13] There are often reports of violations of labor rights by agents and recruitment bodies at home and destinations often reflected in the seizure of personal documents including passports, contract substitution and placement in unsuitable jobs, non-compliance of promised wage level and other working conditions and jobs, and lack of health care and timely payment of wages. The poor and hard-working conditions, lack of access to proper health care and the heat stress on construction sites have caused high death rates attributed largely to cardiac arrest, heart attack, suicide, traffic accidents and workplace accidents. A total of 7,469 Nepali migrant workers have reportedly lost their lives in a period of last eleven years ending in April 2019 while serving in various countries; deaths occurred mainly in Malaysia, followed by Saudi Arabia, Qatar, UAE and Kuwait.[14]

There is a lack of pre-departure information and orientation for rural job seekers. There are reports of 15 percent of migrants abroad without a work permit, and about half of returned migrants do not have contract letters of employment with them. A portion of the migrants, not getting employment immediately after reaching the destination, have to wait for weeks to get the job, while others are compelled to seek alternative jobs. Even more serious problem relates to female labor who are generally exploited more and deprived of basic rights without the proper mechanisms to protect their interest. A review report of March 22, 2015, by Advocacy Forum and National Network for Safe Migration (NNSM) submitted to the UN Human Rights Council sums up the human rights violation of Nepali migrant workers as being high risk victims of recruitment malpractices including forced labor, trafficking, sexual and physical harassments, debt bondage, fraudulent employment offers, racial bias and xenophobia, exorbitant fees, placement in perilous employment, under or non-payment of wages and discriminating laws and policies in destination countries.[15] There are also many cases of family breakdowns and failed marriage relations due to long spousal separation resulting from migration.

Available data collated from the Department of Foreign Employment reveals the migratory pattern of Nepali labor as largely unskilled; 74 percent of the migrant workers who received labor permits in 2013/14 were categorized as unskilled. Therefore, there is an urgent need to improve the quality of labor by enhancing their technical and vocational skills in keeping with the demand trend of the market. Better skills would mean better-paying jobs and improved working conditions with the prospect of a more promising future after returning home. The task of creating vocational and technical skills through appropriate training is important from the point of meeting domestic needs too for which the country is presently relying on migrant labor.

This requires an effective labor market information system to facilitate the development and supply of skills to match with the market demand. Furthermore, the problem arises because of the poor pre-departure orientation of the migrant labor that leads to much of their harassment and exploitation. Despite the provision of compulsory pre-departure orientation training, the cost of training must be borne by the migrants themselves. More than sixty licensed institutions for such training are all located in Kathmandu involving high cost of orientation for those coming from outside. The implication is that only a limited proportion of migrants go through due process, others reportedly 'purchase' the certificates illegally.

Despite the phenomenal growth of remittance earnings in the past and its increasing importance in maintaining the positive balance of payments in the face of mounting trade deficit, its true potential is yet to fully materialize. Until the mid-nineties, the remittance money came mainly through informal and undocumented illegal channels. After the foreign exchange reforms eliminated dual exchange rates and permitted the opening of foreign exchange accounts in Nepali commercial banks in the early 1990s, remittance inflow from banking channels started to increase. Further reforms to incentivize money transfer through formal channels were introduced by permitting money remit agencies and commercial banks to operate in countries employing Nepali labor. The first money transfer licensee was IME in the year 2002 that started remitting money from Malaysia, followed by many more bank branches in the Gulf and other countries. The opening of multiple channels for money transfer also reduced the cost of money transfer to less than 3 percent (of $200 transfer) that compares favorably with the global average.

Despite these positive developments, 5 to 10 percent of the total transfer from Gulf countries and Malaysia is estimated to be taking place through the illegal Hundi channels; 11 to 17 percent of the transfer is estimated to be carried personally and through friends and relatives, as people perceive Hundi as easier, cheaper[16] and quicker than the official channel. As regards the money transfer from India, more than 90 percent come through unofficial channels. It is, therefore, necessary to plug this leakage through strong administration as well as by offering incentives. One possible incentive could be to free the renewal of passport to migrants if the application is attached with bank vouchers of remittance transfer as practiced in some countries like Sri Lanka and the Philippines. Any other facility and privilege including social security, insurance and subsidized business loan provided to migrants and returnees should be linked with the evidence of money transfer through official channels.

Concluding remarks

Remittance has emerged as an important source of livelihood of the people next only to agriculture, and from the macro perspective as the largest source of foreign exchange that has contributed to stabilizing current accounts and maintaining financial stability. It has multiplier effects in the economy spurring economic opportunities and employment creation. The skills and resources of the returning migrants are also an asset to the country that can be utilized for economic development. Therefore, it is important to mainstream this sector in the economic planning process to optimize its contribution to the economy.

It is necessary to initiate measures to make the labor migration more efficient, inexpensive and free of hurdles and malpractices together with the improvement of skills to match market demands, and effective pre-departure orientation training. For the safety and protection of the rights of migrant labor, it is necessary to have bilateral labor agreements with major destination countries, which is presently limited to only few nations including Qatar, Malaysia and

Korea, and strong monitoring mechanism to protect the rights of the migrants by strengthening the concerned government bodies including the diplomatic missions.

Given the crucial importance of foreign exchange earnings for the macro-management of the economy, all possible incentives should be provided to attract official transfer of remittance by drawing upon lessons from good practices of other countries. It is also important to make the best possible use of the remitted earnings to enhance the productive capacity of the country in the long run. Also, the skills and knowledge learnt abroad by the migrants returning home are an important source of knowledge transfer that needs to be utilized for promoting the domestic economy with proper policy measures. The Dutch Disease phenomenon arising from high remittance inflow leading to increased household income and expenditure with negative incentives to raise domestic production as a result of the rising relative price of non-tradable goods also demands special policy responses. The situation has reduced pressure to generate more productive domestic employment leading to loss of the country's competitiveness, with growth of non-productive services.

Notes

1. Thurow, Lester Carl (1996). *The Future of Capitalism*, Chapter 5. Nicholas Brealey Publishing Ltd: London 1996.
2. For details, see Migration and Remittances Team. (April 2019). *Migration and Remittances: Recent Development and Outlook*. World Bank Group and KNOMAD.
3. Caplan (1970), Poffendenger (1980). Quoted in Adhikary, Jagannath. and Gurung, Ganesh. (2009) *Migration, Security, and Livelihoods: A case of Migration between Nepal and India*, (pp. 54-55). Nepal Institute of Development Studies.
4. Government of Nepal and International Organization for Migration(IOM) (2010). *Foreign Employment Remittance and Contribution to Economy of Nepal*, (p. 11). Kathmandu.
5. Kansakar, Vidya Bir Quoted in Adhikary, J. and Gurung, G. (2009). Ibid. (p. 74).
6. CBS Report. Quoted in Adhikary, J. and Gurung, G. (2009). Ibid. (p. 94). There is, of course, some discrepancy between the figures reported in Nepali and Indian censuses. For example, the 1981 Nepal census showed 375,196 Nepali absentee population living in India, while the Indian census reported 501,252 Nepali-born people living there (pp. 74-75).
7. The budget was presented by this author as Finance Minister then under the Premiership of G P Koirala.
8. NIDS/World Bank. (2009). Quoted in Government of Nepal and International Organization for Migration. (2010). *Foreign Employment, Remittance and its Contribution to Economy of Nepal*, (pp. 14-15).

9. Government of Nepal and International Organization for Migration (IOM) (2010). Ibid. (p. 29).
10. Central Bureau of Statistics. *Nepal Living Standard Survey 2010/11: Statistical Report,* Volume 2, (p. 81).
11. Government of Nepal and International Organization for Migration (IOM) (2010). Ibid. (p. 30).
12. Nepal Rastra Bank Research Department. (Ashoj 2073 v.s.). *Bipresan Prapta Garne Ghar Paribarko Bachat Tatha Lagani Prabritti,* (p. 8).
13. Baruah, Nandita. and Aryal, Nischala. (2018, June 6). *Nepali Labor Migration: A Status Report.* Asia Foundation. Retrieved from https://asia foundation.org 2018/06/06
14. *Naya Patrika* (2076 v.s., 4 Srawan). Quoted from the reports of National Human Rights Commission, and Employment Promotion Board of the Ministry of Labour and Employment. The data pertains only with respect to migrant workers gone abroad with labor permit, excluding others who migrated through informal channels without permit.
15. Advocacy Forum (AF) - Nepal and the Member Organizations of National Network for Safe Migration (NNSM). (2015). *Emerging Issues and Challenges of Nepalese Migrant Workers.* OHCHR UPR Submissions. Retrieved from https://uprdoc.ohcr.org
16. GIZ and ILO. (2015). *Analysis of Labor Market and Migration Trends in Nepal,* (p. 57).

Chapter Ten

Foreign Aid and Development Finance

Nepal is a late starter in economic development. It was only after the dawn of democracy following the end of Rana oligarchy in 1951 that the country began a process of institutionalized development with budgetary cycles and economic planning. The post-1945 period was also a new era in global development cooperation. Known as the Commonwealth of Nations prior to 1951, Nepal began availing of external assistance by joining the Colombo Plan for cooperative economic and social development in Asia and the Pacific. Before this, the country's economic situation was extremely poor, and any investments in areas associated with modern development—schools, hospitals, roads, sewerage—were borne out of the charitable whimsies of Rana oligarchs and not as the solemn duty of rulers to systematically serve the people.

External assistance

Given the country's poverty and limited internal resources, it was natural to seek external aid to start the modernization process. The role of foreign aid has been crucial to Nepal's economic development process beset by fiscal and external deficits, savings-investment gap and a rudimentary socio-economic-infrastructural base.

The history of foreign aid in Nepal started just four weeks before the end of the Rana oligarchy, with the signing of the Point Four agreement with the United States. The actual work of this first foreign aid project began in 1952 with the establishment of Village Development Training Center to train community development workers with US instructors. The US government also extended assistance in other fields including agriculture, health, education, malaria eradication and the ambitious Rapti Valley Project. The agriculture program included the introduction of a new variety of crops, livestock centers, improvement of hand tools and land productivity through irrigation. The Indian assistance commenced in 1953 with the construction of Gauchar airport and the road linking Kathmandu with Raxaul. The Indian aid mission was established in 1954 to coordinate support in other fields including health, education, manpower training, drinking water and irrigation. In 1954, India announced a grant of US$1.2 million for irrigation and drinking water projects. The principal objective of both USA and India to assist Nepal in the early 1950s seems to have been motivated by a desire to keep the country outside the influence of Nepal's northern neighbor China, a newly established communist republic. This was made clear in the statement of the US Department of State which said that the fundamental objective of the US aid in Nepal was to maintain in power a non-communist government.[1] The agriculture sector was considered the most vulnerable to communism, hence the early American focus there. While the US was concerned about the fact that the impoverished economy of Nepal could provide a fertile ground for communist influence, the Indians were considering the Himalayas as its defense frontier vis-à-vis China. It is for this reason the Indian assistance was extended also to reorganize and modernize the Nepal army.

The early part of the 1950s saw the emergence of other donors including the United Nations, the Ford Foundation, the People's Republic of China, Switzerland, and the Soviet Union. The UN assisted in malaria eradication, dairy development, geological surveys and nurses training. The Ford Foundation supported the development of cottage industries, handicrafts and domestic science school. A series of dairy and cheese plants were started with Swiss assistance. China provided $12.6 million for the first time in Nepal with $4.2 million in cash and the rest in kind. This was followed by Indian support of $21 million for the first development plan of Nepal. The Soviet Union offered $100,000 plus equipment and technical assistance to build a fifty-bed hospital and scholarships for Nepali students to study in the Soviet Union. British assistance in the 1950s comprised mainly of technical assistance for manpower training. Later, it helped build the Biratnagar-Dharan-Dhankuta highway. The total inflow of foreign aid during the 1950s is estimated at Rs. 474 million, of which the USA and India were the principal donors, contributing 52 and 32 percent, respectively.[2] The bulk of the assistance in the early days was directed towards the development of agriculture, road transport and power development. Other sectors were education, health, communications and industry. Indian assistance helped to build such projects as the Kosi Dam, Trisuli/Devighat power plants, Bir Hospital, Tribhuvan and Siddharth highways, BP Koirala Health Institute in Dharan and some irrigation projects. Grants from China were used to construct Arniko and Prithvi highways, Kathmandu-Bhaktapur trolley bus line, brick and tile and leather and shoe factories and cancer hospital in Bharatpur. External assistance from various donors including the Soviet Union was mobilized to construct part of the East-West highway. Soviet assistance was also availed to build Panauti hydroelectric plant, and sugar and cigarette factories. US aid was mobilized to build Balaju Industrial Estate, Dhangadi-Dadeldhura highway and several agriculture and education projects. Japanese assistance helped in building TU teaching hospital, Kulekhani hydro project, Udaypur cement factory, Karnali bridge and BP highway. German assistance was mobilized to support Marshyangdi hydropower project. This is not an exhaustive list, but a few examples of bilaterally-assisted projects in the earlier days, mainly in the infrastructure sector.

Historical trend

It may be of interest to review the historical trend of the role of foreign aid vis-à-vis that of internal revenue in total government expenditure. Nepal launched its First Five-Year Plan in 1956 with a planned outlay of Rs. 330 million, of which 71 percent was expected from external sources. Subsequent development plans also relied heavily on external sources which were offered largely in the form of grants by bilateral donors. Of the total public expenditure of Rs. 1,780 million during the Third Plan (1965/66-1969/70), external sources contributed 58.4 percent. The Fourth Plan also relied on foreign aid for 58 percent of the total outlay of Rs. 2570 million. The sixth and seventh plans covering the decade of the 1980s relied on external sources for around 60 percent of the total outlay. From the Second Plan (1962-65) until the Sixth, India was the largest donor contributing between 24 to 57 percent of total development assistance. Other major donors were the USA, China, Soviet Union, UK, Japan, Germany, and Switzerland. The role of multilateral donors started becoming important from the 1970s.[3] The Nepal Aid Group was created under the auspices of the World Bank in 1976. By 1987, sixteen countries and six international agencies participated in the group that accounted for the bulk of foreign assistance to

Nepal. The level of commitment from the Nepal Aid Group increased from Rs. 1.5 billion in 1976/77 to Rs. 5.6 billion in 1987/88.[4] The commitment from the Group reached Rs. 56 billion equivalent to US$1 billion in the Paris Meeting chaired by this author in 1996.

The Eighth Plan (1992-97) started by the democratic government after the political change of 1990 also had to rely on external assistance for 65 percent of the ambitious planned outlay of Rs 113.47 billion, given the poor base of internal resources. The general trend in the share of internal revenue and external assistance in the actual total public expenditure since 1989/90 has been presented in Table 10.1. In 1989/90, the last year of the Panchayat regime, internal revenue contributed 47 percent of public expenditure, while foreign assistance contributed 40 percent. At the end of the decade in 2000/01, the contribution from internal revenue increased to 61.2 percent, while the share of external sources declined to 23.5 percent. The declining trend of external assistance in relative terms is reflected in subsequent periods. Although the share in absolute terms increased from nearly Rs. 58 billion in 2010/11 Rs. 107.39 billion in 2017/18, its relative share declined from 19.6 percent to 10.1 percent of the total budget in the same period. The declining share of external sources is accompanied by the increasing mobilization of internal revenue that went up from Rs. 199.8 billion in 2010/11 to 726.7 billion in 2017/18. In relative terms, the share increased marginally from 67.6 to 68.2 percent, respectively.

The data mentioned in Table No 10.1 shows that the actual share of foreign aid in total government expenditure, despite annual fluctuation, remained at around 16 percent on average, for the years since 2000/01. In fact, this is less than the estimated figures in the annual budgets because of the actual expenditure shortfall generally experienced in meeting budgetary estimates. A review of the annual budgetary allocation and expenditure from 2010/11 until 2017/18 shows that the share of foreign aid in the total budgetary allocation varied between 18 and 29 percentage points. The ratio of actual expenditure to overall budgetary allocation during the review period fluctuated between 73 and 91 percentage points with an average of over 80 percent. The ratio of actual expenditure to foreign aid budgetary allocation varied between 66 and 31 percent, with an average of 51.2 percent during the period.[5]

Table 10.1: Foreign Aid, Internal Revenue and Public Expenditure (Rs in ten million)

Sn	Heading	Fiscal Year						
		1989-90	2000-01	2005-06	2010-11	2015-16	2016-17	2017-18
1	Total Expenditure	1966.5	7983.5	11088.9	29536.3	60101.6	83724.8	106618
2	Internal Revenue	928.7	4889.4	7228.2	19981.9	48196.2	60918	72672.5
3	2 As % of 1	47.2	61.2	65.2	67.6	80.2	72.8	68.2
4	Foreign Aid	793.5	1879.7	2204.2	5799.8	7625.2	8994.5	10739.5
a	Grant	197.5	675.3	1382.8	4592.2	3247.8	3193.2	2843.2
b	Loan	596.0	1204.4	821.4	1207.6	4377.4	5801.3	7896.3
5	4 As % of 1	40.3	23.5	19.9	19.6	12.7	10.7	10.1

Sources: Ministry of Finance, Economic Survey Reports, Budget Speeches and Nepal Rastra Bank report Current Macroeconomic and Financial Situation 2018/19 for data on 2017/18.

This indicates that the discrepancy between planned and actual expenditure is higher in external assistance, compared to the overall budgetary performance. This may be attributed to several reasons including incomplete reporting of direct payments, procedural delays in getting reimbursement from development partners and low capital expenditure due to budget overestimation without considering the capacity of implementation agencies. The actual expenditure was particularly low after 2016/17; it reached a mere 31 percent in 2016/17[6] when the volume of development assistance went up significantly in the aftermath of the 2015 earthquake. The ratio of actual aid expenditure recorded some improvement, to 40 percent, in 2017/18.

It is obvious from the data presented above that Nepal has made significant progress in mobilizing internal resources reducing the reliance on foreign aid in relative terms. This can be attributed to post-1990 revenue reforms, expansion of the private sector and higher import growth backed largely by spending from remittance income. The VAT, income tax and customs duties are the principal contributors to revenue generation, representing around 30, 21 and 19 percentage points respectively of the total revenue. Even as the absolute volume of foreign assistance as part of the budget has been rising, the positive growth in the mobilization of internal resources has reduced its relative share in total public expenditure.

Another aspect of the evolution of foreign aid in Nepal is the declining share of the grant component. External aid in the early years was made available almost entirely as grants. It accounted for 98 percent and 87 percent, respectively, of external aid for the Third and Fourth Plans. The emergence of loan as a major part of development cooperation with the corresponding decline of the grant component started with the entry of the World Bank and the Asian Development Bank as major sources after the late 1970s. Loans accounted for 48 percent of external aid in the Sixth Plan; in the last fiscal year of the Seventh Plan 1989/90, the ratio reached as much as 75 percent. The share of loans represented 73 percent of the planned outlay of the Eighth Plan. Data presented in Table 10.1 shows some decline in later years particularly since 2000 when its actual share fluctuated between 64 percent in 2000/01 to 20.8 percent in 2010/11. In the last year under review, 2017/18, loan constituted 73.5 percent of development assistance. The low share of loan component in some years is probably explained by the grant assistance in some projects by the World Bank and the ADB. Even in terms of commitment, the grant commitment of Rs. 116.6 billion in the year 2017/18 was almost equal to the loan commitment of Rs. 117.7 billion.[7] In the recent budget of 2018/19, the grant component has almost halved.

Major development partners

In recent years, while bilateral assistance from the USA, India, Japan, UK, China, Germany and others continue to be important, the major role is assumed by multilateral institutions including the World Bank Group, Asian Development Bank, UN Country Team and European Union for capital and technical assistance.

According to the Development Cooperation Report 2017/18 (Chapter 2) published by the Ministry of Finance, the total volume of ODA disbursement reached US$1622.8 million in 2017/18, up from $1394 million in 2016/17 and $1079.71 million in 2010/11. The top five development partners for the year 2017/18 were the World Bank Group ($533.5 million), Asian Development Bank ($291.7 million), the United Kingdom ($123.8 million), USAID ($117.8 million), the European Union ($116.2 million) and Japan ($106.2 million). Of the total amount disbursed that fiscal year, US$570.3 million (35.1 percent) was in grant form, $819.1 million (50.5 percent) in loan and $233.3 (14.4

percent) in the form of technical assistance. The European Union was the largest contributor of grant ($113.2 million), followed by the World Bank Group ($94.7 million), UK ($59.2 million), USAID ($44.5 million) and India ($39.6 million), China ($36.4 million), UN Country Team ($32.1 million), ADB ($29.7 million), Japan ($21.4 million), Switzerland ($22 million), and Norway ($21 million) among others. Of the loan assistance, the largest contributors were the World Bank Group ($438.6 million) and ADB ($258.2 million), followed by Japan ($76.2 million), China ($18.5 million) and India ($15 million). With regard to technical assistance, the USAID was the largest provider ($73.4 million) followed by United Kingdom ($64.7 million), UN Country Team ($33.5 million), Germany ($19.2 million), Japan ($8.6 million), and Australia ($7 million).[8]

Modalities, forms and sectors

The preferred aid modality of the government is general budgetary support that could be used as per the national priorities. Sectoral budgetary support and Stand-Alone Project support, followed by Pool Fund for small projects, together with humanitarian assistance when needed are other preferred modalities mentioned in the Foreign Aid Policy of the government.

Data published by the Ministry of Finance[9] reveals that of the total disbursement of $1622.8 million in 2017/18, 43.1 percent was delivered for project support, followed by 19.9 percent for humanitarian assistance, 16.3 percent through budget support, 16.3 through program support, and 1.9 percent sector through sector-wide support. Support for Stand-Alone projects is the most popular modality of development assistance accounting for more than 50 percent of the disbursement in all years since 2010/11 until 2015/16. In 2016/17 and 2017/18, its share declined to 48 percent and 43 percent, respectively, because of the increased share of humanitarian assistance for reconstruction in the aftermath of the 2015 earthquake. It may be noted that humanitarian assistance represented 22 percent of aid disbursement in 2015/16 also. In years prior to the earthquake disaster, the share of humanitarian assistance was relatively low ranging from less than 1 percent to 5 percent.

Data on sector-wise distribution of ODA shows that practically all sectors have found access to external aid. The principal beneficiary sectors are energy, education, local development, health, housing, drinking water, road transportation and urban development. The other sectors that benefit from ODA include agriculture, earthquake reconstruction, economic reforms, environment, science and technology, irrigation, livelihood, financial reforms, women, children and social welfare, peace and reconstruction, public administration and others. In the year 2017/18, the top five sectors accounting for 52 percent of ODA disbursement were the economic reform sector (13 percent), followed by education (12.5 percent), urban development (9.2 percent), health (9 percent), and local development (8.4 percent). The other beneficiary sectors were energy, housing, road transportation, agriculture, drinking water, peace, and reconstruction. In the preceding years until 2015/16, energy was the largest recipient sector followed by local development, education and health. The share of education and housing sector increased in 2016/17 owing to a significant amount of ODA disbursed for post-earthquake school and housing reconstruction programs. The dramatic increase in the share allocated for economic reforms in 2017/18 by several-fold represents an exceptional case, explained by the significant amount of ODA disbursed for the World Bank-funded Fiscal and Public Finance Management Development Policy Credit.[10]

Study on the volume and nature of external assistance would be incomplete without capturing the disbursement channeled through international non-government organizations (INGOs) by the donor community. Data on INGO assistance in the past was very limited. In recent years, the number of INGOs reporting has increased since the introduction of the AID Management Platform (AMP) from 2012/13 in the Ministry of Finance. The AMP is a management tool of the Ministry of Finance to centralize information about aid inflows inside Nepal. There were sixty-two INGOs reporting to AMP in 2017/18, operating in Nepal with activities practically in all districts. Their engagement has covered various sectors including service delivery in the social sector, livelihood support for poverty reduction, awareness creation and advocacy, and humanitarian assistance.

In the fiscal year 2017/18, $110 million is estimated to have been disbursed through INGOs in various fields, in addition to the ODA component of $1623 million, making the total disbursement of $1733 million from external sources. The contribution from INGOs increased from $40.8 million in 2012/13 to $76.08 in 2013/14, $116.89 in 2014/15, and $186.53 in 2016/17; but it declined to $110 million in 2017/18. The increased contribution figure until 2016/17 is attributed mainly to larger INGO engagement following the April

2015 earthquake, and also to an increasing number of INGOs reporting since the AMP launching. The lower disbursement figure in 2017/18 could have resulted from fewer INGOs reporting to AMP. Looking at the disbursement by sector, the largest beneficiary has been the health sector, followed by education, livelihoods sector, women, children and social welfare, and reconstruction.

Aid effectiveness

The question of aid effectiveness in developing countries is a matter of global concern attracting the attention of OECD nations. This has resulted in the Paris Declaration in 2005, Accra Plan of Action in 2008 and High-Level Forum on Aid Effectiveness in Busan 2011. The fundamental principles agreed in these forums for aid effectiveness include, among others, ownership by developing countries to set strategies for poverty reduction including institutions building and tackling corruption, alignment of donors behind these objectives, donor harmonization to avoid duplication, and mutual accountability of both donors and partners for development results which should be measurable.

The objective of development assistance from both the donor and recipient perspectives is to contribute towards achieving self-reliance of the recipient nation. One of the guiding principles and objectives, as defined in the Foreign Aid Policy 2002 and Development Cooperation Policy 2014 of Nepal, is to achieve self- reliance to reduce aid dependency in the long run by enhancing domestic resource mobilization. From this perspective, the reduction in Nepal's relative dependence on development assistance as reflected in the sources of public expenditure is a positive development. However, the issue of improving the aid quality and efficiency to enhance its effectiveness remains a subject of national concern.

Notwithstanding the country ownership principle of the Paris Declaration and the imperative of channeling aid through country system, experience in Nepal shows that a significant portion of aid in Nepal is channeled off-budget. In 2017/18, only 78 percent of foreign aid was delivered through on-budget projects. This represented some improvement over the situation in 2015/16 when the ratio of on-budget and off-budget disbursement were 63 and 37 percent, respectively. Based on the Ministry of Finance report on development cooperation, the off-budget disbursement not reported in the government budgetary system comprises of technical types of assistance from development partners including those implemented through INGOs and NGOs, and commodity and humanitarian assistance for reconstruction after the 2015 earthquake.

It may also be relevant here to look at aid disbursement from the perspective of compatibility and alignment with national development plans and priorities. The Development Cooperation Policy 2014 declared that the main objective of mobilizing external resources is to help achieve the development goals stated in the periodic development plan. The priority pillars of the past three-year plans are: social development, infrastructure, macro-economic stability, good governance and human rights, peace, rehabilitation and inclusive development, and cross-cutting fields. Data published by the Ministry of Finance indicate that 35.3 percent of the ODA in 2017/18 was disbursed in the infrastructure sector, followed by 31.7 percent in social development, 24.7 percent in macroeconomic and development policy, 4.6 percent in peace, rehabilitation and inclusive development, 2.5 percent in cross-cutting fields and 1.3 percent in good governance and human rights. This disbursement pattern did not represent any substantial change from that observed in 2016/17.

Another policy issue is associated with aid fragmentation in view of the multiple donors engaged in a number of fields in Nepal, creating problems of management and coordination. Each development partner is reported to have been engaged, on average, with nine different counterpart ministries/agencies in 2016/17 and 2017/18; some of them having more than twenty-four counterpart agencies. Aid scattered in a large number of small projects lead to fragmentation of development cooperation and incur high transaction costs and management burden to government and development partners alike. Realization of this problem prompted the new Development Cooperation Policy 2014 of the government to acknowledge the need to improve the situation through the division of work among development partners on the basis of comparative advantage. The Policy declared that it will not accept the grant assistance of less than $5 million except in exceptional cases like sector-wide approach program, pool fund, co-financing, humanitarian and technical assistance. The document also says it will not accept a concessional loan of less than $10 million and other loans of less than $20 million in stand-alone projects.

The responsibility of mobilizing and coordinating external assistance from the government side lies with the Ministry of Finance, its International Economic Cooperation Coordination Division being the focal point. No government ministry or agency is authorized to formally approach donors without prior approval of the Ministry of Finance. The development partners should pass through this Ministry for providing assistance to any government body. For high-level dialogue and coordination between the government and development partners on development issues, periodic plan and resource requirement, Nepal Development Forum (NDF) has been created since 2000. This forum is the successor to the World Bank-sponsored early mechanism of AID Nepal Group formed in 1976, which was subsequently named Consultative Group; the meetings of these forums were generally held in Paris. In recent years, the meeting of the new mechanism NDF is normally held in Nepal as and when necessary. The forum also acts as the donor pledging forum of development assistance to meet the government resource requirement. Its first meeting in Nepal was held in February 2002, chaired by this author as the Finance Minister then. The donor community extended broad endorsement to the framework of the Tenth Five Year Plan of Nepal, which was also treated as the country's Poverty Reduction Strategy Plan (PRSP), and commended the government efforts to link these with annual budgets through Medium Term Expenditure Framework (MTEF). The partners also expressed support to meet the country's resource gap of about $500 million annually needed to implement the poverty reduction plan.[11]

At the local level, there is a mechanism of Local Development Partners' Meeting, generally held every four months for regular dialogue between the government and the donors. They facilitate the implementation of development cooperation projects by resolving emerging problems. Meetings on portfolio performance are also held periodically between individual donors and government ministries bilaterally.

Another policy issue relates to grants and loan assistance. Generally speaking, the preferred modality is the grant, particularly in sectors like health, education, drinking water, human development, and sustainable development, and agriculture, humanitarian and technical assistance. Loan component is accepted for infrastructure creation and income-generating projects only on soft and concessional terms, not tied to fixed suppliers without competitive bidding. It is not the policy of the government to resort to commercial loan from the market. Adherence to this policy has resulted in relatively low and manageable status of Nepal's external debt. Nepal's outstanding public debt including internal borrowing that exceeded 60 percent of GDP in the previous decades showed a declining trend, particularly since 2005 to reach 25 percent of GDP in mid- 2015, which further rose to 30 percent of GDP in 2018. It is projected to rise to 35 percent in the medium term and further to 42 percent in the next two decades, owing to continuing fiscal and current account deficits against the need to implement fiscal federalism and to put the economy on a higher growth path.[12] But if the budgetary structure presented for the fiscal year 2019/20 is any indication, the national debt will rise much higher than this. The estimated reliance on borrowing for the year is around 14 percent of GDP, the highest in recent years.

The outstanding *external* debt that stood at $3.6 billion (16.9 percent of GDP) at the end of the fiscal year 2015/16, rose to $4.8 billion (17.3 percent of GDP) in the following year.[13] Multilateral sources including the World Bank, ADB and IMF account for more than 90 percent of this external debt. Japan is the largest bilateral lender of soft loan, followed by South Korea, India and China. The loan from Japan is of a highly concessional nature payable over a period of forty years, where procurement is based on global competitive bidding. The payback is often returned to Nepal in the form of development goods under the Debt Relief Fund. The loans from India and China in recent years are channeled through their Export-Import (Exim) banks where interest rates, terms and tenure of repayment, and procurement conditions are less favorable than those of multilateral lending institutions like the World Bank and the Asian Development Bank. Lately, both countries have extended increased amounts of loan from Exim banks for the development of infrastructure projects like roads, airports, and hydropower. Furthermore, Nepal's participation in the Belt and Road Initiative of China could lead to additional loan undertakings. Similarly, the Indian offer of a large volume of Exim Bank loans for various projects could also raise Nepal's stock of foreign debt. While it is within the declared national policy to resort to such external borrowing for the development of physical infrastructure to support high economic growth, it is important to make a thorough techno-economic appraisal of concerned projects before negotiating loans. Recently in 2018, the government of Nepal reached an agreement with China and India for the railway connection to Kathmandu from both sides, through the extension of Shigatse-Kerung railway from China and Indian railway from Raxaul. These are high-cost projects, with preliminary estimates of more than $5 billion in total. The detailed project reports, including their techno-economic appraisal and the mode of financing, are awaited to gauge if these projects are viable in terms of returns and payback potential. Obviously, caution must be exercised while resorting to external debt to support such projects. Indebtedness has become a prominent casualty of South-South aid, once seen as a benign alternative to the Organization for Economic Cooperation and Development (OECD) paradigm of official development assistance. From Sub-Saharan Africa to Latin America and Pakistan to Sri-Lanka, debts incurred in politically-driven projects have begun to haunt and bite.[14]

Concluding remarks

The external aid landscape has undergone significant change over the past seventy years. Despite increasing aid inflow from a large number of development partners, the degree of aid reliance for public expenditure has declined significantly with impressive progress in the mobilization of internal resources. The share of bilateral grant aid which dominated development financing in the early days started declining with the growth of concessional loan from multilateral financial institutions. In recent years, there is also a growing availability of procurement-tied bilateral loan offers.

Because of past progress in internal revenue mobilization, the ratio of total public debt to GDP that showed a declining trend in the past has now registered growth from 25 percent of GDP in 2015 to 30 percent in 2018, of which external debt amounts to 17 percent of GDP. Sound fiscal management and careful selection of projects for multilateral loans in the past have kept Nepal's external debt obligation low, within sustainable limits. Nevertheless, the external assistance requirement is still high; it is needed to upgrade the country's poor infrastructure for balanced regional development, to optimize the natural resource utilization and facilitate higher economic growth. The country still requires generous grant and concessional loan support from bilateral and multilateral development partners to supplement domestic resources, together with efforts to improve aid quality and management to maximize its productivity and effectiveness. While resorting particularly to source-tied debt financing, careful prioritization of projects—based on socio-economic rationale and financial sustainability including payback potential—is required so that the country will not face the risk of debt stress, incurred through politically dictated projects.

Notes

1. Quoted in Khadka, Narayan (1991). *Foreign Aid, Poverty and Stagnation in Nepal,* (p. 138). Vikas Publication.
2. Ibid. (p. 179).
3. Ibid. (p. 207).
4. Foreign Aid to Nepal. *Wikipedia*. Retrieved from https://en.wikipedia.org/wiki/Foreign_aid_to_Nepal
5. Ministry of Finance. *Development Cooperation Report 2017/18,* (pp. 58-59).
6. Ibid. Chapter 2.
7. Ibid. (p. 60).
8. Ibid. Chapter 2.
9. Ibid. Chapter 3.
10. Ibid. (p. 12).
11. Nepal Development Forum 2002. (2002, February 4-7). *Report of the Proceedings.* Kathmandu and Pokhara.
12. IMF. (February 2019). *IMF Country Report No.19/60. Staff Report for the 2018 Article 4 Consultation.* Washington DC.
13. IMF. (2017, March 13). *IMF Staff Report.*
14. For example, the $1.3 billion Sri-Lankan maritime port of Hambantota built with the Chinese loans, has recently been handed over to a Chinese company for 99 years because of insolvency arising directly from under-utilization.

Chapter Eleven

State of the Economy

Some contemporary aspects of the country's political economy have been discussed in the preceding chapters. The objective here is to dwell on the overall state of the macro economy and allied topics not covered so far. The country has passed through difficult times in the recent past, marked by unstable politics, decade-long violent conflict, ethnic turbulence, trade disruption, an extended period of political transition and natural disasters all of which have dampened the pace of its economic change.

Macro performance

Prior to the start of the reform process—particularly after the beginning of the democratic era in 1991—the development policy was protectionist, state-led with public sector domination and a limited role of private sector initiatives and investment. Because of low levels of investment and productivity, the average growth rate during the period between 1965 and 1985 was estimated at less than 3 percent and that of per capita income at 0.8 percent. The low growth rate, poor export performance and expansionary fiscal policy of the government leading to budget deficits as high as 12 percent of GDP in 1983 resulted in a full-blown financial crisis. By 1985, the widening current account deficit shrank the total foreign exchange reserves so much that they could only cover three months of imports. The precarious macro-economic situation prompted the government to start a stabilization and adjustment program aided by the IMF and the World Bank to extricate the economy out of the stability crisis.

The reform process received a big impetus after the formation of the Nepali Congress government led by Girija Prasad Koirala with a popular mandate from the 1991 general election. As explained in Chapter 3, the sweeping reforms introduced in the early 1990s liberalized the economy with market-oriented measures giving broad space to private investment including foreign capital, non-government organizations and cooperatives by opening up many economic sectors which had hitherto been the exclusive preserve of the state. The objective was to spur investment and growth, together with increased public investment in rural development, social sector and human capital for poverty reduction and regional development. There was further deepening of the reform process including the introduction of the Value Added Tax, reforms in public administration, public expenditure and revenue, and promulgation of the Local Governance Act. The reforms resulted in a spurt of economic activities which led to the growth of tax revenue and consequently the public expenditure.

These reforms and consequent acceleration of economic activities made a positive impact on the country's economic growth, which exceeded an average of five percent between 1986 and 1996. The fiscal year 1993/94 registered a 7.9 percent growth rate, still considered to be the highest in recent memory.

The economy diversified further with an increased share of trade in GDP. The share of trade in GDP and exports doubled (exports of goods and services rose from 11.5 percent of GDP in 1985 to 23 percent in 1996). The share of manufacturing also nearly doubled from 5 percent of GDP in 1986 to 9 percent in 1996.[1] There were significant improvements in macro-economic and fiscal indicators including a rise in private investment from 10.8 percent to 13.7 percent and gross domestic savings from 10.5 percent to 15 percent of GDP during the period leading up to 2001. Improvements were recorded in other indicators relating to the fiscal deficit, export-import ratio and inflation.[2]

The economy began to suffer after the start of the Maoist insurgency in 1996 with its intensification after 2001 resulting in a serious law and order problem and disruption of development activities and normal governance that took a serious toll on the economy. Political turmoil worsened with the midnight dissolution of the House of Representatives in May 2002 and subsequent usurpation of power by King Gyanendra in February 2005.

The Maoist violence and the civil conflict following the royal takeover manifested in street protests, labor unrest, *Bandhs* and strikes resulting in disruptions of economic life. They affected the economy severely. Meanwhile, the phasing out of quotas as part of the WTO Agreement on Textiles and Clothing (successor agreement to the Multi-Fiber Arrangement) led to a steady loss of share for Nepali garment exports in the international market. Nepal's merchandise export which had peaked at 14 percent of GDP in 2001 plummeted to 5 percent by 2010. The share of the manufacturing sector which had reached

9 percent of GDP in 1996 steadily declined. The growth rate that had averaged 5 percent in the previous decade slowed down by one percentage point between 1996 and 2005.

Nepal's historical growth trend shows the annual growth that averaged a mere 1.98 percent during 1965-74 and 3.22 percent in 1975-84, rose to 5.16 during 1985-94, which further declined to the average of 4.10 in 1995-04 and 4.18 in 2006-13.[3] The return to peace in 2006 could not bring about the expected peace dividend. The average growth rate remained only around 4 percent in the following decade too, thanks to the rocky and protracted political transition marked by unstable politics, prolonged controversy on the nature and content of the new constitution resulting in two national elections for a constituent assembly. During the period of ten years since 2005/06, the annual growth rate did not reach 5 percent in any fiscal year, except in 2006/07 and 2013/14.

The failure to revive economic growth widened the per capita income gap between Nepal and the rest of South Asia including India, Bangladesh and Pakistan which experienced strong and sustained growth during the period. The per capita income of Bangladesh which was $35 higher than that of Nepal in 1995 widened to $100 by the end of the conflict in 2005, which further reached around $200 after seven years because of the failure to maintain growth at par with faster-growing neighbors.[4]

Data presented in Table 11.1 reveals some macroeconomic indicators, particularly since 2011/12. The growth rate which was 4.61 and 3.76 percent respectively in 2011/12 and 2012/13 shows a spurt of 5.72 percent in 2013/14 further plummeting to 2.97 and 0.2 percentage points in 2014/15 and 2015/16. The sharp fall in the two years is attributed to the April 2015 earthquake and the unofficial Indian blockade lasting four and half months since 23 September 2015 that not only resulted in large-scale physical devastation and losses but also halted economic activities creating a humanitarian crisis and national turmoil. The return to normalcy after the end of the blockade in February 2016 and consequent rekindling of economic activities, massive post-earthquake reconstruction program accompanied by favorable monsoons raising agricultural production in two consecutive years against the background of poor economic base of the preceding two years helped raise the growth rate to 7.39 percent in 2016/17 and 5.89 in 2017/18.

Table 11.1: Macro-Economic Indicators (2008/9-2017/18)

S. No.	Headings	2008-09	2011-12	2012-13	2013-14	2014-15	2015-16	2016-17	2017-18
1	GDP Growth Rate	3.9	4.61	3.76	5.72	2.97	0.2	7.39	5.9
2	Agri. GDP	3.02	4.63	1.1	4.55	1.1	0.23	5.2	2.82
3	Non-agri. GDP	4.34	4.53	5.01	6.41	3.89	0.38	8.5	7.1
4	Consumer P. Index	12.62	8.3	9.9	9.1	7.2	9.9	4.5	4.2
5	Gross Capital Formation as % of GDP	21.35	20.77	22.59	23.52	27.97	28.73	31.81	34.1
	a) Public	4.48	4.68	4.45	4.83	5.18	7.12	6.42	7.8
	B) Private	16.87	16.08	18.15	18.68	22.79	21.6	25.4	26.3
6	Gross Domestic Saving as % of GDP	9.43	10.99	10.55	11.92	9.21	4.07	11.95	15.0
7	Gross National Saving as % of GDP	35.87	39.47	40.69	45.73	44.14	40.11	45.35	43.9

*Source: Ministry of Finance, 2018: Macroeconomic Indicators Dash Board

It may be relevant to note that Nepal relies heavily on private sector investment for economic growth. As revealed by the data presented in the Table 11.1, the contribution of the private sector accounts for the bulk of the annual capital formation averaging around 79 percent, the remaining 21 percent coming from the public sector. The gross domestic savings ratio rose from 9.43 percent in 2008/9, with some fluctuations to reach 15 percent over time in 2017/18, while the gross national savings showing an increasing trend from 35.87 percent in 2008/09 to 43.9 percent in 2017/18. The high share of national savings compared to domestic savings reflects the contribution of remittance inflows.

One interesting development in recent years is the decline in the consumer price index. It has hovered around four percent in the last two years, representing a sharp drop from an earlier period, 2008-2016, when the index fluctuated between 7.2 to 12.6 percent. The low inflation in the last two years is attributed mainly to a restrained increase in food prices compared to non-food items. Curiously, this low inflation rate is not reflected in the general perception of consumers who complain of rising costs of production and consumables. The paradox is probably explained by the differential weightage given to 496 food and non-food goods and services items of CPI basket which may not reflect generally the current living cost of an average citizen.

Sectoral performance

The economy has undergone a structural shift away from the traditional pattern dominated by agriculture. Its contribution to GDP declined from around two-thirds in the early seventies to 46.5 percent in 1990/91, 34.6 percent in 2007/08 and further to 27 percent in 2018/19. The changing occupational structure with a reduced share of agriculture is a natural phenomenon in the process of economic transformation, but it did not follow the path normally experienced in other fast-growing economies. In the 1990s, both the industrial and services sectors gained importance almost equally from the relative decline in agriculture. The share of industrial sector including electricity, gas and water and construction increased from 19.4 to 22.5 percent, while that of services sector grew from 34.2 to 38.3 percent. Within the industrial sector, the share of manufacturing rose from 7.5 to 9.4 percent. But in subsequent years the industrial share declined to 14.2 percent in 2017/18, while that of the services sector reached 58 percent of GDP. The share of manufacturing subsector of industry has plummeted to around 6 percent. Thus, the structural shift in Nepal's economy is atypical, as the change is represented by a shift from agriculture to services, rather than manufacturing. The services sector is largely dominated by wholesale and retail trade, followed by transport, storage and communications, education, financial services, real estate community and social services.

Agriculture

The agriculture sector grew at around 2.4 percent when the economy was growing at a rate of 4 percent. Its contribution has shrunk dramatically in relative terms as the services sector expanded. Despite a sharp decline in its value-added, agriculture still accounts for three-fifths of employment, reflecting low productivity in the sector. The growth in the sector remains highly volatile ranging from 0.23 to 5.22 percent as seen in Table 11.1, driven mainly by its variable dependence on the monsoons. The high GDP growth in the last two years 2016/17 and 2017/18 was contributed by timely rainfall. Generally speaking, the average productivity of principal cereal crops, rice and wheat, which occupy most of the cultivable land and account for the bulk of agricultural production in Nepal is much lower than in neighboring countries. Nepal's yield in rice is lower than in Bangladesh and India; wheat yield is lower than in Bangladesh, India and Pakistan. A World Bank study revealed that the rise in agricultural income is attributed mainly to gains in price, rather than yield. Of the total increase of 21 percent in crop income from 2004 to 2011, only 5 percentage points was contributed by yields, while 18 percentage points was due to an increase in food price. The reduction in the land area reduced the crop income by 2 percentage points.[5]

Nepal's comparative advantage in agriculture lies in non-cereal items like dairy processing, poultry, tea, coffee, vegetable seed, horticulture products, herbal and aromatic plant products, spices and fisheries, which have contributed most to the output growth of the agriculture sector. This has encouraged farmers to diversify production away from cereal grains to fruits and vegetables. This development together with increasing urbanization and housing construction in farmland has led to a reduction of land allocation to major cereal crops. Despite this, the land allocation to grain staples is ten times higher compared to land occupied by fruits and vegetables, but the contribution of the former to agricultural GDP is disproportionately lower. The country which was once a net food exporter has now become a net food importer because of inadequate domestic supply to meet the increasing food consumption of various categories in response to changing consumption patterns resulting from rising incomes of the people. The import bill of agro products has shown a consistently rising trend, registering a five-fold increase from Rs. 44.43 billion in 2009/10 to reach Rs. 215 billion in 2017/18. Ironically, the country is importing even basic cereal food grains including husked rice, maize, wheat, barley and buckwheat which now accounts for 20 percent of imported agro-products. A variety of factors are responsible for inhibiting the growth of agricultural productivity in Nepal. These include unsophisticated technology, insufficient coverage of irrigation and fertilizer use, manpower shortage, land fragmentation and low prevalence of mechanization.

Industry and FDI

The industrial sector languished during the conflict years. The value-addition of the manufacturing sector which had peaked at 9 percent of GDP at the end of the 1990s stands presently at 6 percent. Investment in manufacturing did not get a boost even after the peace process commenced. Nepal's private sector is largely dominated by small firms, and a few large- scale family-run conglomerates involved in trade, manufacturing and services sector. Only 18 percent of the registered firms have more than twenty employees, which is low compared to other South Asian countries like Bangladesh, India, Sri Lanka and Pakistan.[6] The subdued share of the secondary sector of the economy because of the low level of investment is a matter of concern attributed to turbulent and unstable politics, prolonged political transition, infrastructure deficit, and institutional shortcomings leading to a weak investment climate.

Foreign direct investment (FDI) plays a catalytic role in economic growth by bringing capital and technology, enhancing productivity and competitiveness, and facilitating integration with the international economy. Nepal has undertaken a number of initiatives in the past including the enactment of Foreign Investment and Technology Transfer Act in 1992 (updated in 2019), membership of WTO, SAFTA and BIMSTEC together with the signing of bilateral investment protection and promotion agreements and avoidance of double taxation agreements with a number of countries. However, FDI inflow into Nepal remains meager. Of the total FDI flows into developing countries, $646 billion, in 2016, South Asia received 3.1 percent going mainly to India, Bangladesh, Pakistan and Sri-Lanka. Nepal's share was only 0.1 percent of this flow. During the period 2013-17, the annual FDI inflow averaged 0.4 percent of GDP, compared to 1.3 percent in Bangladesh, 1.8 percent in India, 0.8 percent in Pakistan and 1.2 percent in Sri Lanka.[7]

Despite the various policy announcements and the hosting of occasional investment forums and summits inviting foreign investors to attract FDI, Nepal still has to go a long way to become an attractive destination. The annual FDI inflow averaged a modest Rs. 3.37 billion in the last decade between 2001 and 2017. The total FDI stock comprising of paid-up capital and reserves along with foreign loans from investors as of mid-July 2017 stood at Rs. 151.2 billion, up from Rs. 52.1 billion in mid-July 2013, Rs. 75.4 billion in 2014, 106.2 billion in mid-July 2015 and 137.7 in mid-July 2016. The uptick in the total outstanding FDI stock was mainly due to accumulated reserves.[8] The FDI in Nepal is concentrated largely in the services sector comprising of telecommunications, transport, financial intermediation and hospitality sub-sectors accounting for more than 70 percent of the total stock. The share of manufacturing and hydropower was around 30 percent as of mid-July 2016.

Tourism

Blessed with unique ecological diversity ranging from icy peaks of the tallest Himalayan mountains to steamy jungles of the *Tarai* flat land, unique natural beauty, multi-ethnic and multi-cultural human diversity and world-famous architectural heritage of cultural and religious significance, the tourism sector's importance to accelerate growth and development is well-accepted. It also generates strong spillover effects on other sectors including agriculture, aviation, transportation and hospitality. According to the annual report of the London-based World Travel and Tourism Council (WTTC), the direct and indirect revenue generation from travel and tourism in Nepal was Rs. 240.7 billion in 2018 (up from Rs. 195 billion in 2017), representing 7.9 percent of GDP of which 56 percent was contributed by domestic tourists. The sector's contribution to job creation, directly and indirectly, was estimated at 1.05 million jobs and projected to reach 1.35 million by the year 2029.[9]

Despite some progress, the sector has yet to capitalize its full potential. The arrival of foreign tourists, which declined during the long period of insurgency began reviving after the peace process, reaching 1.2 million in 2018. In 2015, the year of the earthquake, tourist arrivals plummeted to 539,000. Competing destinations across South Asia like Sri Lanka and the Maldives attract more tourists than Nepal despite their smaller size. Nepal's foreign exchange earnings from the sector are also low at around $600 per international visitor, just about one-third of that in India and Thailand.[10] The average spending by foreign tourists has shown a declining trend lately reaching as low as $44 per day per tourist in 2018 (a drop from $68 in 2015).[11] The country's total foreign exchange earnings in the fiscal year 2017/18 from tourists was equivalent to 67 billion rupees, lower than the foreign currency amounting to Rs. 79.6 billion spent by Nepali nationals travelling abroad in the same year.

A new development in the sector is the tourist growth from neighboring countries, India and China, as well as domestic tourists. According to WTTC, domestic tourism accounted for 66 percent of the sector's share in GDP in 2016. The future prospect of the sector has created an investment surge in hotels, airlines, tours and travel industries. There exist in operation 136 hotels of various star ratings and luxury resorts across the country. Of the fourteen five-star hotels, eight operate in Kathmandu, and the rest in Pokhara, Bhairahawa and Nepalganj. A large number of new luxury hotels and resorts are under construction to cater to high-end tourists in places like Kathmandu, Chitawan, Lumbini, Pokhara, Nepalgunj, Dhangadi, Mahendranagar, Biratnagar, Biratnagar, Dharan and Jhapa.

Transport and communications

The underdeveloped state of economic infrastructure happens to be one of the major constraints for economic growth in Nepal. Basic infra-structure lowers cost of production and helps augment labor productivity by boosting health and education outcomes. Starting from a poor base, significant progress has been made since 1990 in creating economic infrastructures such as road transport, electricity, irrigation and communications; but relative to peer countries, Nepal lags woefully behind.

The road subsector plays a dominant role in the transportation sector in the absence of other means except for limited air service. Therefore, road development was treated as a high priority in the past decades, has registered significant quantitative progress from a total of around 7,000 kilometers in 1990 to exceed 88,000 kilometers, including 29,639 km built by the central Roads Department linking all districts headquarters; local bodies have built another 58,398 kms. But of this total, quality remains the problem, as only a total of 15,815 km is black-topped and all-weather, the remaining roads being earthen and graveled. The other problem is the quality of construction. Most road and other infrastructure projects suffer from high cost and time overruns, together with quality constraint leading to maintenance problems. Furthermore, the hill and mountain topography of the country makes construction costs high and excess rainfall during the monsoon period causes landslides, further pushing up the maintenance cost. Consequently, most parts of the country remain inaccessible during the monsoon time. As far as the railway service is concerned, at present only two railway lines exist: the 28 km Jayanagar-Janakpur and 6 km Raxaul -Sirsiya. The former is to be extended further to Bardibas and Simara. The latter is used only for container traffic of cargo imports to Sirsiya dry port container depot. The project to develop 945 km East-West Railway is at a preliminary stage, for which detailed feasibility reports on various segments are yet to be completed.

The air service has undergone significant expansion after the government adopted an 'Open Air' policy allowing private airlines to operate domestic and international services. At present, the country has three airlines operating international flights and twenty airlines operating domestic flights. In addition, thirty international airlines operate flights to and from Nepal with whom the country has bi-lateral air service agreements. There are thirty all-weather airports in the country including one international airport in Kathmandu. The country has witnessed a significant rise in air passenger traffic in recent years causing air traffic congestion, particularly at the single airport in the capital city, which serves both domestic and international flights. Two other international airports under construction, Gautam Buddha Airport in Bhairahawa and Pokhara Airport are expected to relieve the Tribhuvan International Airport (TIA) of some congestion. The former is expected to be completed in 2019 and the latter in 2021. The other major international airport proposed as an alternative to TIA is planned at Nijgadh, Bara, for which land acquisition and extension of an expressway from Kathmandu are both under process.

It may also be mentioned that the availability of new and advanced technology in the communications sector has helped expand the quantity and quality of telecommunication services in Nepal, as the number of service providers and users has multiplied. At present, six companies provide services, of which the state-owned Nepal Telecommunications Corporation and the Malaysian-owned NCell account for the bulk of the operation. The total number of telephone users including basic, mobile and GMPCS now exceed 38 million, with the telephone density reaching 130.3 percent. The access to telephone services has reached all seventy-seven districts of the country and cover 90 percent of the geographical reach. The use of internet service has also become part of daily life among the educated people. According to the report of the Nepal Telecommunication Authority, 250 new users were added every hour to internet service in 2017, the total internet users reaching 16.7 million Nepalis in October 2017. The internet penetration ratio is 63 percent.

Public expenditure and revenue

Data presented in Table 11.2 summarizes the historical growth trend of public revenue and expenditure as a proportion of GDP since 1991. The total government expenditure increased from Rs. 26.4 billion in 1991/92 to 46.5 billion in 1995/96, 110.9 billion in 2005/6 to 1066.2 billion in 2017/18, registering an annual growth of 15.3 percent during the period. In relation to GDP, the expenditure registered a growth from 18.2 percent in 1991/92 to 35.7 percent of GDP in 2017/18. The noteworthy aspect of the expenditure trend is the increasing share of recurrent expenditure from a mere 6.8 percent to 23.1 percent of GDP during the period. The share of capital expenditure declined from 11.4 percent of GDP in 1991/92 to between 3 and 5 percent from 2005 to 2016. The ratio increased further in the last two years to reach 8.8 percent in 2017/18.

This is explained by an investment spurt associated with post-earthquake rebuilding and reconstruction. It may also be relevant to mention that the increased ratio of recurrent expenditure in later years is partly attributed to the reclassification of public expenditure according to IMF's Government Finance Statistics (GFS) since the fiscal year 2010/11. Public expenditures prior to this were classified into regular and development expenditure. Some expenditure items of recurrent nature spent in such sectors like health and education, capital grant and subsidy given to local bodies included in the development expenditure earlier were reclassified under recurrent expenditure. The definition of capital expenditure includes only spending on physical assets like land, building, furniture and fittings, civil works, vehicles, plant and machinery, capital research and consultancy.

Table 11.2: Expenditure Revenue Indicators (1989/90-2017/18)
Rs in 10 million

S. No.	Heading	1991-92	1995-96	2005-06	2010-11	2015-16	2016-17	2017-18
1	GDP (current price)	144931	24891.3	65408.4	136695.4	225316.3	264259.5	300724.6
2	Total Expenditure	2641.8	465.4	11088.9	29536.3	60101.6	83724.8	106617.5
3	2 as % of GDP	18.2	18.7	17.0	21.6	26.7	31.7	35.5
4	Recurrent expenditure	9905.4	2156.2	6701.8	21016.8	37129.7	51861.6	69345.7
5	4 As % of GDP	6.8	8.7	10.3	15.4	16.5	19.6	23.1
6	Capital Expenditure	16512.8	2498.1	2960.7	4732.8	12325.1	20874.8	26354.7
7	6 as % of GDP	11.4	10.0	4.5	3.5	5.5	7.9	8.8
8	Total Revenue	13512.7	2789.3	7228.2	19981.9	48196.2	60918	72672.5
9	8 as % of GDP	9.4	11.2	11.1	14.6	21.4	23.3	24.2

Note: Recurrent expenditure and capital expenditure do not add up to total expenditure, the table does not include expenditure in financial management (loan repayment).

Source: Economic Survey reports of the Ministry of Finance. 2017/18 data sourced from NRB report of February 2019.

The most positive historical development in public finance has been the rising trend of public revenue. In absolute terms, it increased from 13.5 billion in 1991/92 to 27.9 billion in 1995/96, 72.2 billion in 2005/6 and Rs. 726.7 billion in 2017/18, registering an annual growth of 16.6 percent. As a percentage of GDP, it increased from 9.4 in 1991/92 to 24.2 in 2017/18, of which tax revenue including income tax, value-added tax, customs and excise duties represent around 90 percent of the total. VAT introduced in 1996 is the largest source contributing around 30 percent of the total tax revenue followed by income tax, customs and excise duties, respectively. The progress in internal revenue mobilization in Nepal has received appreciation from the international community including the IMF whose 2017 country report based on Article 4 consultations stated:[12]

> *Nepal has achieved strong growth in revenue in recent years. That was facilitated by growth of the tax base with rising remittances propelling consumption of imports- alongside sustained efforts to strengthen tax administration including at customs. There is considerable scope to raise the revenue further. This would be important to finance the current and capital spending needed to achieve the Sustainable Development Goals SDGs) and address infrastructural bottlenecks to boost the medium-term growth and raise living standards throughout Nepal. The authorities' ongoing efforts to modernize the tax system and strengthen core tax and customs administration have the potential to substantially raise collections.*

The report also complimented the strengthening of tax administration by the Inland Revenue Department with the implementation of Strategic Plan (2012/13-2016/17) and the supporting Reform Plan, and the Department of Customs for making significant strides in modernizing customs administration.

Public debt and external sector

The subdued capital expenditure of the government while the economy has been experiencing strong revenue growth has kept the budget deficit within manageable limits in recent years. There has been a cash surplus in the last few years at the end of the fiscal year because of the shortfall in capital expenditure, which has led to large government cash balance at the central bank.

Table 11.3: Public Borrowing and Outstanding Debt
(As percentage of GDP)

Fiscal Year	Internal Borrowing	Outstanding Internal Debt.	External Borrowing	Outstanding External Debt.	Total Debt Received	Total Outstanding Debt
2011/12	2.38	14.01	1.03	20.25	3.41	34.26
2012/13	1.12	12.5	0.98	19.67	2.1	32.17
2013/14	1.03	10.65	1.09	17.86	2.12	28.51
2014/15	2.00	9.49	1.38	16.16	3.38	25.65
2015/16	3.90	10.63	1.95	17.29	5.85	27.92
2016/17	3.34	10.74	2.20	15.67	5.54	26.41
2017/18	3.6	13.0	2.5	17.4	6.1	30.4

*Source: Government of Nepal, Financial Comptroller General Office, Annual Consolidated Financial Statement 2015/16, 2016/2017. Data on 2017/18 sourced from IMF country report no. 19/60, February 2009.

Nepal's public debt stands at 30 percent of GDP, low by international standards. The debt to GDP ratio of 60 percent is treated as a prudential limit for developed countries, while 40 percent is the suggested ratio for developing countries, not to be breached frequently. Despite this general rule of thumb not to cross this limit to ensure fiscal sustainability in the long run, most economies in both developing and developed choose to defy this norm. Against this backdrop, Nepal's present debt ratio is considered low and manageable. But there are other associated ratios and indicators relating to export earnings and revenue linked with the issue of debt sustainability. Obviously, Nepal's modest debt level has kept the debt management within a sustainable limit, however, the large current account deficit resulting from huge export-import gap could add to external sector vulnerability.

In the latest Country Report of February 17, 2019, based on the 2018 Article 4 Consultations,[13] IMF has cautioned about external economic and financial vulnerabilities in the coming years, despite favorable growth driven by post-earthquake reconstruction, investment in hydropower projects, rebound in agricultural production and tourism-related activities. The widened current accounts deficit of 8.2 percent of GDP in 2017/18 due to strong import demand and higher oil price is expected to persist in the near term because of increasing government spending and loose credit policy to achieve a moderately high growth target. Growth might be attained at the expense of worsening external and internal imbalances. The result will be a rapid decline in reserves projected to reach US$ 6.8 billion in 2019/20 sufficient to cover only 4.4 months of imports, which could force a disruptive adjustment.

One worrisome aspect of the Nepali economy is the mounting trade deficit with sluggish exports in the face of skyrocketing import of goods and services. In the SAARC region, Nepal faces the second-highest deficit in the external balance of goods and services equivalent to 30 percent of GDP, after Afghanistan's deficit of around 40 percent of GDP. The overall external trade of Nepal which was Rs. 171 billion in 2000/01 increased to Rs. 1.32 trillion 2017/18. But the export-import ratio during the same period plummeted to 1:15 from an earlier 1:2. The actual deficit which stood at 91 billion in 2004/5 peaked at Rs. 1.16 trillion in the fiscal year 2017/18. The total exports in 2017/18 stood at Rs. 81.6 billion with 11.8 percent growth from the previous year, while the value of imports surged by 36 percent to reach Rs. 1.2 trillion. As percentage of GDP, exports represented less than 3 percent in the year, compared to imports at 41 percent. The trade deficit in the first ten months of the new fiscal year 2018/19 between mid-July and mid-May 2019 widened by 19.7 percent to Rs. 1099.7 billion. The export-import ratio also declined to 6.7 percent from 6.8 in the corresponding period of the previous year.

Nepal has trade relations with more than 150 countries, but the major trade partners are India and China accounting for more than three-fourths of Nepal's trade. In the year 2017/18, India's share in Nepal's total export and import was 57 and 65 percent, respectively, while China accounted for 3 percent of exports and 13 percent of imports. Other partners in Nepal's export trade include USA, Turkey and the UK representing 11 percent, 6 percent and 4 percent of Nepal's exports; other destinations accounting for more than 1 percent each of Nepal's exports are Italy, France, Bangladesh, Japan and Canada. The top ten exports (as per 4-digit HTS codes) from Nepal in 2016/17 were coffee, tea, spices (10.6%), manmade staple fibers (10.1%), textile floor coverings (9.3%), clothing, accessories (7.9%), vegetable, fruit nut preparations (6.1%), iron and steel (5.8%), miscellaneous textiles (4.4%), manmade filaments (4.2%), food industry waste, animal fodder (4%) and paper yarn, woven fabric (3.6%). The top ten product groups accounted for roughly two-thirds of the total global shipment from the country.[14]

The widening trade deficit resulting in a huge foreign exchange liability was largely shouldered by remittance inflows amounting to Rs. 864.7 billion in 2017/18. The current account deficit that year was Rs. 245.2 billion compared to a narrow deficit of Rs. 10.1 billion in the previous year. The surge in current account deficit is largely attributed to growth in the import of petroleum products, transport equipment and parts, and industrial goods. The overall balance of payments registered a surplus of Rs. 960.2 million compared to a surplus of Rs. 82.1 billion in the previous year, contributed mainly by capital transfer of Rs. 17.7 billion and FDI of Rs. 17.5 billion.[15] However, in the first ten months of the new fiscal year 2018/19, further worsening of the current account deficit by Rs. 221.4 billion and low level of capital transfer and FDI, resulted in a BOP deficit of Rs. 68.20 billion. Consequently, the gross foreign exchange reserves of the country decreased to reach Rs. 1,060.70 billion as of mid-May 2019 from Rs. 1,102.6 billion at mid-July 2018. In dollar terms, the total foreign exchange reserve stood at $9.42 billion as of mid-May 2019 from $10.08 billion at mid-July 2018, sufficient to cover the prospective merchandise imports for nine months, and merchandise and services imports for less than eight months.[16]

The abysmal state of Nepal's export trade in the face of a sharp acceleration in imports is mainly responsible for the worsening current account deficit despite the significant contribution from remittance inflows. This is not a sustainable solution in the long run. Nepal has preferential trade arrangements with major economies. India has offered duty-free market access to Nepali products meeting the minimum value-added threshold except for some items in the negative list. China has offered preferential trade arrangement with zero-tariff to more than 8,000 items in six-digit customs classification. Nepal negotiated its membership of the World Trade Organization in 2004, and many developed economies have offered duty-free access for various products under such arrangements like Generalized System of Preferences (GSP), Everything But Arms (EBA) by European Union and Trade Facilitation and Trade Enforcement Bill (TFTEB) of USA. Also, Nepal's membership of the South Asia Free Trade Agreement provides an opportunity for export growth in the SAARC region. The country's ability to benefit from these opportunities depends on improved competitiveness with higher productivity based on comparative advantage for which increased investment with higher technology from friendly nations is the key. Unfortunately, Nepal's ease of doing business ranking as presented in the 2018 Doing Business Report of the World Bank has slipped further to 110th position from 105th position in the previous year. This does not send a favorable message to potential investors. Under this circumstance, to attract external investment particularly from neighboring India and China, the country will have to make serious efforts to improve not just investment enabling conditions, but also be ahead of peer countries.

Poverty and social sector

The most conspicuous achievement of Nepal's development performance in the past few decades has been in the social sector and poverty reduction. A number of surveys measuring the living conditions of Nepali households conducted have come to this conclusion. Three rounds of Nepal Living Standards Surveys (NLSS) were conducted in 1995/96, 2003/04 and 2010/11 using a standard survey model developed by the World Bank. The surveys found the poverty level at 42 percent in 1996, 31 percent in 2004 and 25 percent in 2011. Using the new poverty definition, the poverty rate in 2010 stood at 25 percent at the national level but marked by urban-rural and regional disparities. The poverty rate was found to be 15.5 percent in urban areas and 27.4 percent in rural areas. The poverty incidence is higher in the Mid-West and Far-West regions. The recalculation of poverty across federal provinces under the new constitution shows the level of poverty incidence ranging from 17 percent in Province One to 46 percent in Province Seven.[17] For the year 2017, the National Planning Commission estimates the overall poverty level at 18.7 percent.

While the estimates from the first two surveys are comparable because of uniform methodology, the third one has revised the poverty definition with methodological improvements to reflect the overall improved economic wellbeing in Nepal since 1995. The new poverty line was fixed at Rs. 19,262 using consumption data from the 2010 survey, which represented a 35 percent increase in real value over the original poverty line of 1995. If the poverty line of 1995 with adjustment for inflation had been applied, the poverty rate estimate in 2010 would have been as low as 12.5 percent. Measured by the international extreme poverty line of US$ 1.90 in PPP terms, the proportion of Nepali households living in poverty fell from 46 percent 1996 to 15 percent 2011, the lowest in South Asia.[18]

In addition to poverty reduction in terms of income and consumption expenditure of households, the NLSS have shown significant improvements in the quality of life in terms of educational, health, literacy and access to other economic services. The UNDP Human Development Report (HDR) of 2010 ranked Nepal as one of the top ten fast movers globally in non-income human development index (HDI) because of impressive progress in health and education despite modest income growth. The report lauded Nepal's impressive progress in health and education sectors traced to major public policy efforts, despite difficult circumstances and the spread of conflict. The latest UNDP HDR puts Nepal in a medium human development category, ranking 149th out of 189 countries and territories, with a score of 0.574 HDI in 2017. This represents an increase of 52 percent from the HDI of 0.378 in 1990. Despite gradual progress, the country is still behind the South Asian average score of 0.638. The HDI status of Nepal is ahead of only two South Asian countries, Pakistan and Afghanistan. Nepal's progress in life expectancy and child enrollment of schools is higher than the South Asian average, but it lags behind in mean years of education among adult population and per capita income.[19]

Another remarkable success was in meeting most of the Millennium Development Goals ahead of schedule. The time-bound targets in its major MDG components including poverty alleviation, reduction in child and maternal mortality, progress in school enrollment and gender equality in education, access to drinking water and sanitation were fully achieved. The country has also recorded strong progress in shared prosperity, despite persistent inequality of opportunity. The Gini coefficient estimated by the World Bank in the year 2010 stood at 32.8 in December 2010, registering a sharp decline from 43.8 in December 2003.[20] Between 2004 and 2011, the consumption level of the bottom 40 percent of the population grew almost twice as fast as the consumption level of the upper 60 percent, making the country one of the best performers globally on shared prosperity.[21]

The 2016 World Hunger Index released by the Washington DC-based International Food Policy Research Institute (IFPRI) ranked Nepal at the top position in South Asia for progress in hunger reduction resulting from a sharp decline in undernourishment, child stunting and child mortality.[22] Its 2018 Hunger Index report of 119 countries has ranked Nepal at 72nd position, above Bangladesh (86), India (103), Pakistan (105) and Afghanistan (111), and slightly below Sri-Lanka (67) and Myanmar (68).

In view of the limitation of income-based poverty measure, the concept of the Multidimensional Poverty Index (MPI) has been introduced. Studies have been undertaken using this concept to measure poverty in Nepal, in cooperation with Oxford Poverty and Human Development Initiative of Oxford University. The new approach is designed to complement the conventional income poverty approach and captures various dimensions of health, education and living standards with multiple indicators carrying varying weights following the global MPI framework. The MPI combines the headcount poverty representing the percentage of poor people with the intensity of poverty. The poverty analysis of data since 2006 based on this approach shows that the value of MPI dropped sharply from 0.313 in 2006 to 0.127 in 2014. The headcount ratio declined from 59.35 percent to 28.62 percent during the period, while the intensity of poverty came down from 52.7 to 44.2 percent.[23] The intensity of poverty is measured in terms of the level of total deprivation faced by the people across all dimensions.

Disaggregation of 2014 poverty data makes the substantial urban-rural disparity evident, with 7 percent of urban and 33 percent of the rural population being multi-dimensionally poor. The status of MPI across newly restructured federal provinces shows that the headcount ratio of 12.2 percent is the lowest in province 3, followed by 14.2 and 19.7 percentage points in province 4 (Gandaki) and 1 respectively, compared to 28.6 at the national level. The ratio of multi-dimensionally poor households is the highest in province 6 with 51.2 percent, followed by provinces 2, 7 (Sudur Paschim) and 5, with 47.9, 43.5 and 33.6 percentage points respectively.[24]

Concluding remarks

It is obvious from the data presented in the preceding discussion that Nepal's growth performance has been sluggish, much lower than that of peer economies in the region since 2001, attributed to various factors including turbulent and unstable politics, prolonged political transition affecting development administration, and natural disasters, making the country an economic laggard in the region. The overall size of investment is low, largely from the private sector that is channeled mainly to the services sector. The public investment that stands around 5 percent of GDP is not only low but also inefficient as reflected in the high incremental capital-output ratio (ICOR) of 4.9, the highest in the region. Inefficiency is also manifested in underspending of capital budget due to prolonged delays in completion of projects.[25]

Exports have slowed down to historically low levels accompanied by ballooning imports, resulting in the unprecedentedly high trade deficit. The overall growth performance was mediocre particularly in fiscal years 2014/15 and 2015/16, in the aftermath of the 2015 earthquakes, civil conflict and border blockade. Against this backdrop of low base years, the growth rate of subsequent years has been positive, contributed mainly by normalization of economic life after the end of trade blockade, favorable monsoons, improved power supply, steady inflow of remittances and the massive launch of post-earthquake reconstruction programs. The positive growth rate is expected to be sustained in the near-term. Meanwhile, the IMF has cautioned that the pursuit of higher growth with the expansionary policy could lead to fiscal and external imbalances. To ensure sustainable growth in the medium-term, the need is to raise productive capacity through higher investment and greater competition.

Even in the face of the slowdown of economic growth in the 2000s except the year 2005/6 amid an intensification of violent conflict and turbulent politics prior to 2014/15, the economy witnessed positive developments in a number of areas. As presented above, the growth rate in internal revenue has been impressive reaching around 24 percent of GDP, the highest in South Asia, which has contributed to increasing economic self-reliance for public expenditure. The ratio of public expenditure to GDP has been rising largely financed by internal resources. But the disturbing part is the increasing ratio of recurrent expenditure at the expense of capital expenditure; the trend is likely to continue further in the context of expanded administrative super-structure under the new constitution.

The most positive development in the recent past particularly after 1990 is the substantial progress in poverty reduction and social indicators as reflected in the human development index, hunger reduction, the fulfillment of MDG targets and other aspects as reported in different international reports. The decline in Nepal's poverty is reflected both in terms of income poverty and multidimensional poverty. Nepal has been ranked 22nd among seventy-seven developing countries in the Inclusive Development Index of the World Economic Forum report (2018), up from the 27th position in 2017, well ahead of several BRICS countries such as Brazil, India and South Africa.[26] The Nepal Country Economic Memorandum of 2017 by the World Bank also highlights other aspects including the significant decline in income inequality in recent decades, low unemployment rate and strong female labor force participation in the country. Contrary to the experience of most other economies characterized by high economic growth with limited impact on poverty alleviation, Nepal represents a unique case of modest economic growth with remarkable performance in poverty reduction. It is against this background that the World Bank report termed Nepal a 'leader in poverty alleviation but a laggard in growth'.

The improved social indicators and the remarkable progress in the reduction of multi-dimensional poverty are contributed mainly by the increased investment in the social sector and infrastructure building following the restructuring of public expenditure started since the early nineties as part of the reform process. This resulted in increased access of households to basic social and economic services like education and health services, drinking water, transport, communications, irrigation, electricity and banking facilities.

One of the most important factors behind poverty amelioration resulting from increased household income has been the growth of remittance inflow to the country. This phenomenon has, however, led to the loss of productivity at home affecting growth. There is growing feminization as well as a shortage of labor for farming, public works and industrial activities. Over the past decade, there has been a sharp deterioration in export competitiveness, while imports have surged on the back of rising inflow of remittances. The massive transfers have likely induced a Dutch Disease with the expansion of the non-tradable sector and its spending effect, leading to contraction of the manufacturing sector and the rise in real exchange rates. As Nepali Rupee is pegged to Indian Rupee, the pressure on the Nepali rupee to appreciate against foreign currencies other than India's has aggravated the problem of competitiveness.

Notes

1. World Bank Group. (May 2017). *Climbing Higher: Towards a Middle- Income Nepal*, (p. 9)."
2. Mahat, Ram S. op cit . *In Defence of Democracy*, (pp.161-162)
3. World Bank. (June 2014). *Nepal Policy Note:* 3 'Is' for Growth, (p. 5). South Asia Chief Economist Office.
4. World Bank. Ibid. (p. 6).
5. World Bank Group. (May 2017). *Climbing Higher: Towards A Middle –Income Nepal*, (pp. 36-37).
6. Quoted in World Bank Group. (2018). *Creating Markets in Nepal: Country Private Sector Diagnostic*, (p. 22).
7. World Bank Group. (2018). Ibid. (p. 230).
8. Nepal Rastra Bank. (June 2018). *A Survey Report on Foreign Direct Investment in Nepal.*
9. Estimates by World Travel and Tourism Council 2019 Annual Research Report. Quoted in *The Kathmandu Post.* (2019, May 27).
10. World Bank Group. (November 2018). *Creating Markets in Nepal- Country Private Sector Diagnostics*, (pp. 35-36).

11. This is attributed to several reasons. The increasing number of tourists visiting overland from India to the birth place of Buddha Lumbini, brought by Indian tour operators, reportedly stay for only a few hours. Non-resident Nepali visitors with foreign passports generally spend only in local currency. Another factor for low spending is the online payment methods primarily by Chinese tourists via Wechat and Alipay transferring money from one Chinese account to another bypassing formal banking channels in Nepal, according to a report by *The Kathmandu Post.* (2019, May 17).
12. International Monetary Fund. (March 2017). *IMF Country Report No.17/74,* (p. 32). Washington DC.
13. International Monetary Fund. (2019). *IMF Country Report No 19/60, 2018 Article IV Consultation*—Press Release Staff Report and Statement by the Executive Director for Nepal. Washington DC.
14. Workman, Daniel (2018, August 18). Nepal's top ten exports. *World's Top Exports.* Retrieved from http://www.worldstopexports.com/nepals-top-10-exports/
15. Nepal Rastra Bank Research Department. (February 2019). *Current Macroeconomic and Financial Situation,* based on annual data of 2018/19, (pp. 4,9). Kathmandu.
16. Nepal Rastra Bank Research Department. (June 2019). Ibid. Based on the first ten months data of 2019/20.
17. The figures are based on the World Bank staff calculation using 2010/11 Nepal Living Standard Survey. National Planning Commission, Government of Nepal and Oxford Poverty and Human Development Initiative. (2018). *Multidimensional Poverty Index, 2018: Analysis Towards Action,* (p. 2). Kathmandu.
18. The World Bank Group. (February 2018). *Nepal Systematic Country Diagnostic: A new approach for a federal Nepal,* (p. 3).
19. *The Kathmandu Pos*t. (2018, September 16).
20. https://ceicdata.com.nepal
21. World Bank Group. (February 2018). *Nepal- Systematic Country Diagnostic,* (p. 3). Washington DC.
22. Nepal has been ranked at 72 position among 118 countries, compared to Myanmar (75), Sri-Lanka (84), Bangladesh (90), India (97), Pakistan (107) and Afghanistan (112).
23. National Planning Commission. (2018). *Nepal Multidimentional Poverty Index-Analysis towards Action 2018,* Chapter 4, (p. 25). In partnership with OPHI, University of Oxford.
24. Ibid.
25. The ICOR at 4.9 is estimated by the Approach Paper for the Fifteenth Plan, lower than the 5.2 estimate of the Approach Paper of the previous Fourteenth Plan. The estimated figure from 2001 to 2007 was 5.7, the highest among comparator countries. World Bank Group (May, 2009*), Climbing Higher: Towards A Middle- Income Nepal.*
26. World Bank Group. (2017). Nepal Country Economic Memorandum - *Climbing Higher Towards Middle Income Countries,* (p. 1). Washington DC. This World Bank report has quoted the 2017 report of World Economic Forum which had ranked Nepal at 27the place, but the position was upgraded to 22nd position in WEF report of 2018.

Chapter Twelve

Challenges and Tasks Ahead

After decades of political turmoil and post-conflict transition, Nepal entered a new phase of political development after the promulgation of the 2015 Constitution. The recent political history is marked by frequent changes in political regimes and governments, from family autocracy and absolute monarchy to representative parliamentary democracy with a constitutional monarchy and a democratic republic with decentralized federalism. This was the outcome of a long period of political struggle for popular sovereignty, violent conflict and popular uprising resulting in constitution-making by elected representatives of the people. The constitution reflects popular aspirations for a just and egalitarian society through democratic means and institutions. The Constitution has also institutionalized the popular will through the incorporation of extensive fundamental rights to expand human freedoms, removing major sources of suppression and exploitation including state tyranny and denial of basic needs. The federal political structure with three tiers of government decentralizes power to the people's doorstep. The new governance structure has now taken shape following elections of approximately 37,000 representatives at all levels.

National goals

The focus of the national agenda at present is the full implementation of the constitution, together with economic growth and socio-economic development. The goal is to meet the rising aspirations of the people that are further reinforced by democratic institutions and practices including periodic elections and the communication revolution. In a globalized world, awareness of the quality of life in other parts of the world is rising even among people living in remote corners of the country. To accelerate economic growth for general wellbeing, it is necessary to unshackle and optimize the use of the country's resources and external opportunities.

The foremost resource in any country is its people. In Nepal, we are abetted by unique natural beauty, biodiversity, abundant water resource and geographical location between two fast-growing major economies of the world. The country's unique human mix and ecological diversity with natural beauty and pleasant climate not only attracts tourists but also has the potential of making the country a high-value agro-power. Nepal has the prospect of becoming a clean energy powerhouse of South Asia substituting imported fossil fuel with hydro-electricity. The fast-growing neighboring countries offer the prospect of a huge market next door, as well as sources of capital investment and technology. But the economic performance to date, as elaborated in previous chapters, has been mixed and far short of the country's needs and potential. The failure to capitalize on these assets is attributed to a number of factors which deserve attention to attain fresh economic impetus to reaching a respectable middle-income target over the next decade.

Nepal, currently categorized as one of the forty-eight least developed countries (LDC) of the world, aims to graduate to a developing country status by 2022. To attain this objective, it has to meet two of the three criteria, in two consecutive triennial reviews, relating to gross national per capita income, human assets and economic vulnerability set by the United Nations. The human asset index includes indicators on education, health and undernourishment, while the economic vulnerability index relates to the country's ability to cope with susceptibility to external economic and environmental shocks. Nepal met the second and third criteria in 2015 and 2018, therefore becoming eligible for graduation.

With respect to the first criterion, Nepal's per capita gross national income in 2018 stood at $745 (averaged between 2014 to 2016 using the Atlas method) which was substantially below the threshold of $1230 fixed by the UN. Despite the inability to meet the income threshold, Nepal was technically qualified for graduation; but the country abandoned the plan to graduate in 2018 based on non-income criteria alone, fearing that such a graduation, not undergirded by a firm economic foundation, could be reversible. Further, a non-LDC status might curtail trade preferences and concessional aid flow that Nepal currently enjoys. The government plan at present is to be considered eligible for graduation at the next triennial review in 2021 and plan for a smooth and sustainable transition thereafter. By 2030, the country expects to meet most of the SDGs and become a middle-income country. The seventeen SDGs cover a wide range of goals and targets including ending poverty and hunger, infrastructure and social development, quality education and health services, climate action, innovation, industrialization, sustainable consumption and decent life.[1] The National Planning Commission estimate of the investment required to meet SDG goals is around Rs. 2 trillion investment per annum, which is equivalent to 58 percent of GDP of the year 2018/19.

Growth and investment

The country successfully attained almost all MDGs and targets between 2000 and 2015. Building on this foundation, the country should expedite the process of achieving the SDGs which are much more ambitious and comprehensive. Even in the midst of slow economic growth over the past few decades, the country made remarkable progress in poverty reduction and human development. The main challenge at present is to accelerate economic growth by raising investment. Together with Afghanistan, Nepal remains the poorest country in the region. Only with increasing productivity and growth can the country uplift the living conditions of the people and meet rising aspirations. To quote the famous economist duo, Jagadish Bhagwati and Arvind Panagariya, growth is necessary for alleviating poverty in a country that starts from a low income base, since it reduces poverty directly by pulling the poor into gainful employment, and facilitates additional poverty reduction by generating revenues that enable the financing of redistributive programs principally aimed at the poor. To achieve this double-barreled outcome, they suggest a two-track strategy: one, reforms to accelerate and sustain growth while making it more inclusive, and two: reforms to make redistributive programs more effective as their scope widens.[2]

In the process of facilitating growth, the country should be able to capitalize on the country's resource endowment, goodwill and partnership with the international community, including the two big neighbors. To rekindle growth, it is necessary to vigorously address the challenges and constraints the country is facing at present. Although the present government has set itself a fanciful target of double-digit growth for the twenty-five years, a feat no other country has ever achieved in human history. With the right policy and institutions inducing a favorable investment climate, Nepal can position itself on a sustainable growth trajectory of at least 7 percent over the next decade. This would double the size of the economy, in real terms, in a decade.

The country's endowment of water, land and forest resources, agro-ecological diversity and natural beauty represent one potent source of growth if optimally utilized. Prof. Lester Thurow of MIT has observed that natural resources have ceased to be the major source of competitive advantage, as new technologies and institutions alter the traditional sources of competitive advantage. Having them is not a way to become rich, and not having them is not a barrier to becoming rich: Japan does not have them and is rich; Argentina has them and is not rich, to put simply.[3] Nepal's experience until today substantiates this theory. Despite the immense potential of Nepal's water resources, the country depends on external sources for almost half of its basic power need. Similarly, there is an increasing import bill of agro and forestry products even to meet the basic requirements because of the failure to make optimal use of one-third of the country's territory under agriculture, and 40 percent under forest cover.

The political issues dominated the national agenda over the last few decades. Economic policy was not growth-enhancing as the state assumed a predominant role and shrunk the role of the market and the private sector. The post-Panchayat period in the 1990s witnessed the liberal reforms opening up the economy which recognized the need for a creative partnership between the government, private sector, non-governmental organizations and local bodies in nation-building. The role of the state became pronounced in creating an enabling environment for the private sector in production and business activities, and in expanding social infrastructure activities and anti-poverty programs. But the unstable politics, decade-long insurgency and the protracted transition took its toll on the economy. The continued preoccupation with power politics, the debate over the future political system and unresolved issues of the peace process dominated the national debate, sidelining economic priorities. In the new political context after the promulgation of the constitution, the economy should be the primary national agenda involving an unequivocal commitment and action from all sides.

The first priority is to raise investment in areas with potential for generating growth and economic opportunities. The investment ratio in Nepal remains relatively low compared to regional peers. Gross fixed capital formation has registered growth in recent years reaching 34 percent of GDP in 2017/18. But the economy suffers from poor productivity and low public investment accounting for only around one fifth of the total, which is below the average of South Asian and other low-income countries. The output growth is driven mainly by factor accumulation rather than by productivity growth owing to diminishing returns on capital. The ratio of public capital spending increased only in the post-earthquake years driven by reconstruction. The public investment inefficiency is reflected in the high incremental capital-output ratio (ICOR) estimated to be 4.9 in the government's latest plan document. The investment concentrated mainly in infrastructure projects that suffer from poor construction management leading to low quality work with high cost and time overruns. The poor infrastructure resulting from this is the constraining factor for private investment and productivity. Therefore, the obvious requirement is to boost infrastructure investment with greater efficiency. Public investment in infrastructure can be raised by limiting the rising trend in recurrent and unproductive spending. Increased and efficient public investment in infrastructure networks to provide road access and other services like electricity in remote areas not only enables private investment but also acts as GDP magnifiers by raising labor and capital productivity, economies of scale and human capital development. Similarly, private sector investment also needs to be encouraged in infrastructure projects that are commercially viable offering a reasonable rate of returns, through legislative and other reforms.

Given the low and inefficient investment level in the country, it is important to attract FDI which could be a game-changer, with the ultimate objectives of improving productivity, competitiveness and integration to the global market boosting the export sector. The present FDI inflow in Nepal is very low, at around $100 million per annum focused mainly in energy and services sectors. Investment in the productive sector is limited. Boosting FDI is crucial to harness the immense hydropower potential with which the country can transform itself into a clean-energy based economy, replacing the heavy import of petroleum products. FDI is also necessary to play a key role in materializing Nepal's potential of becoming a global player in the value chain of high value herbal and aromatic products by linking to lucrative foreign markets. Given Nepal's panoramic beauty, favorable climate condition and friendly people, possibilities also exist to make the country an attractive hub for investment in high-quality education, medical treatment and outdoor sports. The huge trade deficit resulting from the poor export sector in the face of mounting import of goods makes it necessary to attract investment in the manufacturing sector for export augmentation as well as substitution of imports. This calls for a favorable investment climate with suitable amendments in prevailing laws. There must be a realization of the fact that foreign investment is required not just for capital investment, but also for new and innovative technology, management know-how and market linkages. Therefore, there is a need to waive protectionist policy in small, medium scale manufacturing industries and agriculture sector on a selective basis. To expand the manufacturing base, it is necessary to adopt a more liberal industrial policy.

Infrastructural gap

Infrastructure development is a precondition for growth. It plays an important role in promoting inclusive development with shared prosperity through its impact on the lives of the poor and marginalized populace, particularly in a situation like Nepal's where a large part of the population lives in remote regions with poor access to economic services. Efficient infrastructure also helps raise labor productivity, economies of scale and human capital through contribution to education and health. It is this sector that raises agricultural income by connecting farm producers with the market, enables better delivery of services, and lowers production cost of firms to improve competitiveness.

Despite some progress made in the recent past, there is an acute deficit of quality infrastructure. This has deterred private investment. Nepal ranked 130th out of 138 countries on the 2016 Competitive Index of Infrastructure of the World Economic Forum and is ranked 114th out of 160 counties on the 2018 Logistic Performance Index.[4] The principal infrastructure constraints in Nepal compared to regional peers remain electricity and roads. A World Bank study in 2014, estimates the investment need equivalent to 8 to 12 of GDP per annum until 2020 with a total of thirteen to eighteen billion US dollars to address the quantity and quality deficiency of Nepal's infrastructure. But the gross public investment in infrastructure is below 5 percent, less than the average of other South Asian and all low-income countries. Despite the abundant potential of hydropower production, population living in many remote rural areas have no access to electricity, and the overall level of electricity supply and consumption remains very low. The per capita consumption in 2014 was a mere 139 KWh, compared to the South Asian average of 707 KWh and Indian average of 806 KWh. It has reached 198 KWh in 2018.

The government has recently announced the ambitious target of generating 15,000 MW in the next ten years. Currently, more than 200 projects are in the pipeline with a cumulative generating capacity of 8,000 MW. The progress is slow with rising costs due to numerous problems. Private sector power producers complain of difficult and cumbersome processes to get licenses and to sign power purchase agreements. One important factor behind this problem is attributed to the double role of the Nepal Electricity Authority (NEA) in power generation as well as transmission and dispatch. NEA is the sole authority for power transmission to load centers and distribution across the country, while also accounting for around 50 percent of the domestic power production. This creates a significant advantage for NEA over the private producers due to conflict of interest while planning and building transmission lines for projects developed by its subsidiaries vis-à-vis the private sector. Development of transmission and distribution lines has been slower than power generation, a problem which has affected the power dispatch from some completed private sector projects. The need for separating the operational and regulatory roles through unbundling of NEA was felt more than a decade earlier. Despite government pledge, this reform is yet to materialize.

The country also suffers from poor transport connectivity. The difficult topography and geology, together with the scattered population predominantly in rural areas make transport connectivity a costly development imperative. The road network representing practically the only surface means of transport is inadequate and suffers from poor maintenance, impacting the competitiveness and spatial concentration of economic activities. Almost 40 percent of services inputs to processed food exports are reported to be transport-related, as are 30 percent for leather and 25 percent for beverages and tobacco exporters.[5] One contributing factor to high transport cost arises from poor enforcement of state legislation against anti-competitive practices such as collective price-fixing and other market distortions from transportation syndicates and cartels. The country faces the problem of frequent road traffic accidents taking a heavy toll of human lives and physical injuries. On average, 2,000 people are killed in road accidents in Nepal every year, a total of 2,541 in the fiscal year 2017/18 caused by various factors including poor road condition, mechanical failure and human negligence.[6] In the first six months of the fiscal year 2017/18, 1,176 persons succumbed to deaths in road accidents.[7] Under these circumstances, transport is one of the most-cited top business constraints in Nepal.

Against this backdrop, the high priority imperative for public and private investment in infrastructure is obvious. The investment status in the power sector has been discussed earlier in a separate chapter. Successive governments have accorded priority to road construction resulting in expansion of the road network to 88,000 km in 2018, but only 18 percent of this is blacktopped and all-weather. There has been no private investment in the road sector so far. Of the total network, 53,938 Km represents local level rural roads, which are seasonal in use. Various ambitious projects including the Kathmandu-Tarai multi-lane fast track, Tarai Postal Road, Mid-Hill Highway and various other projects including upgradation of existing roads are at different stages of implementation. The Nepal Army has also been deployed in road construction, particularly to develop road access into remote and backward regions since the early 1990s. Recently, the government has assigned the responsibility of constructing even the modern Kathmandu-Tarai multi-lane highway to the Nepal Army. But the overall sectoral progress has been slow because of public investment inefficiency. The average life of ongoing projects is more than eleven years, and in the case of larger projects even more. Even the 'national pride projects' are not implemented more swiftly than other projects, and have been ongoing for more than thirteen years on average, with the longest project ongoing since 1988.[8]

A recent investigation by the CIAA reports disarray in construction contracts leading to Rs. 118 billion at risk involving 1,848 projects under seven different ministries without progress in construction, as the contractors have abandoned work without time extension, while others have failed to make progress despite repeated time extensions. It is reported that procurement regulations relating to monitoring, supervision in quality control, construction deadlines and penalty for non-performance are not strictly adhered to due to administrative softening of the government agencies[9], which is attributed to corruption factor and weaknesses in state apparatus. This is just an example of the poor quality of construction management including in the large 'national pride projects'. The mega projects where the time and cost overrun has more than doubled include such projects as Sikta Irrigation, Melamchi Drinking Water, Mid-Hill and Tarai Postal highways and Babai Irrigation. The Mid-Hill Highway was started in 2006/07 with the estimated cost of Rs. 33 billion. The cost has more than doubled, and the project duration extended from the original ten years by five additional years.

The governance shortcoming is also echoed in politically driven projects without basic preparation and necessary techno-economic appraisal. The recently announced government plans for Kerung-Kathmandu and Raxaul-Kathmandu railway projects represent a case in point. The preliminary cost estimate of these projects is about $5 billion. It may be noted that there are a number of highways[10] including those under construction and upgradation connecting Kathmandu with central Madhes/Tarai of Province Three that would contribute to boosting trade with India. Similarly, connectivity with China is being enhanced by opening road links from Hilsa of Humla district in the Karnali Province, Korala of Mustang district of Gandaki province and Kimathanka of Sankhuwasabha of Province One in the East to open new trade routes. If the estimated amount of investible fund required for the proposed railway projects were available for the transport sector through mobilization of internal and external sources, the immediate priority should have been to upgrade and extend highways and quality roads throughout the country that would not only be investment enhancing by lowering production cost and expanding market but also contribute to balanced development by opening up new economic opportunities in most parts of the country. Both the proposed railway projects are technically complex in view of difficult geography, limited reverse cargo traffic, security and other unforeseen implications that will add to costs and strain management capability. No serious study covering techno-economic and other aspects including estimates of two-way traffic volume in relation to various ongoing and planned roadways with both neighbors and prospective payback has been undertaken to justify the mega investments in railways on both sides. Similarly, the government announced the plan for inland waterways and river navigation from the Bay of Bengal through the Ganga to major rivers like Kosi and Narayani of Nepal for cargo and passenger traffic, even before undertaking basic techno-economic feasibility studies and appraisal. Shipping is definitely an energy-efficient and cost-effective mode of cargo transport, but before taking any decision on the project, detailed techno-economic studies including a cost-benefit analysis, volume of trade estimate along the route, standard of shipping vessels with tonnage capacity, environmental aspects, navigability in the context of the depth of river water, taking into account the diversion requirement for irrigation and other uses is necessary.

Given the country's diverse terrain within a limited distance, road is the most suitable mode of transportation. It is cheaper, offers flexibility to transport in short distances, feeder service and in handling passengers in low number and goods in short distances. Investment in quality infrastructure including roads and hydropower is required not only to encourage private investment but also to enhance labor productivity, economies of scale, human capital development, and for service delivery and assistance during an emergency. Therefore, the need is not only an investment augmentation in infrastructure but also addressing quality deficiency through efficient use of resources. Policy and planning reorientation is also required for prioritization and sequencing of projects based on socio-economic justification and financial sustainability analysis, rather than being driven by emotion and populist consideration. It is also necessary to emphasize the maintenance and upgradation of existing road and airfields network to improve connectivity, while being selective with proper sequencing with regard to the construction of new projects, based on socio-economic rationale. The most conspicuous deficiency remains in the procurement and contract management in the implementation processes of infrastructure projects that have hindered performance quality. Furthermore, the present confusion over overlapping of responsibilities and mandates between different tiers of government must be resolved through appropriate legislation and clear policy guidelines, followed with efficient execution.

Fiscal federalism

Nepal has adopted a highly decentralized federal constitution with three tiers of government, one central, seven provincial and 753 at the local level. The government at each level is constitutionally empowered to execute a broad set of tasks. The immediate challenge is building up the extensive institutional capacity practically from scratch, at local and provincial levels. The requirements include enactment of necessary legislation, provision of manpower and necessary physical facilities including office buildings in all administrative centers. The transitional cost of this new political and administrative superstructure is estimated at three to four percent of GDP for four years. Even after nearly one and a half years of the formation of provincial governments, there has been no decision on the majority of the provincial capitals because of conflicting positions on their locations. Conflicts also continue to exist over the division of authority between three levels of government, arising in the absence of appropriate legislation and conflicting interpretations of constitutional provisions. The federal government is often blamed for centralizing power in maintaining local security and selecting civil servants, neglecting the constitutionally federalized and decentralized power to sub-national and local governments.

The weak institutional capacity due to systemic deficiencies and lack of proper manpower with experience and expertise is creating risks in the use and management of funds at subnational levels. There is an implementation problem of the Medium-Term Expenditure Framework (MTEF) which has been in practice at the central level. Reform measures are required to create institutional capacity for planning, budgeting and execution including systems for tracking and monitoring expenditure and physical progress. At present, the country is facing excessive fiscal pressure for recurrent spending at all levels, while the public capital investment suffers from under-spending. The country is already under stress of high share of recurrent spending in the federal budget, at around 26 percent of GDP, driven mainly by growing wage bill, rising non-contributory social security spending and various other distributive programs, driven by populist interest rather than economic consideration and sustainability. The recurrent expenditure as a percentage of GDP proposed in the federal budget for the fiscal year 2019/20 has further risen to 28 percent of GDP.

The recurrent spending will further increase after the formation of a full institutional structure with necessary manpower at all levels. The size of the civil service under the new structure is estimated to reach 137,371 comprising of 47,920 at the federal level, 22,685 at the provincial level and 66,766 at the local level. This will be in addition to the size of elected members, executive body including the council of ministers at the provincial and federal levels; the total membership at legislatures and executive councils at the local level alone exceeds 36,000. A preliminary estimate of the annual operational cost of provincial and local governments stands at Rs. 60.6 billion annually, including 8.2 billion for salary and associated costs of administrative staff, Rs. 22.06 billion for salary and other associated costs of elected representatives and Rs. 30.3 billion for other operational expenses. Thus, the operational cost of the new administration, excluding central government expenses, will be approximately 2 percent of GDP. As it is within the authority of the subnational governments to decide on the wage bill, perks and privileges of these institutions, there are reports of reckless and brash spending on unwarranted unproductive and consumptive items for personal and partisan uses. In some cases, there are reports of gross misuse of resources in various perks and allowances of elected representatives at local levels amounting to more than the annual revenue generated locally. On the other hand, the capital budget suffers from serious under-execution and misuse, attributed to several factors including capacity gap, procedural hurdles and arbitrary budget allocation to ill-conceived projects without adequate preparation. Allegations are also often heard of investment choices being driven by potential for illicit gains and graft, rather than by the rate of returns and contribution to national output.

The weak institutional capacity to implement development programs is evident from the large shortfall in development expenditure both at federal and sub-national levels in 2018/19. The federal government was able to spend only 47 percent of the capital budget in the first eleven months, while provincial governments could spend only around 20 percent on average. Thousands of infrastructure projects approved and initiated by central administrations under the previous constitution have been left in limbo, resulting from their disownment by the central government without proper handover to sub-national levels. The lower-level governments, on the other hand, suffer from multiple capacity constraints.

The increasing recurrent expenditure is driving the fiscal deficit, financed largely by domestic debt. In the fiscal year ending 2018, total public debt increased by 4 percent of which domestic debt accounted for 72 percent.[11] The reliance on debt financing to fund the estimated budget deficit for 2019/20 is projected to reach as much as 14.2 percent of GDP of which 40 percent will be funded by domestic borrowing and the remaining 60 percent from external borrowing. The overall budget structure proposed for the year shows that almost the entire amount of internal revenue will be spent on recurrent expenditures, while the capital spending will have to rely on internal and external borrowing. The new trend will push the outstanding national debt to a higher level, creating a generational burden.

Given the need to make the transition to federal structure sustainable, sound and prudent fiscal management is necessary to ensure austerity in administrative spending and institutional strengthening to build capacity to plan, budget and execute development programs, while raising domestic revenue. The current debt distress of the country is low resulting from prudent macroeconomic policies, together with careful selection of projects and funding sources, while resorting to debt financing in the past. Caution must be exercised in the coming days against the misuse of the available fiscal space for unproductive and populist programs driven by short term political interests without a thorough appraisal. To achieve a long-term sustainable growth path, it is also important to strengthen the macro-economic policy framework and to tighten monetary and fiscal policy relative to the expansionary policies of the past two years.

Reforms are also required in public financial management (PFM) to deal with the problem of under-spending of the capital budget. The country has a well-designed PFM framework including the system of Medium-Term Expenditure Framework (MTEF) and Public Expenditure and Financial Accountability (PEFA) as per international practices and standards. PEFA offers an opportunity to review the PFM reform progress offering strategic directions.[12] Nepal's overall performance as measured by the first PEFA benchmark was at the lower range of the spectrum, though at par with countries at similar levels. The second PEFA assessment in 2014 concluded that Nepal PFM is relatively strong by making substantial improvements by deepening the structures and processes of public finance, particularly with the use of information technology. Nepal's PEFA rating was found better than the average of fifteen fragile states and twenty-seven low-income countries. The rating in four dimensions was better or equal to those of fifty-one middle-income countries.[13]

Notwithstanding the improvements recorded in Nepal's PFM system by PEFA assessment, there remains still a gap between the design of PFM systems and budget planning, formulation, execution and oversight.[14] Therefore, there is a need for institutional strengthening and capacity building of PFM practitioners. To improve budget implementation with better utilization of resources, the bulk allocation for execution should be limited to only ready-for-implementation projects with finalized feasibilities, work plan and procurement timeline. The budget calendar needs to be restructured separating planning, formulation and executive phases with strict adherence.

One reform introduced with the promulgation of 2015 Constitution was advancing the date of budget presentation by one and a half months before the start of the new fiscal year to create some space for preparatory work for speedy implementation of development projects proposed in the budget. There is a statutory provision under clause 3 of article 119 of the constitution to present the annual budget by the federal government on *Jestha* 15 (end May/early June), prior to the start of the fiscal year on *Shrawa*n 1 (mid-July). This provision has been brought into practice from the fiscal year 2016/17. But the phenomenon of under-execution and under-spending of capital budge continues, the spending ratio in the last three fiscal years being less than 80 percent. This results from the problems associated with project selection, approval, authorization, release procedures and project management, compounded by political interference in decision making. Furthermore, despite some progress made in the PFM at the central level, the practice is yet to trickle down at lower levels. To improve capital spending capacity, reforms are also required to develop national norms for project costing and minimum standards for contracted works and provide technical and institutional support to local government capacity for monitoring and supervision.

Security concerns

The economy still suffers from the legacy of the Maoist conflict, manifested in sporadic terrorist activities engineered by Maoist breakaway groups posing security threats in the country. There were several incidents of bomb explosion during the last general election aimed at candidates including this author.[15] In recent months, there are news reports of widespread extortion from businessmen and industrialists through life threats, bomb blasts at Arun 3 hydro project, and at the corporate office of Ncell telephone company and dozens of its communication towers in various parts, in which one civilian was killed and others injured. There are frequent news reports of detonated improvised explosive devices with death toll and human injuries, sometimes killing the rebels themselves carrying such devices due to self-explosion. The rebel faction is operating in a semi-underground manner setting up the paramilitary structure and even claiming parallel 'people's government' reminiscent of the outfit during the period of the past Maoist insurgency.

It has been reported that the breakaway Maoist outfit led by Netra Bikram Chand is in possession of a large number of weapons that were not stored in the cantonments as per Agreement on Monitoring of the Management of the Arms and Armies (AMMAA) during the Peace Process after signing the Comprehensive Peace Agreement in 2006. During the search operation in the wake of the bomb blasts on February 22, 2019, the police seized a cache of arms and ammunitions.[16] The Home Ministry is reported to be in a dilemma whether to deal with the problem as a security issue or seeking a political solution through dialogue. This lackadaisical approach even in the face of a security threat with blatant violation of law and order represents a negative development in the way of creating a conducive investment climate in the country. In March 2019 the government took a decision to ban the Chand-led Communist Party of Nepal, but the decision did not deter the outfit to further their extortion drive. Following the government decision, the outfit issued a circular to all their party units with instructions to forcibly collect 'taxes' from businessmen, local representatives, community forest committees and individuals for its so-called people's government. The situation calls for effective government action in maintaining law and order to protect the lives and property of people while making political efforts to bring the rebels to a peaceful process.

Productivity and work culture

Growth is primarily a function of human resource and capital formation, amplified by technological progress. It is generated not only by the deployment of inputs but also by better allocation of resources and the use of productivity-enhancing elements. One of the reasons behind growth differences among nations is rooted in the varying levels of total factor productivity. A study by Klenow and Rogriguez based on a cross-country sample from 1960 to 1985 concludes that the difference in total factor productivity is the primary determinant of growth differences between countries.[17]

Nepal's overall factor productivity performance in key sectors is very low even by the standards of developing countries. Its position in terms of total factor productivity (TFT) level and TFT growth is the lowest in South Asia. The country's long-term economic growth has been driven almost entirely by capital and investment with very little contribution from productivity growth. The TFT growth for the aggregate economy was observed in the post-liberalization and stabilization period contributed significantly by labor productivity growth in the services sector. The TFT growth in the manufacturing sector declined, while the agriculture sector showed a mixed result.[18] The key productivity-constraining factors are: limited technology transfer, high infrastructure and transaction costs, labor market rigidities and unpredictable business climate. The change in employment structure normally observed in the course of economic transformation of low-income countries is the shift from low productivity agriculture sector to manufacturing, and then to services. But in Nepal employment growth is highest in the services sector rather than manufacturing.

The expansion of the services sector of non-tradable activities like retail and wholesale trade, real estate and housing is driven mainly by increasing public expenditure and remittances income. Tradable sectors like agriculture and industry do not attract workers. The large outflow of labor to other countries and the remittances they send home have helped to reduce poverty, but have led to the loss of productivity and competitiveness at home causing low growth. There is growing feminization, as well as a shortage of labor for farming and industrial activities, that has led to high production cost, affecting investment growth. Many sectors including construction and some manufacturing subsectors rely largely on foreign labor due to limited availability of domestic skills. Labor productivity is affected also by the militancy of unionized labor often resorting to strikes and factory close-down demanding a wage increase and other perks disproportionate to the inflation rate and productivity growth.

Minimum wages are reviewed every two years and fixed with a trilateral agreement between unions, employers and the government. The minimum wage of Nepal in the manufacturing sector is considered one of the highest in the region, linked not with productivity, but with the cost of living. Also, survey data until 2012 shows that Nepal's wage overhead cost is highest in South Asia. This disconnect was observed between wage growth and productivity growth per employee in the manufacturing sector between 2007 and 2012 when wage and other benefits increased at an annual rate of 12.25 percent while the productivity increased at the rate of 11.4 percent.[19] The national salary and wage index also rose faster at the rate of 9.3 percent compared to the increase in consumer price index by 4.6 percent as of mid-January 2019.

An important factor affecting productivity in Nepal is the high degree of politicization in society, as a large section of the population gets involved directly or indirectly in the activities of political parties, their affiliates and interest groups. Partisan politics dominates the civil service, labor and student unions, teaching profession, trade and industry and practically every profession including the local level school management committees and users' groups of different services affecting the work culture and productivity at every level. The various groups are involved in politics in the hope of addressing their interests through political channels. The prolonged political instability, conflict and struggles for democratic rights in the country have also developed a culture of strikes, blockades, lockouts, street protests and similar activities putting forth demands or in protest of a specific policy or action of the government.

This culture is naturally prevalent in the labor front also. A total of 4,451 events of general strike were recorded in the Nepal Office of UN Department of Safety and Security from 2008 to 2013. The initiators included political parties, rebel groups, transport unions, local communities, ethnic and alliance groups, business communities, student unions, struggle committees and trade unions.[20] Naturally, the consequence of such events is reflected in poor factor productivity ultimately leading to heavy economic cost in terms of loss of output and reduced growth. According to a study by Nepal Rastra Bank for the period, between 2008/9 and 2013/14, the total accumulated output loss in this period of five years was estimated to be Rs. 117 billion at an average of Rs. 27 billion per annum at current prices. The output loss represented 1.38 percent of annual output.[21]

The deterioration in productivity and loss of export competitiveness has led to import surge backed by rising remittances. Nepal's productivity growth has oscillated around zero percent between 1970 and 2015, contributing nothing to overall growth, when adjusted for human capital, employment and labor force participation.[22] The imperative of productivity-enhancing measures is, therefore, necessary to promote growth, as faster growth in productivity will result in higher GDP growth with the same amount of capital investment. With the creation of right skills, there are sectors like commercial agriculture, construction and manufacturing industries where labor can be absorbed with higher productivity. There is, therefore, an urgent need for state policy to produce skilled manpower through training programs in response to market demands. There is a large scope for higher productivity in agriculture with mechanization, advanced technology and introduction of high-value crops including vegetables, fruits, herbs and aromatic plants with high export potential after substituting imports. There are instances of many migrant returnees engaged in such and other activities generating income much higher than they earned abroad. There are also a number of other sectors like construction, manufacturing and others which are presently employing a large number of foreign manpower. The overall need is to improve the generally politicized value system towards productivity and output-oriented work culture and ethics with an emphasis on hard work, entrepreneurship, creativity and innovation to accelerate factor productivity and growth.

Similarly, attracting FDI with new technologies, business and management practices and markets is vital to raise productivity and competitive advantage. Niall Ferguson, the Harvard professor and the author of the book Civilization: the West and the Rest,[23] argues that the rise of the Western civilization over the past five centuries is the outcome of six 'killer applications' one of which is the Protestant work ethic, meaning sober, conscientious and capable workers devoted to work as a divinely willed purpose of life. It required an increase in intensity and duration of work, combined with the accumulation of capital through saving and investment. The mixture of hard work and thrift is the essence of this culture. He argues that in recent years this work culture is alive and well in China that lifted millions of Chinese out of abject poverty and made the economy the second strongest in the world, while the Western world is slowly abandoning this work ethic.

Excessive preoccupation with political issues, limiting the economic agenda in rhetoric only is one factor that explains low economic growth in Nepal. I recall an interesting observation made by Mahbub Ul-Haq, the architect of UNDP Human Development Reports, during the SAARC Finance Ministers meeting in New Delhi while launching the South Asia Human Development Report in the mid-1990s. Explaining the major factor behind the widening per capita income differential between South Asia and East Asia (excluding China) in PPP terms from a mere $200 in 1960 to $11,000 in 1993, he said all state priorities including first, second and third of East Asian counties revolved around economic issues, while those of South Asian countries revolved only around political matters. The phenomenon has undergone some change with the start of the economic reform process of South Asian countries including Nepal in the 1990s. But politics still reigns supreme in case of Nepal' national life,

Human development and disparity

Nepal's impressive progress in human capital formation with gains in health and education sectors, together with a reduction in poverty compared to regional peers is well recognized by the international community and development partners. The life expectancy above seventy years, youth literacy rate at 85 percent and access to clean water and sanitation exceed regional averages. However, disparities exist between urban and rural areas and among provinces and regions. There has been impressive progress in school enrollment in all regions, 97.1 percent at the basic level and 44 percent at higher secondary level, on average. Disaggregation of data by province reveals uniformity at the basic level. Net enrollment at the higher secondary level is the highest at 48 percent in Province 3, compared to 39.6 percent in Province 2 and 40.5 percent in Province 5. This shows the minimal spatial disparity between provinces in access to education at the lower level. But the problem remains in inequities in access to quality and a higher level of service, as reflected in the low level of attendance at higher secondary education, a phenomenon explained by poverty, geography and ethnic traditions. Provision of quality health and education service is lacking in remote areas that lack proper infrastructure and suffer from inadequate manpower and supplies of medical drugs and educational materials. The problem is further compounded by the politicization of service providers including teachers and health personnel indulging in frequent absenteeism. The generally low quality of education and health service in such situations creates space for the private sector to play a stronger role in providing services; which is not reachable to poor families. In fact, the public sector spending per student in community schools is found generally higher than the individual spending in private schools. There is an inefficient use of government expenditure leading to low productivity because of the factors discussed in the preceding section that result in low quality of government services.

The Nepal Human Development Report 2014 measured the trend in the Human Development Index (HDI) and Human Poverty Index (HPI), together with trends in regional access to facilities, household wellbeing and individual ability indices between 2001 and 2011 across regions (classified into Kathmandu Valley, Eastern and Central Hills, Western Hills, Mid-Western and Far-Western Hills, Western, Mid- Western and Far-Western Mountains, Eastern and Central Tarai, and Western Tarai). According to the report, the trends in HDI and HPI have been positive across all regions, but the relative positions of disparity among regions remain unchanged, although there are signs that the gap could be narrowing. The Kathmandu Valley remains the top-ranking region, while the Western, Mid-Western and Far-Western Mountains continue to be the lowest ranking regions in all indices. There has been rapid improvement in HDI and HPI scores of Western Hills and Western Mountains, with strides in literacy and education, and increased earnings from remittances in tourism income. The Eastern and Central Tarai present a unique position where labor and total factor productivity, as well as access to facilities index, are among the highest in the country, but the HDI and HPI, as well as household wellbeing, are among the lowest.[24] There also exist socio-economic inequalities in caste and ethnic dimensions, the most disadvantaged groups being the *Dalits*, Muslims and some groups of *Janajatis*.

It may also be noted that Nepal's social assistance program has evolved and expanded in the last two and a half decades. This program includes old age allowance, single women's allowance, child grants, disability allowance, public works and scholarships to marginalized and vulnerable communities. Nepal's spending in such social assistance is estimated to be approximately 2 percent of GDP, the highest in South Asia. The total social security expenditure including cash transfers has increased to more than 4 percent of GDP. Such schemes have proliferated as a result of competitive populism between political parties at the central level in the past and between multiple governments under the new constitution. The program is uncoordinated and fragmented with the involvement of a number of government agencies and suffers from weak delivery leading to widespread leakages, gaps and duplication of beneficiaries. The poverty reduction impact of such cash transfer program is limited, as the benefits accrue equally across all income groups. Under the circumstances, there is a need for reforming the social protection program to make it more efficient, poverty-focused and fiscally sustainable. Rather than spreading such schemes, a sound social protection policy framework must be formulated at the national level targeted to the poor and vulnerable within which to take future decisions and reform the current ones. At the same time, there is a need for reforming and strengthening the administrative mechanisms for effective implementation of the schemes with the identification of real target groups.

Governance factor

After all is said and done about Nepal's development challenges and constraints, the most imperative factor towards contributing swift progress henceforth under the federal democratic framework of the present constitution is to improve the quality of governance with strong, efficient and well-functioning public institutions. A strong state with capable institutions to enforce the rule of law and maintain work discipline without arbitrary actions is necessary while committing itself to reduce all forms of corruption. In view of the country's vulnerability to frequent natural disasters, strong state mechanisms are also required to deal with shocks and to mitigate the risks of areas prone to disasters like drought, floods, tornado, GLOFs and landslides, with appropriate preventive policy measures. The loss of hundreds of lives and destruction of property and physical assets resulting from mainly floods, inundation and landslides from the southern plains of the country to the hills and mountains in the north happens to be normally an annual phenomenon in Nepal, as experienced in the current monsoon season of 2019 also. Such a condition of the country calls for building state capacity with strong institutions for disaster preparedness for prevention, mitigation, response and recovery actions against such hazards. Institutional preparedness is required with necessary capacities for rescue and relief works during disasters as well as for post-disaster rebuilding and rehabilitation efforts.

The investment climate for the private sector including FDI would depend on the credibility of state institutions relating to the security of property rights, predictability of policies and rules, reliability of the judiciary, freedom from corruption and the quality of bureaucracy. The civil service and development administration must be strictly merit-based and free from the malaise of political prejudice and affiliation prevailing at present. Public officials must be incentivized to perform better by ensuring accountability placing checks on arbitrary actions. A well-functioning bureaucracy capable of providing key inputs for political decision making and delivery of services is the key to promote growth and reduce poverty.

But Nepal's administrative institutions suffer largely from excessive favoritism based on partisan prejudices rather than merit, a problem which has become more pronounced in recent years. Selection of managers in key positions generally reeks of cronyism. Even appointments in state-run centers of excellence in education, health and other sectors, embassies abroad, and constitutional bodies including the judiciary and other autonomous institutions like the anti-corruption authority are largely guided by partisan and parochial considerations. There are frequent reports of grand corruption at various bureaucratic, political, and even constitutional bodies. The Corruption Perceptions Index averaged 127 between 2004 and 2018 among 175 countries. Its ranking worsened to 124th in 2018 from 122nd in 2017. Corruption factor has pernicious effects on the delivery of public services, and debilitating impact on productivity, economic growth and development.

Allegations of corruption have become more pronounced even inside political parties when it comes to nominating candidates in elections, especially under the safe provision of proportional representation. The problem has now percolated down to lower levels of government. The cost of competing in elections has been rising dramatically every cycle. Despite expenditure ceilings prescribed under the election regulations, tens of millions of rupees are reported to be generally spent even by candidates at the local level.

Under the circumstances, it is absolutely necessary to have strong, effective and fair public administration to enforce rule of law, upgrade the quality of governance and management ability to ensure efficient and optimal use of public resources to attain the goals of economic development and social justice. The effectiveness of governance would first depend on the quality of decision making on development policy and priorities, and the institutional capability to implement policy decisions. The political leadership and policymakers should restrain from overestimating their knowledge and ability in major decision-making, management and delivery. It is important to have a long-term vision and to overcome the penchant for populist approaches and short-term political gains. This involves sound economic policies, well-conceived priorities and strategies, together with administrative and management capabilities for effective implementation. In today's globalized world, the pursuit of economic goal involves the imperative of strong and capable institutions manned by competent human resources. These institutions are also required to deal with the increasingly complex and sophisticated negotiations with bilateral, multilateral agencies and transnational companies on issues like trade, investment and technology transfer. It would be pertinent to quote here the World Development Report 1997 that good government is not a luxury, it is vital for economic development:[25]

An effective state is vital for the provision of goods and services –and the rules and institutions—that allow market to flourish and people to lead healthier, happier lives. Without it, sustainable development, both economic and social, is impossible. Many said much the same thing fifty years ago, but they tended to mean that development had to be state-provided. The message of experience since then is rather different: that the state is central to economic and social development, not as a direct provider of growth but as a partner, catalyst and facilitator.

This suggests that we need a strong state that knows its boundaries. The country presently suffers from the syndrome of setting excessively high targets with little consideration of the implementation capacity and resources.[26] The other part of the strategy is to raise state capability by reinvigorating public institutions to check arbitrary state actions and combat entrenched corruption. To improve institutional capabilities and effectiveness, there is a need to boost internal competition in the civil service through merit-based recruitment and promotion sans favoritism.

Concluding remarks

The country has entered a new political set-up under the new constitution bringing the government closer to the people with promises for a just, egalitarian and prosperous society. To achieve these goals, Nepal will need first and foremost to make functional the new federal governance structure which it has adopted. The country's Achilles heel is the all-encompassing capacity deficit it has in implementing the written laws and executing policies, rooted in deteriorating political culture. The immediate need is to build and strengthen institutions at subnational levels to enable them to perform their constitutional duties. There are serious problems and challenges in governance, development planning, and financial management that require fresh approach for good governance with emphasis on ensuring rule of law, prudent and efficient fiscal management, strong and capable institutions with merit-based bureaucracy, rational planning and decision-making based on proper appraisal of implementation capacity, rather than populist swaying.

To sustain the new political structure, meet the fundamental rights to ensure freedom from poverty and deprivation, and provide opportunities for economic wellbeing and upliftment to attain its socialist aspirations, it is necessary to raise factor productivity, reorient social protection program making it more poverty-focused and accelerate economic growth with increased volumes of quality investment. Public investment needs to be scaled up and made more efficient, particularly to close the infrastructural gaps, while restraining the growth of recurrent public expenditure. At the same time, domestic and foreign private capital is essential to rekindle and reinvigorate growth and to transform the economy. Only an investment-friendly climate with liberal policies, strong rule of law ensuring the security of property rights, improved infrastructure and business-friendly regulations can lead to a higher flow of FDI in a sustained manner to expand Nepal's industrial base. FDI also brings in new technology, know-how and captive foreign markets.

In sum, for the country to graduate to higher levels of development and be on a course of equitable prosperity under the new political dispensation, it is necessary to reorient our work ethic, value system and public policy. The excessive preoccupation with politics and factional interests must give way to a shared economic vision with an emphasis on productivity, formalization, social mobility, quality governance, meritocracy and social justice. A state can emerge to become self-legitimizing only when freed from partisan interests and parochial affiliations. This is the least that a country as proud as Nepal, South Asia's oldest nation-state, can hope to aspire in a new century that has brought unprecedented opportunities for a rapid catch up with peers, while also confronting the existential peril posed by climate change.

Notes

1. See https://www.un.org/sustainabledevelopment/sustainable-development-goals/
2. Bhagawati, Jagdish and Panagariya, Arvind (2013). *Why Growth Matters,* Chapter 7. Public Affairs: New York.
3. Thurow, L. C. (1993). *Head to Head- The Coming Economic Battle Among Japan, Europe and America,* (pp. 40-42). Nicholas Brealey Publishing House: London.

4. World Bank Group. (November 2018). *Nepal Development Update,* (p. 15).
5. World Bank Group. (February 2018). *Nepal-Systematic Country Diagnostic,* (p. 15). Washington DC. Quoted from Trade Policy Notes, World Bank 2016.
6. *The Kathmandu Post.* (2018, August 12). Kathmandu.
7. *The Himalayan Times.* (2019, January 7).
8. World Bank Group. (May 2017). *Climbing Higher: Towards a Middle- Income Country,* (p. 19).
9. *Annapurna Expess.* (January 2019). Kathmandu.
10. The roads are Kathamndu-Nijgadh fast track, Kanti Rajpath, Dakhinkali-Hetauda, Prithvi Highway,Muglin-Narayan Gadh-Hetauda and old Tribhuvan Rajpath.
11. World Bank Group. (November 2018). *Nepal Development Update,* (p.9).
12. The World Bank. (June 2014). *The Vision for Nepal: Synthesis Policy Note.* South Asia Chief Economist Office.
13. Government of Nepal. Ministry of Finance. (May 2015). *Public Expenditure and Financial Accountability (PEFA) Assessment as of 2013/14,* (p. 8).
14. World Bank. (June 2014). *Nepal Policy Note:* 3 'Is' for Growth, (p. 20). South Asia Chief Economist Office.
15. An improvised explosive device was hurled at the fleet of vehicles carrying myself and others during election campaign in Danda Goan of Kakani rural municipality of Nuwakot district on November 17, 2017. The blast caused serious damage to one of the vehicles causing serious injuries to five political cadres in it. Similar attacks were hurled targeting many other candidates including NC candidates Gagan Kumar Thapa in Kathmandu, Narayan Bahadur Karki in Udaypur, and NCP candidates Krishna bahadur Mahara and Barsa Man OPun in Rolpa.
16. *The Kathmandu Post.* (2019, March 8). This included two sub-machine guns (SMG), three of its magazines, a pistol and hundreds of bullets together with other accessories seized from the house of a rebel leader in Sivaraj Municipalty in Kapilbastu district.
17. Klenow, P. J. and Rodriguesz-Clare, A. (1997). The Neo-Classical Revival in Growth Economics: Has It Gone Too Far? (pp. 73-103). In *NBER Macroeconomics Annual,* Volume 12. University of Chicago.
18. Karmacharya, Binod K. (2015). Partial and Total Factor Productivity in Nepal: A Review and Policy Implications. In Pyakuryal, B. (Ed.), *Macro Economics: Radical rethinking in Growth, Inequality and Inclusiveness in Nepal.* Kathmandu.
19. Sapkota, Chandan (2014, August 28). *Labor Productivity and Wages in Nepal.* Retrieved from sapkotac.blogspot.com.
20. Quoted in Shrestha, Min Bahadur and Chaudhary, Sashi Kant (2013). *The Economic Cost of General Strikes in Nepal.* In *NRB Working Paper No.20.* Nepal Rastra Bank.
21. Ibid.
22. World Bank Group. (May 2017). *Nepal Counrty Economic Memorandum-Climbing Higher: Towards Middle Income Country,* (pp. 21-22). Wasinghton DC.
23. Ferguson, Niall (2011). *The Civilization: The West and the Rest,* Chapter 6. Allen Lane Penguin Books.